How to Teach Life Skills

to Kids with
Autism or Asperger's

JENNIFER McILWEE MYERS
Aspie at Large

How to Teach Life Skills to Kids with Autism or Asperger's

All marketing and publishing rights guaranteed to and reserved by:

FUTURE HORIZONS INC.

721 W. Abram Street
Arlington, Texas 76013
800-489-0727
817-277-0727
817-277-2270 (fax)
E-MAIL: *info@FHautism.com*
www.FHautism.com

Book design © TLC Graphics, *www.TLCGraphics.com*
Cover by: Monica Thomas; Interior by: Erin Stark

Myers, Jennifer McIlwee.
  How to teach life skills to kids with autism or Asperger's / Jennifer McIlwee Myers.
    p. ; cm.

  Includes bibliographical references and index.

  ISBN: 978-1-935274-13-1

  1. Autistic children—Education. 2. Autistic children—Life skills guides. 3. Autism—Popular works. 4 Asperger's syndrome—Patients—Education. 5. Asperger's syndrome—Patients—Life skills guides. 4. Asperger's syndrome—Popular works. I. Title.

RJ506.A9 M94 2010

618.92/858/8

Printed in the United States of America

This book is dedicated to the two people who made me make it happen: Temple Grandin, Ph.D., who has provided inestimable help, and Gary C. Myers, who believes in me.

Table of Contents

Section III: Specific Life Skills

Section IV: Really, Really Big Skills
That Everyone Needs

Foreword

By Temple Grandin, Ph.D.,
author of *Thinking in Pictures* and *The Way I See It*

Jennifer Myers provides practical ways to provide structure and guidance so that individuals on the autism spectrum can lead productive, fulfilling lives. Jennifer's parents did many of the same things that my mother did to teach me how to live independently. When both Jennifer and I were children, there was a heavy emphasis on learning manners and learning how to listen and be considerate to others. At the dining room table, my mother reminded me to give another person a chance to talk when I chatted too long. I had to learn this through many specific examples. Consideration for other people was also taught by many specific examples. One example was when I woke mother up to open a tube of glue with a stuck top. She was annoyed, and explained that waking her up was not considerate. Another time I was making a lot of noise close to mother when she was on the phone. This was another example of not being considerate. Jennifer's book provides lots of SPECIFIC examples of how to teach important skills for daily life. She has divided her book into many short chapters that offer practical advice on how to teach specific skills.

Today Jennifer has become an accomplished speaker and has had successful employment in computer programming and technical writing. For this introduction, I interviewed Jennifer to obtain an overview of her professional life. Before she went to college she was successfully employed at Bloomingdale's as a sales clerk in the gourmet food section.

She almost lost her job due to "meltdowns" at work. She didn't snap at customers, but snapped at other employees in the stockroom. To keep her job, she figured out new ways to cope. She hid in more secluded parts of the backroom and she stopped eating sugar-laden food from the gourmet food section that made her more prone to meltdowns. She also learned how to have totally quiet "meltdowns." In my own case, I switched from anger to crying when I got upset. At every job site, I found secluded places to hide, such as under the basement stairs or in the electrical rooms. I went to these places to pull myself together after I had problems interacting with people who were mean to me.

Jennifer kept the job at Bloomingdale's for a year before going to college. Her first attempt at college did not go well because she had no clear goals, and she was short on life skills for living away from home. She majored in four different subjects over four semesters, then dropped out to get married and became a housewife for five years. To figure out how to run a house, she read *Hints From Heloise* and other books on housekeeping. Being a housewife with no kids and no goals was boring, so she decided to go back to school with much more specific goals—goals that would lead to employment.

One of the things she had to learn was how to ask other people for help, which was a vital skill for earning her B.S. degree from California State University, Fullerton in computer science. She had two internships that used her computer programming skills and taught her work skills. Her first internship involved creating report programs and helping manage marketing data. Unfortunately, she had to quit the first internship because the company was using unfair business practices. I had a similar experience where one of my employers was having financial problems and I was told to buy advertising space, when I knew that my employer would probably not pay for it. I quit this job because I was being asked to engage in the totally dishonest practice of buying advertising space and not paying for it.

In her second internship, she helped maintain a software library for a massive application the company had developed. She obtained this second internship through a contact she made through socializing with people her husband worked with.

After college, Jennifer did freelance technical writing. In these jobs she used BOTH her computer science skills and her writing skills. Like me, she never got jobs through the typical "front door" method of interviewing. She got referrals to new clients because they liked her work. In my own case, I had to sell my work and not myself. I sold jobs by showing a portfolio of pictures and drawings of completed design projects.

WHAT HELPED THE MOST AFTER COLLEGE?

I asked Jennifer what factors helped her to be successful after college; both in her work and personal life. One important factor was mentoring from her father. He is a sales engineer for a company that makes air pollution control equipment. His job involves visiting plants and determining which pollution control equipment would work best for them. He used the Dale Carnegie book, *How to Win Friends and Influence People,* to develop the people skills he needed to do this. This helped him to be successful, because it taught him how to listen to other people's needs. It is very positive and it gave lots of concrete examples. The Dale Carnegie book was also helpful to Jennifer. She realized that listening to other people is important because you can learn from them. One must never be an arrogant "know it all." Listening to other people's ideas also helps with accepting new ideas and becoming more flexible.

In my own work, I was originally going to limit my design projects to cattle until a client begged me to design a large stockyard for pigs. This client helped me broaden out and expand my business, and become more flexible. There were not enough design projects to stay hyper-focused on projects for cattle. However, I had to be careful not to spread out so much that I would not know what I was doing. I had to become competent in a large enough area to find enough work, but not so broad an area that I would not be knowledgeable. I had to establish some boundaries, and there were things that I would not design, such as feed mills or water distribution systems. It took me three years of hard work to learn cattle handling systems. Learning how to design feed mills would take another three years. However, handling pigs had enough similarities to cattle handling that only a few weeks of learning was required.

FLEXIBILITY OF THINKING

I developed a system for updating both my livestock handling knowledge and my knowledge about autism, to keep my information up-to-date. When I read new scientific articles or any other new information, I asked myself if I needed to modify or change the advice that I had been giving. For example, I used to think that all individuals on the autism spectrum were visual thinkers like me. I have learned from others on the spectrum that some of them are not visual thinkers. Unlike me, they learn best through the auditory sense, and their ability in drawing and visual spatial tasks is poor. Therefore, I now make it very clear to parents and teachers that some individuals think in pictures and others do not. However, most individuals on the spectrum tend to be specialized thinkers who are good in one area, but have weak skills in another. Therefore, the emphasis needs to be on building strengths. If a child is good at math then let him/her take advanced math. If he/she is good at art, then develop the child's drawing and artistic skills. My career in designing livestock facilities is based on the use of my excellent visual skills. A career in computer programming would have been impossible for me, because the symbols were too abstract for me to visualize.

LESSONS I LEARNED AS A CHILD

Today I see too many fully verbal children who have absolutely atrocious manners. I went out to dinner with a family where a nine-year-old was combing his hair with his fork. I told him to put the fork on his plate.

When I twirled my fork in the air mother made me put it back on the plate. Another time I saw another child walking around a hotel lobby with his finger in his nose. Mother would have made it very clear that this was not acceptable. This little boy had good speech and was fully capable of learning that a finger up the nose was not acceptable around other people.

I was always encouraged to learn how to do tasks by myself, such as shopping. By the time I was nine I could shop by myself and buy kites and model airplanes. I knew the rules—don't touch things in stores unless you are going to buy them. Miss Edson, the owner of the local toy store made it very clear what the rules were, and all the neighborhood kids obeyed her.

In conclusion, parents and teachers have to allow time for kids to learn to do things by themselves. Jennifer provides lots of examples of how her parents expected her to do household chores even though it took her a while to learn to do them correctly. Her parents knew that the only way she could learn was by doing and she had to be given lots of opportunities to learn.

Acknowledgements

There are a bunch of people who have contributed to this book with their time, talent, or sheer wonderfulness.

In fact, an insane number of people who have been of help to me should be acknowledged here, but I'll have to omit many of them due to space, time, and my overloaded brain. Many days it seemed that the whole autism world was clustering around me, giving me advice, support, and all sorts of interesting bits of information and feedback, which is cool, but hard to pin down in words or names.

I've also gotten a lot of help from anonymous parents whom I happened to stumble across when they were experiencing their worst moments. Otherwise intelligent, loving parents who are lost and bewildered on a hot day at Disneyland have helped me to see what results when good parents go nuts. You can learn a lot from watching what parenting moves do and don't work at a crowded theme park. (Hint: Giving in to tantrums has serious negative repercussions.)

And just in case some of those kids read this: it's okay; Mickey will not be mad at you if you don't finish all of your French fries. And they will not put you in Small World and glue your feet to the floor and make you sing if you don't stop crying. Honest.

Just a few of the many, many others who helped:

My family: Mom and Dad, who blatantly demonstrated that you can teach the thickest little Aspie in the world to look after herself, dress reasonably decently, and even return a hideous sweater for store credit.

Catherine, my "stealth sibling." She rocks.

My brother Jimmy, without whom I'd never have been diagnosed. Also, he's awesome.

My nephew Pete, who has played a key role in Jimmy's education. And mine.

Paula Petersen, who gave me my start in educating parents about ASDs in the coolest ASA support group imaginable.

You would not believe the bunch of crazy people who are not even related to me who have purposely encouraged me to write. Not least among these are the denizens of "Wayne's World," aka Future Horizons. Wayne Gilpin is an amazing show-runner, as well as a tireless chief cook and bottle-washer. The man is astonishing.

Kelly Gilpin, editrix supreme. If anyone gets in her way, I will come after them with a sledgehammer.

Jennifer Gilpin. Amazing feedback and endless useful information. Hilariously funny, but that seems to be true of the Gilpins in general.

Katherine "Dash" Gilpin. Giving me hope for the youth of America while providing tons of insight and entertainment.

Alex Gilpin. A much-missed source of inspiration. Without him, none of this would be happening.

Veronica Zysk. Another editrix of note. She helped me understand better how to communicate with the non-autistic part of the autism world.

Even crazier than the FH crew are the many people who have plenty of work to do and are very busy educating the world about autism and Asperger's but still helped me out. They almost make me think that this "altruism" thing actually exists.

Like Temple Grandin. There's a reason the book is dedicated to her.

Tony Attwood. The man knows more about Asperger's and about the Beach Boys than anyone. Not that the topics are related. Okay, maybe a little related, but that's a whole other book.

Oh, and Carol Gray. The woman is scary: her blood must be naturally about 75% caffeine, and she is so darn optimistic and cheerful that it's unbelievable. She has chosen to be optimistic and cheerful around me repeatedly, and it has helped.

And Ellen Notbohm. Smart, useful, thoughtful, encouraging. Read her books. Seriously, read her books.

Oh, and read Tony's stuff and Carol's too. Google them.

Stephen Shore is just cool and has given me a lot of insight. Another person to Google.

Many people with ASDs and many family members of people with ASDs have helped as well. They ask me questions, they write to tell me how wrong or right I am, and there are dozens and dozens of them. Any list would be endless.

The insights and ideas of many members of the Orange County Interagency Autism Group have been useful and fascinating. Special shout-outs to Vera Bernard and Marcy Melton, but there are many others.

HyeKyeung Seung, for teaching me so much about language acquisition.

Important: I would never have gotten through the period of writing this book without my awesome pals at the Unitarian Universalist Church in Fullerton. Too many to list, but they rock!

Gary Myers, here's a kiss. I chose you to end this list.

Introduction

Temple made me do it.

After years of giving presentations on various aspects of the autism spectrum, I'd had many, many people ask why I didn't write a book about autism and Asperger's Syndrome. Various publishers and authors had suggested various topics, and I actually had three different books underway. My normal level of disorganization is such that they all were growing but not getting much closer to being finished.

Then I called Temple up one evening in June of 2009 about something completely different, and she asked what I was working on. I mentioned that I wasn't really sure what to write about or which book to focus on.

"Your life skills talk," she told me, "you need to write a book about that."

I started to protest that I already had started other books and wanted to finish one of those, but she cut me off.

"Your life skills talk is good, that's what people need. You need to do an outline from that."

For roughly the next hour, she walked me through the topics in my talk, while I frantically scribbled notes on bits of scrap paper. She gave me strict instructions for creating an outline based on those topics.

Finally, she told me, "Get the outline to me by Tuesday morning so I can tell you whether to go ahead with it."

It was Sunday evening.

I got the outline to her by Tuesday morning.

She approved the outline and I started going. The result is the book you are holding in your hands.

The moral of the story is to not ask Temple for help unless you really want her help, because she doesn't mess around.

Thank heavens.

So this book is based on my various talks about life skills, which means it is written more or less the way I speak. Grammarians take note: this means the language use is casual, with plenty of non-standard usage. This means that sometimes the awkward but correct use of "he or she" and "his or her" is replaced with the incorrect but readable "they" and "their." The usage changes with the flow of the language, just as it would in a talk. Also, there are sentences that start with "so," "but," or "and," which is also going to drive the grammarians nuts but is, again, really quite normal in speech.

Additionally, this book contains quite a number of asides or quick references that are based in geek-think. Don't worry if those asides don't completely work for you: they aren't vital to the meaning of the text, but they may make things a little clearer to my fellow geeks. Consider them tiny shout-outs to my fellow Aspies, and if you aren't into the "geek world" you can just let them pass.

Thanks for reading this. And yes, I am aware that I owe Temple big-time.

— JENNIFER MCILWEE MYERS

Read Me First

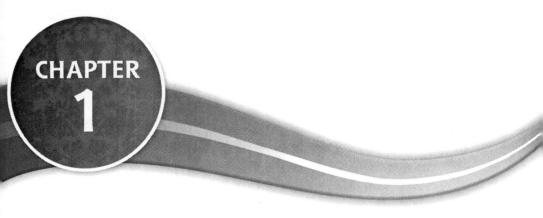

Why You? Why Me? Why Life Skills?

Hi, my name is Jennifer and I'd like to provide you with tons of information, hints, and ideas about how to teach life skills to children, teens, and/or humans with autism spectrum disorders.

I have Asperger's Syndrome (AS), which is an autism spectrum disorder. That alone certainly does not qualify me to teach you or anyone else about Asperger's and autism, but getting diagnosed with AS turned out to be the starting point for a journey that led me here, to you, and to the hope of sharing with you what I've learned on that journey.

In addition to having AS, I am an extraordinarily lucky person, and my incredible amount of sheer dumb luck has led me to experience and discover a lot of great stuff about how learning life skills can greatly enhance not just the lives of children with autism spectrum disorders, but also the lives of those who live with them, care for them, and teach them.

You are, I hope, a person who would like to understand more about teaching, reaching, and helping someone with an autism spectrum disorder. Or you may just be someone who got stuck in the bathroom and this is the only thing in there to read.

Parents and teachers of children on the autism spectrum have a huge ability to affect that child's functioning in the world. A parent or caregiver who is willing to take on the job of teaching life skills can lift that child to his or her best possible level of functioning in the world.

Not all of us on the spectrum are destined for greatness; nor are all of the children with autism who struggle actually "secret geniuses" who will blow the world away with their brilliance someday. But we are all human beings who need to be able to get by from day to day with some small measure of independence and strength.

I hope this book will help you to move yourself and your child towards better day-to-day functioning. I really, really, really hope that it will give you some insight into how people with autism think and feel, and what it is we need extra help to learn.

At the very worst, if you are stuck in the bathroom with this book, and after you wash your hands, you find there are no dry towels in the bathroom, you might use this book to blot them on. Glad to be of service.

WHY LIFE SKILLS?

There are so many things involved in parenting any child, and so many things for a child to learn in order to function as an adult: the alphabet, how to ride the bus, calculus, frugal shopping, putting on one's own socks, and deciding whether you should or shouldn't change your own oil.

The problems and tasks of parenting often are doubled or tripled when a child has any autism spectrum disorder (ASD). Suddenly, parents have to face the ins and outs of IEPs, figure out what exactly an occupational therapist is and whether their child needs one, and determine which of the many proffered treatments are mad, bad, or just plain dangerous.

So why should parents (or teachers, OTs, speech pathologists, and psychologists) put "teaching this child life skills" high on the list of things to deal with? How can anyone make time for life skills when so many children with ASDs are woefully behind in academics, speech, or social skills?

What's more, many parents have hopes or fears that make life skills a low priority. Many tell me that their child either is or is soon going to be "cured" and therefore doesn't need special intervention for day-to-day skills. Others fear that their child is so low-functioning, so hard to educate, that there is no point to trying to teach him to do laundry, make a simple meal, or even pick out his own outfit in the morning.

But no matter where a child is on the autism spectrum, and no matter where he or she is likely to wind up, life skills count!

Yes, there are children with autism (and people in general) who may have little chance at being independent in later life. But there is a huge difference between an adult with autism who is used to being waited on hand-and-foot and one who is able to get dressed on his own, help with the dishes, or successfully use simple stress-busting techniques.

Similarly, no matter how smart a child is, or how "recovered" he may wind up, if he can't go out to lunch with the guys from work, choose his own outfits, or deal with other people's mistakes calmly, he's going to wind up living in a very small, sheltered world.

Not only are people with ASDs less likely to pick up skills like this on their own, but we also take a lot longer to learn them. Simple exercises like crossing the street or taking the bus may be completely non-obvious to us, regardless of IQ. And learning how to deal with mistakes calmly and appropriately takes us a long, long, long time. Heck, I'm forty-four, and I'm *still* working on it!

The nature of schooling and our society mean that children are often judged and ranked by their academic skills. But there are jobs you can hold if you can't read. There are jobs you can hold if you can't write. There are even jobs you can hold if you can't talk.

There are few or no jobs you can keep if you yell or scream when you don't get what you expected. There are very rarely jobs you can hold if you can't stop talking when your boss is trying to tell you something. Being on time and being dressed right for that activity are so important to employment that being late to or dressing badly for an interview are job-killers.

Sure, a few people get away with yelling, being late, dressing wrong, and so forth—if those people are such huge money makers that it is worth it for folks to put up with them. But even super-geniuses will have an easier time getting on with life if they learn a few basic skills.

And even kids who will probably never be independent adults get more respect and more support if they can do the little things that inform the people around them that they are human beings. A guy who has occasional meltdowns but mostly understands the idea of doing his fair share and of apologizing for causing others pain or inconvenience is simply more likely to be treated with a modicum of respect and friendliness than one whose behavior constantly triggers defensive responses from those around him.

Even social and support groups that are specifically for adults with ASDs have to have standards. A group that includes people with super-sensitive ears, noses, and hearts is not going to be happy to include people who yell, smell, and raise hell.

THE GEEK WORLD

Many parents and teachers, even some with very high-functioning children, believe that there is not much out there for a child with autism. They feel it is okay to skip teaching skills like functioning in a grocery store, doing household chores, and other daily tasks, because they believe their child is always going to need constant daily care.

This makes sense only if you think the socially oriented "neurotypical" (NT) world is the only real world there is. That's the world that most elementary school teachers, occupational therapists, marketing executives, and a disproportionate number of women inhabit.

In the NT world, *Star Trek* fans are geeks, and people do things like stocking up on greeting cards and buying gifts for no occasion "just in case" something comes up and a gift is needed. That same world involves a wide variety of behaviors that I find rather incomprehensible, from the use of decorative towels and soaps that cannot be actually used to (shudder) "manscaping."

These are the folks who enjoy dinner parties and social dancing, who believe that every opportunity for schmoozing is good, and who, given the choice, choose work that brings them into contact with other humans most of the day.

These people naturally come to believe that the child with autism—the child who prefers solitude to clamor, who loves to focus on one problem or activity for hours at a time, who loves organizing objects infinitely more than organizing social activities, and who has no innate urge to attend a playdate—well, they come to believe that this is a child who will never find a way in the world.

What these folks don't know is that there is a whole world of us already out there. It's the geek world, and it's hidden right under their noses.

Yes, one of the most vital reasons that children on the autism spectrum need to learn life skills is that there is a whole geek world out there waiting for us to find it. The kinds of skills that are discussed in this book are the ones that make it possible for us to find, interact with, and develop lives in that world.

And yes, the geek world is real and valid. There's a reason that Temple Grandin refers to NASA as a sheltered workshop for people with high-functioning autism. There's a reason that some people's work cubicles are decorated with action figures and *Doctor Who* calendars. There's a reason that Hollywood can make a killing off of elaborate boxed set releases of *Lord of the Rings* that have twenty or more hours of behind-the-scenes extras per movie.

This geek world is almost invisible to "typical" parents, teachers, therapists, and peers. It is the world of engineers, computer programmers, research scientists, animal experts, writers, artists, and many others. It's a place where the "geeks" hang out, and it exists both within and in parallel to the one where you who are typical live.

There are college dorms full of engineering and science majors where every other person will love trains. There are break rooms at NASA where arguments about the relative merits of comic book superheros are de rigueur.

It's not just the "brainy" geeks who can benefit from living, working, and making friends in the geek world. Model train clubs, Lego™ clubs, and other special interest groups often are places where kids who can't fit in anywhere can fit in.

Heck, I live in Orange County, California, USA, where we have a thriving Lego Model Railroading club. That's right, a club for people who like to build model train sets out of Legos. Not incidentally, this is a club founded, run, and populated by adults who can afford to buy their own Legos. Thousands and thousands of Legos.

Parents of the most introverted autistic children often despair of ever finding a way to draw those children out. They might find a way by venturing into the geek world as it exists near you. Folks who love model trains may be able to help you figure out how to work trains into all of your child's social-skills and life-skills training.

Children and adults who are considered "low functioning" can really benefit from contact with people in the geek world. The world of a teen or adult who is obsessed with Thomas the Tank Engine™ can be greatly expanded by adults who speak the language of trains.

Most important, I want you to know and remember that there are grownups—functioning, employed grownups—who have massive doses of the traits associated with the autism spectrum. This is one of the most vital reasons that teaching life skills is important—because we geeks, wonks, and nerds are living fulfilling lives throughout the world. People with autistic traits who learn to be polite, hardworking, and generally functional have the best chance to join in. It can be done. We exist. There's a whole world of us out there.

Please teach your child the life skills needed to join us.

Frames of Reference

This book is definitely not intended to be an "autie-biography." There are enough fine autobiographies by people with autism and Asperger's Syndrome out there already. The world can do quite well without one from me.

However, it would be helpful for you to have enough background information about me (and my brother Jimmy, who has autism) to know where the stories and examples herein are coming from, and why they may well be quite useful to you.

When I do talks on teaching life skills around the US, people tell me that the most useful insights they get are from the stories I tell about myself and my brother. Here's how it all got started.

MY DIAGNOSIS

As I mentioned before, I have Asperger's Syndrome.

Some years ago, around 1993, my younger brother Jimmy got diagnosed with autism. Or rather, he had an official diagnosis of PDD:NOS, which later became an official diagnosis of autism.

After Jimmy got diagnosed, for some years my mom kept saying things to me like, "They say he does such-and-such because he has autism, but *you* always did that too."

I didn't think much of it at first. After all, I was trying to live my life and figure out how to function as adult, which for me was a very tricky process. And I certainly did not look into getting diagnosed with anything. I'd already had a bunch of diagnoses—too many, too often, and without any good effect.

Yes, like a lot of people with autism spectrum disorders, I spent a good swath of my childhood getting diagnosed, re-diagnosed, judged, poked, and prodded without anyone coming up with any thoughts that were helpful to me. Everyone around me seemed to agree that "something is wrong with Jennifer," but no one came up with any explanation or information that made any sense.

Many children with autism spectrum disorders (ASDs)—autism, Asperger's, or PDD:NOS, to name the most notable—go through this. The diagnoses kids receive vary from bi-polar disorder to schizophrenia to "nothing that a good spanking wouldn't fix." If you've got a child who has been diagnosed with an ASD, there's a good chance that you are familiar with this drill.

After years of hearing my parents tell me that various attributes and activities of my brother's were just like mine had been, after hearing over and over that the very things that were officially labeled "autistic traits" were often identical to my childhood behaviors, well, after enough years of that I decided to look into things.

I got online, searched for information on "autism and related disorders" and found out about Asperger's Syndrome. I sought out a psychologist who was an expert not only in ASDs, but also in a few of my previous diagnoses, and he confirmed my suspicions. At the age of thirty-six, I was diagnosed with Asperger's Syndrome.

That diagnosis opened the world up for me. But I would not have had the skills to use that diagnosis to open doors if it weren't for my parents' insights and how they raised me.

BRINGING UP BABY

When I was a small child, my parents didn't have a real diagnosis or label for what was happening with me, yet my mom noticed that something was "different" very early on. She knew that there had been some relatives, great aunts on my father's side, who had never really been able to fend for themselves. She absorbed as much information about the family quirks and foibles as she could, observed me closely, and developed strategies for teaching me all of the things she knew I would need extra help with.

So at an age when most children with Asperger's are getting ooohed and ahhed over for their "little professor" characteristics, I was being shoved into learning life skills at an accelerated, or speeded up, rate.

This is important: many, many children with ASDs get seriously shielded from life, much more than they may need to be. Kids with autism who use PECS perfectly well are never asked to use them with anyone other than teachers and parents, so they never communicate with anyone else at all. Aspies who can speak super-fluently at age two are never prompted to ask for directions to the bathroom themselves.

In other words, children with autism spectrum disorders are seldom given the practice they need to successfully go through even the smallest daily interactions that other children learn intuitively with only a little prompting. We have a greater need, yet we get less instruction.

My mom saw that whatever it was that was going on with me, she was going to need to teach me life skills earlier, more often, and with more frequent repetition than most kids needed. Instead of dialing back the level of teaching for a child who wanted to avoid doing those things, she cranked it up.

Mind you, she didn't just "throw me into the deep end" and expect me to swim. She worked carefully on building up my skills in vital areas, such as asking for help, finding things I needed, taking care of myself and my possessions, understanding what money is for and how we get it, and all of those little things that had to be taught with a special amount of effort if she ever expected me to get out of the nest and go!

Vitally, she taught me the same lessons over and over, used multiple approaches in multiple situations, and seldom assumed that I "got" something if there wasn't blatant evidence that I did. You can't assume that a child with an ASD knows how to do something just because they can rehearse it, pick out the right options in a workbook, or even give a good verbal account of the right thing to do. Getting a child to actually do the thing they are learning in multiple real-life situations (with appropriate adult support and protection as needed) is the gold standard for life skills.

Oh, I also got uncannily lucky in the nature of my dad and his approach to teaching. He really had little idea of what is "age appropriate" or what it is that a child can or can't do, so he answered my questions honestly, instead of in "age appropriate" ways, coached me on adult life skills like how to shake hands in a business situation (as opposed to the ridiculous practice of teaching disabled children to shake hands with other small children), and generally assumed that, if I was interested, it was worth his trouble to teach me.

Then I had a sister, four years my junior, who was amazingly socially savvy. By watching her, I could learn appropriate social behaviors that I had totally missed. For a child with Asperger's, observing the social behaviors of a very socially adept child four years younger is a great way to find out huge amounts of information about how the social world works.

My sister also taught me the value of lying low. Many girls with Asperger's become "invisible" as they get older, especially in their teens. This is an insanely great way to avoid bullying, although I never got really good at it. My natural noisiness, bossiness, and general lack of social awareness meant I could not implement all the cool stuff my sister did. But I still learned a lot from her.

Then, waaaaaaay after all of the agonies of going through school with undiagnosed Asperger's were over, *then* came my brother's diagnosis and subsequently awesome progress.

Mom and Dad applied the same skills and concepts they had used with me to Jimmy's problems, but this time they had some even greater advantages. First, they had an accurate diagnosis and, therefore, access to some really good professionals such as OTs, speech therapists, and teachers who knew a lot about ASDs.

Second, they had had me. I was, as my dad says, the beta baby. All of the stuff they'd learned from me somehow seemed to apply to Jimmy.

There were other things too. My sister Catherine and her son Peter (less than a year younger than Jimmy) were—and are—amazingly great for Jimmy. And for me.

But the main thing, the most important thing, was my parents' belief that children need to learn life skills, and disabled or "different" children need to be taught life skills even more than average, typical, or adept children do.

MY LEARNING CURVE

After I got diagnosed, I became somewhat obsessed with learning about autism and Asperger's. I busied myself with buying books, looking up various issues in Asperger's, and so forth. I also decided to go to a local Autism Society of America group's meeting to see if I could learn even more there.

I learned a *lot* from that ASA group. Not only did I learn about ASDs from the parents gathered there, I also learned that many parents of children with ASDs really struggle to understand how their children look at the world and what they are thinking and experiencing.

I wrote a little talk on sensory issues for the group. When I presented it, the feedback was super. I got an invitation to do another, and various people let other various people in other groups know that I was a resource to contact.

It was awesome. I got to meet, talk with, and interview a lot more parents, teachers, OTs, speech therapists, and others who lived with, worked with, or had some special attachment to people with autism spectrum disorders of all kinds.

Additionally, as I did more talks, wrote more articles, and generally got to share what I'd learned with more people, I had opportunities to meet a lot more adults and kids on the spectrum, and to learn from them too. Once in a while, I was even able to help them out.

Since then, I've never stopped reading, attending conferences, and generally trying to insert as much information about the autism spectrum into my brain as possible.

That's where I have the advantage over a lot of parents and others whose days are filled with someone on the autism spectrum. I have the luxury of taking in more books, conferences, and first-person information than most people have time for.

LUCKY KIDS

So that's how I bring the best information I can to you: I read as much as I can, attend as many conferences as reasonably possible, interview professionals in the field of autism, and then I talk to regular parents and teachers to see how the research, theory, and concepts fit into the real world of raising kids with autism.

So why tell you so much about me? And why is the book full of first-person examples about my family?

It's partly because my brother and I got so lucky. Because after years of taking in all of the best data about autism I could find, what I found is that, in one way or another, my parents did a lot of the things that are now the latest and greatest concepts in teaching children on the autism spectrum. My dad says this is because my mom is smart and he is lucky. I say it's because they are both smart and both lucky.

It's partly because I wasn't so lucky all of the time. I went through some of the worst parts of growing up with undiagnosed Asperger's, and experienced in grueling detail the problems, misunderstandings, and sheer agony of dealing with people who did not understand—as well as the sheer agony of not understanding them.

It's also because I've had a lot of contact with a lot of people who have taught me by their actions, by their successes and failures in the process of raising children with ASDs. Heck, a lot of the time the failures lead to the successes. People who are willing to keep trying rather than give up experience both the pain and the triumph of trial and error. No pain, no gain.

But mainly it is because when I speak or consult on autism, no matter how good my raw data is, no matter how thorough my research may (or may not) be, I've found that what people learn the most from, and get the most help from, is the stories that I tell.

Writing up these stories for you is the most effective way I know of giving you concrete insights into the world of autistic learning. These insights will (hopefully) give you the chance to learn from others' mistakes and successes, and thus save you some time and grief in the process of learning to communicate vital life skills to kids who truly need them.

ONE SIZE DOES NOT FIT ALL

Your child, grandchild, sibling, student, or friend will probably not "fit" exactly into the examples herein. There's no set of rules for how to apply every idea to every child.

Fortunately, it isn't necessary to have exact directions for every child. The concepts in this book work across the board; for example, the idea of teaching a life skill like traffic safety involves teaching the same rules in multiple places where they apply, and giving the same information in multiple ways to find out what kind of input the child can process best. This is true whether a child is an "involved case" with classical autism or a hyper-bright kid with Asperger's.

Examples herein include those with children (and occasionally adults) who are nonverbal, highly verbal, visual thinkers, math thinkers, and verbal thinkers. The gang's all here!

Success Comes From Life Skills

Since most of the examples in this book are from my own and my brother's lives, I feel it would be good to give you yet a little more info on our diagnoses and limitations—but most importantly, about how our parents' rigorous life skills training has led to success for both of us.

MY DIAGNOSIS AND LIMITATIONS

As previously mentioned, my official diagnosis of Asperger's came when I was thirty-six, but that would have been my diagnosis all along if Asperger's had been understood. I started talking early, developed a huge vocabulary, and wouldn't shut up.

I also had severe problems learning in a normal classroom. Sensory issues made it very difficult to process what the teacher was saying in a room full of kids, many of whom were moving in their seats, rustling papers, opening books, using scratchy pencils, or whispering and passing notes.

Fluorescent lighting, "busy" classroom decorations, and teachers who believed that the classroom should be full of colorful educational input were also big interferences.

Socially and emotionally, I was always a few years behind my typical peers, and with little skill for reading faces and body-language, I was socially isolated and clueless as to why.

And then there were the meltdowns, the literal thinking, and all of those little things that conspire to make Asperger's invisible but crippling.

I struggled in school most of the time, never learned to study, or even to really figure out what I was supposed to be learning, managed to get through high school anyway, got into college, and promptly crashed and burned.

I'm no genius, but I'm bright enough—I just didn't have the social, emotional, and personal skills needed to be able to continue my education in college. I didn't understand how to get help in my classes or with dorm life, didn't have any idea of how to study, and was bewildered and upset by the strange social behaviors of college students. I only connected to people when classes truly threw me into working on projects with them—but promptly lost the connection due to my own inability to understand friendship maintenance.

However, my parents had taught me enough life skills that I was able to keep my head above water and struggle through life. I had severe problems from undiagnosed Asperger's, and it was my parents' emphasis on and teaching of life skills that got me through life to the point that I was able to keep going and have some really good things in my life despite the struggles.

My parents had taught me many basic skills that a lot of Aspies lack. They taught me about basic self-care, from bathing to making regular dental appointments. They taught me to be on time for work, and never to carry a balance on my credit cards.

They taught me to be polite, and to try my best to be thoughtful towards others. They taught me to dress appropriately, act decently, and to take morals and ethics seriously.

All of this meant that when I was having problems, I was often able to get help by asking politely and persistently.

It also meant that, even without a diagnosis, I was able to pursue relationships and eventually marry my husband Gary. Basic good manners, good hygiene, and knowing concrete ways to show caring made that possible.

Even without a diagnosis, I was able to (eventually) get through college. I knew how to be on time for my classes, how to introduce myself to professors early in the semester, and how to behave in class. Those were all early, simple lessons in life skills that paid off in a big way.

I'm a walking example of how life skills training can make life better for someone on the autism spectrum, even when undiagnosed Asperger's and misunderstood problems are causing serious failures and struggles. If the failures and struggles are punctuated by successes and determination, then it is absolutely possible to have a decent life.

But what, you may ask, does all this have to do with kids who are not so likely to be college bound? Well, the same techniques that worked for me were tweaked by my parents to help my brother as well.

MY BROTHER'S DIAGNOSIS AND LIMITATIONS

My brother Jimmy is what is often called "more involved." His official diagnosis has changed from PDD:NOS to autism to Asperger's to autism. He lives on the opposite coast from me (I'm in southern California, he's in the suburbs of Philadelphia), which affects what his diagnosis is.

That's right, exact diagnoses of where a child (or adult) is on the autism spectrum may vary according to where he lives. Different school districts and different social structures profoundly affect how autistic traits are seen and labeled. But that's a whole other book.

To be more straightforward about it, Jimmy has autism. He had a lot of the now-recognized symptoms from infancy on.

For example, as an infant, Jimmy was what they call "tactile defensive." That just means that he couldn't cope with certain kinds of touch, especially light or unexpected touch. In fact, he recoiled from light touch as an infant; my mom figured out quickly that firm touch worked better than light, and that giving Jimmy some control over when he was touched made him calmer and happier.

Jimmy did start saying words at roughly the right time for a child to start saying words, but he didn't use them as a typical toddler would. He was dependent on using gestures and on the fact that his family pretty much knew what he wanted and when.

He did all the classic autistic-kid things: spinning, obsessing on one topic, reacting really badly to changes in schedule, and failing to generalize information.

Then again, Jimmy and I both still obsess, dislike sudden or unexpected changes, and have difficulty with generalization.

It took a while to get Jimmy diagnosed, mainly because when doctors evaluated him, they would ask my mom things like "Does he obsess/spin/dislike change more than a typical child?"

Of course, my mother's frame of reference included me. As her first child, I got to set her idea of a "normal" range of behaviors. So, since the doctors really never defined what a normal amount of obsessive repetition or spinning was, she kept putting down that he did those things maybe just a bit more than normal. Because, heaven help her, I had partly formed her idea of normal.

So Jimmy's path and struggles have been very different than mine. However, my parents have continued to emphasize life skills in his upbringing.

Jimmy is now twenty-one years old. For years it has looked as though he would never get a high-school diploma, but he graduated in June of 2010. We were unsure whether he would ever be able to hold a job; he has a job and is a conscientious, hard worker.

Okay, so Jimmy is twenty-one, and yet I still occasionally have trouble figuring out whether he is talking about himself or relating an episode of *Arthur*. You would not mistake him for a "normal" twenty-one-year-old.

But he's come farther than we had any right to hope, and a large part of that arose from my parents' conscious decision to work on life skills, social skills, and functionality rather than on trying to jam every last scrap of academic knowledge he could possibly hold into his brain.

A guy can only do so much. My parents understood that teaching him life skills and developing the good habits that would make it possible for him to be a successful worker, successful at socializing, and able to cope with as much of life as possible, was infinitely more important than spending countless hours teaching him algebra.

I envy Jimmy. My parents were aware of his autism very early, they understood his deficits, and they focused on teaching him what he needed for *life* rather than on just academic learning. No, he doesn't "get" algebra, but he does know how to grocery shop, compare prices, and is thrilled to have a job and get an actual paycheck.

At Jimmy's age, I did not desperately want to get a job in my chosen industry, did not understand how to keep a friend, and was utterly unqualified to manage my own class-work. He got those things because my parents knew ahead of time that he would need them badly.

Jimmy's job, by the way, is working for food services at Villanova University—the first university I dropped out of. Twenty bucks says he'll be there longer than I was!

So that gives you a rough idea of where many of the examples in this book are coming from—and also some idea of how life skills relate to success in life and work. Life skills are about getting a life.

The Wacky World of Autism Terminology

I'd like to interrupt your regularly scheduled book here to address the issue of words about autism.

While there is a short glossary at the end of this book, I wanted to just give you a few quick words about the terminology used before we get started. There are a lot of words that are used to refer to or identify autism, and I'd like to mention the ones that are likely to be used here.

This book is about teaching life skills to children, teens (and possibly adults) who are "on the autism spectrum." Being on the autism spectrum means having one of several syndromes or disorders that are neurological in nature but have profound psychological, social, and academic impacts.

Some of the diagnoses included in the term *autism spectrum* are: autism, Asperger's Syndrome, PDD:NOS, and high-functioning autism. Sometimes children are diagnosed with "autism-related traits" or "autistic tendencies," or even just plain "autism spectrum disorder."

In contexts where autism is the main topic (such as this book), people with ASDs are sometimes just said to be "on the spectrum" with the word *autism* dropped out.

Exactly where one bit of the autism spectrum ends and the next begins is difficult to say. Depending on who is doing the diagnosing, the same child might be diagnosed differently under different circumstances. If you are not sure where "autism" ends and "Asperger's" begins, you are in good company.

All of those diagnoses that are considered to be "on the autism spectrum" can be referred to as "autism spectrum disorders" or ASDs for short. So, if a trait or problem is common in people with autism *and* those with Asperger's *and* those with PDD:NOS, then I might say the trait is common in people with ASDs.

To add to the confusion, sometimes people with a diagnosis of autism are called "people with autism" and sometimes they are called "autistics." There are tons of arguments on the Internet about why each of these terms is better, worse, or intolerable. Since part of my aim with this book is to help parents help their kids who have ASDs to be more able to assert their own humanity, I usually will use the term "person with autism."

There are also slang terms for autism: folks with autism or Asperger's may refer to themselves as "auties" or "Aspies," respectively.

I also use a lot of extra terms, including some that I've made up, just because I can. Terms like *Aspergians* and *autoids* (we're curiously curious) may pop up once in a while just because I like them and also because I feel the need to avoid being repetitively redundant.

I would be remiss if I didn't mention that many of the people who are doing cutting-edge research on autism (especially on the genetic and biological underpinnings) have been using the term *the autisms* instead of saying *autism*. This is because autism is not just one thing, and different bits of the spectrum can vary widely in their manifestations, treatments that are needed, and long-term prognosis. I don't use the term in this book, but it is something to note: we are not dealing with something that we have a nice tidy definition of. We are dealing with something we are only beginning to really understand.

Of course, there are terms used for people who do not have autism spectrum disorders. One frequently used term is *neurotypical,* which is short for *neurologically typical.* Sometimes neurotypicals are referred to as "NTs," if only because it is shorter.

The term *neurotypical* is to some extent lacking. We don't really have any really clear demarcation of what the full range of "typical" neurological traits is. And there is no reason to assume that all people who do not have an ASD are neurologically typical. There could be many variants in neurological makeup, both common and rare, that are not autism and not "normal."

Oh, that word: *normal.* Some folks still use *normal* to describe non-autistic people. Thing is, I know a *lot* of people who are not at all normal who are also not on the autism spectrum. In fact, I'm not really sure what a normal person would look or act like. And at all of the schools where I've done observations, I've never once seen a normal child. Frankly, they are all a little nuts.

Like the t-shirt says, "Normal is just a setting on a dryer."

The word more commonly used for "normal" people is *typical.* This term is often used in the phrase *typical peers,* which means children of the same age who are considered to be socially normal (whatever that is). So if someone tells you that a social skills class for children with autism includes typical peers for modeling, what that means is that there are children who do not have ASDs who will be "modeling" appropriate behavior—that is, acting like regular kids. Or rather, they will be acting like kids who are being prompted by adults to do certain things in a very artificial situation.

People who are not on the autism spectrum may also be called "normies" or "normals." Sometimes Aspies and auties use these terms in a friendly sort of way, and sometimes they are derisive. Usually you can tell from the context, but I don't use the terms because if you can't see my face or hear my voice, you won't know whether I am being facetious or insulting. This is something that most people with ASDs who are online don't seem to know. Scratch that: most people who are "talking" online don't seem to understand that their words can easily be misread. But again, that's a whole other book.

The biggest disadvantage of the words *normies* and *normals* is that the exact same terms are used by other groups in completely different contexts. For example, some bodybuilders will refer to non-bodybuilders as "normies."

Once in a while you will run into people on the spectrum who refer to NTs as "mundanes." It's a term out of the world of science fiction and fantasy fandom, and it refers to people who are not fans. If you did not count down the days until the release of the *Lord of the Rings* films, if you do not know who Joss Wheedon is, if you have no strong feelings one way or the other about any given episode of *Star Trek,* and if you don't have a painful love/hate relationship with George Lucas, you might well be a mundane.

And if you do care deeply about *The Lord of the Rings*, Joss Wheedon, *Star Trek*, and/or George Lucas, you should probably have your children screened for autism spectrum disorders, just in case.

Teaching Life Skills to the Spectrum Child:
Ideas and Examples

Learning How
We Learn

THINK REALLY DIFFERENT

Those of us who are on the autism spectrum can learn life skills, but differently. You and I know, or at least have been told, that children with autism spectrum disorders learn differently than typical children do. When teaching life skills, it is vital to understand and remember these learning differences.

No, you do not have to have a perfect, or even near-perfect, understanding of the autistic mind to be able to teach, support, and help your child. But having a good general idea of the kind of thinking differences that are likely to be there can help a lot.

I promise this whole section will be full of practical real-life examples of teaching life skills that will not only help you understand how autism affects the learning process, but also give you concrete ideas and insights. This is not a bunch of theory about thinking; this is about practical teaching ideas.

CHANGE YOUR MIND, CHANGE YOUR CHILD'S LIFE

This isn't minor stuff. When you look at your child from an autism-eye's perspective, you can change your relationship with your child and his or her disability.

When I was first diagnosed with Asperger's, my husband was supportive and interested in learning more. When I asked him to read Liane Holliday Wiley's *Pretending to Be Normal* so that he would learn more about ASDs, he did so willingly.

After he read the book, he came to me and told me it had really changed his point of view. He said, "It's as if for years I've been viewing you from a distance, seeing you walk along in the most peculiar way, and wondering why you walked so oddly. The book helped me see you closer up, and it's as if I suddenly could stand where I could see clearly that you are walking on a tightrope across a vast cavern, and you are acting as you do, not because you have a peculiar gait, but because that's how you have to walk to survive."

A HINT TO START YOUR JOURNEY

Please remember, as we go over the various aspects of autistic thinking, that many of the "bugs" in the mind of an autistic person may be, under other circumstances, a positive "feature."

No, not all problems are also strengths. We live in a society where having a low testable IQ is a major pain in the tuckus, and certainly self-destructive behaviors and lashing out at others don't have an upside, regardless of whether the person with those problems has an ASD or not.

But it will help you and your child a lot if you can look for the good parts, the strengths, and any benefits you might be able to find in your child's way of being. Children on the spectrum often get an endless round of appointments and lessons aimed at fixing them. It can get pretty grueling to be seen as more or less just a bundle of problems with feet on it.

This has major practical applications: a person who does not get any positive feedback for hard work will tend to give up. A person who believes that he or she is basically screwed up may well give up on being anything other than screwed up.

I know, an example is worth a thousand words of explanation. Here is one that touched me deeply, so deeply I can hardly tell you.

Two things my mom frequently told me matter a great deal. First of all, she often told me how nice it was that, from the time I was a baby, I could always amuse myself and be contented to play alone. It was wonderful, she said, that as a young mother she could put me in my crib or playpen with a few toys and I would be completely contented all by myself, so that she could easily write the checks to pay the bills or do other paperwork without being disturbed.

Over and over, I hear parents with kids with ASDs complain that their child wants to be alone too much and isn't interested in others. They don't see that the ability to flourish in solitude is a good thing; it's not a matter of making the child stop loving solitude, but of making sure the child can function with or without it.

Similarly, the second of the two things is that my mom often mentioned to me, "You are very stubborn. It's a really good thing to be, even though you are still learning what is and what is not important enough to be stubborn about. I know you'll work it out over time.

"What's really great about your stubbornness is that you won't do what people tell you to do unless you want to. That's great. I never have to worry about you giving in to peer pressure. No one can make you smoke or drink or do anything you don't want to."

The thing is, she was right. Being stubborn is a great trait if it means you don't give in when people try to push you around or want you to join in those oh-so-charming behaviors that many super-social teens (and adults) wind up participating in.

I'm absolutely *not* advocating a pollyanna-ish approach. I don't expect that when you get a call from the school about your child biting other children, you'll say, "Oh, well, at least that means he's got healthy teeth." No, not at all.

This is about appreciating any little things you can. Find things you can genuinely like about your child.

And please realize, as we go through these examples of how the autistic brain learns differently and what the difficulties here are, that there are some "bad" traits—like being a stubborn loner—that have real-life value. Value your child for whatever he or she is right now, and you'll get farther than if you are focused solely on the difficulties.

HOW WE DO AND DON'T LEARN

When I attend social skills classes and other training sessions designed to help children with autism/ASDs learn to deal with the world, I often see the telltale fragments of a common problem.

Most of those people who are trying to teach life skills and/or social skills to kids on the spectrum are speech pathologists, occupational therapists, and schoolteachers. These are, by and large, people with strong intuitive social skills and a really good ability to generalize information. Not only that, but these are folks who know a lot about child development and how children learn.

Poor bastards. They never see us coming.

Those of us who are on the spectrum (emphatically including me) learn differently than other children. Regardless of IQ, degree of sensory issues, ability to understand and use language, and all of those other variations between us, we all have some common problems with the learning process.

We are far less likely than normal to "get" implicit information. If we are able to understand and use implicit information under one circumstance, we may not be able to do the same elsewhere. A skill that we can produce in one classroom/building/situation may be completely useless once we are a few feet away from that situation.

Knowledge of context—understanding when and where a behavior is appropriate—and generalization—applying knowledge of the overall situation to the small parts of the situation—are not our strengths.

Here's an example of how context may or may not mean a lot to us: When I was a girl, I had a dollhouse that came with molded plastic furniture. The beds all had something odd about them: at the head of each plastic bed, there was a little molded-on plastic butter-mint. You know, like the ordinary butter-mints that are often used in favors at bridal showers and in candy dishes.

For years, this puzzled me. I knew from an early age that it was common for some hotels to leave mints on the pillow, but why would furniture for a dollhouse have that? It wasn't, after all, a doll motel. Plus, the butter-mints were in a far larger scale than the beds—the beds were tiny doll beds, the butter-mints were about the same size as real ones, only flatter.

I was in my twenties when it finally struck me that there were, in fact, no plastic butter-mints on the little doll beds. The flattened butter-mint shapes were actually the pillows on the doll beds!

I should mention that I am not one of those people who was non-verbal or who scored poorly on aptitude tests as a child. I was the classic Aspergian who spoke early and had a testable IQ a bit above average. If, at the time I was confused about the doll bed, you had asked me about the Revolutionary War, classical mythology, or how the Great Depression affected the content of popular films in the US, I would have been able to give you a quite a little oral dissertation.

None of that mattered when it came to connecting basic, practical knowledge from one area to another. Those little plastic pillows weren't actually shaped like pillows that I had seen, they were shaped like butter-mints I had seen, and so that is the category I put them in. The context—the fact that I was looking at a plastic bed with little plastic blankets— did not affect my inference.

AN (IM)PRACTICAL EXAMPLE

But of course, correctly labeling the parts of doll furniture isn't all that vital in childhood. Let's take an example of a very practical—in fact, vital—life skill.

It is an ordinary part of early teaching to make sure that all children know how, when, where, and whether to cross the street. Little kids are taught never to cross the street without holding an adult's hand, and it is a big leap towards "growing up" to be permitted to cross streets alone.

Of course, kindergartens often work with children in teaching street signs and safety, so it is generally considered that a child who has gotten up to, say, third grade in good academic standing will know how to cross the street successfully.

When I was in fifth, sixth, and seventh grade, I was absolutely qualified to cross streets where there were stop signs, but stoplights were a very different matter.

You see, I, as a 'tween and young teen, was a logical sort of person who tried to draw information from various sources to make sense of my world. Very sensible, very smart, right?

From when I was very young, when I crossed a street aided by an adult, I let the adult handle the details. I'm sure some of those adults made an effort to explain the whole walk/don't walk thing to me, but I wasn't necessarily interested in those details. The system seemed very self-explanatory to me.

What was obvious to me was this: when the sign says "WALK" or has the picture of a walking person, you should walk across the street.

Just as obviously, when the sign flashed a red light reading "DON'T WALK," it was absolutely imperative not to be in the street. Flashing lights mean EMERGENCY. Flashing lights on police cars, ambulances, and fire trucks mean "get over to the side and out of the road as much as possible NOW!!!!!!"

And on *Star Trek,* red flashing lights mean you're being shot at, possibly by Klingons or Romulans, so obviously you don't want to be out in the open during that!

Equipped with this absolutely logical, sensible knowledge, I was faced with a dilemma. If I started walking on the WALK signal, I would be in the street when the DON'T WALK light started blinking.

Obviously, when the DON'T WALK signal started, I could not continue to be in the street. I had to get out of the street, which meant running like heck for the closest curb.

With some streets, I could get far enough on the WALK signal to be close to the other curb and dash there upon the DON'T WALK signal. But often I had to run straight back to where I had come from, to avoid breaking the law.

It is, after all, against the law to continue driving down the middle of the street when a fire truck is flashing those lights behind you. Flashing red lights mean that it is not only imperative to get out of the street, but also legally required.

It could take a *lot* of light cycles to get across the street this way. A whole lot.

Eventually, I was able to work it out. After all, sometimes the medians in the center of the road were painted on instead of being raised and having curbs. This clearly meant that the painted lines between the lanes of the road were not actually *on* the road, but were, instead, functionally and legally, curbs.

So, when the DON'T WALK sign came on, I'd head straight for the nearest painted line and stand on it, as if it were a balance beam. If both of my feet were fully on the paint, then I was well within my "legal limits," and could wait there for the next WALK sign.

I cannot begin to tell you of the strange looks I got from the drivers in the lanes near me when I crossed the street. I didn't like being stared at, and felt confused when they vehemently gestured me to continue crossing, so I figured out another way.

Fortunately, I had heard of Schrödinger's Cat. I have been informed by several people who proofread an early version of this that using Schrödinger's Cat is too obscure and weird for a book on autism. Let me reassure the reader that you do not have to really totally understand the cat thing to get the idea I'm trying to communicate, and that this is the only such metaphor that is used anywhere in this book.

So, as I was saying, Schrödinger's cat is a physics parable involving a cat in a sealed box shielded against quantum decoherence. This feline may or may not have been poisoned depending on the state of a subatomic particle. Your local encyclopedia or Wikipedia can fill you in on the details.

This parable, this thought experiment, gives a mental picture of a case in which something is in two opposite states at the same time. The cat does not become specifically either alive or dead until it is observed (although, one might add, from the cat's point of view it is a moot point). This is because there are circumstances under which a subatomic particle takes on a definite state only after being observed.

Don't worry if you don't get it. Physicists were pretty weird even before the 20th century got underway, never mind after.

The point is that I decided that it could be logically argued that the sign did not say DON'T WALK in my frame of reference until I observed that it said DON'T WALK.

So what I started doing is this: as soon as I saw the sign say WALK, I'd start walking as fast as I could but *with my head down, eyes fastened to the ground, with my hands up beside my eyes like blinders.* No, I'm not kidding.

I felt I had a valid argument that made it not-illegal for me to continue walking when the sign blinked DON'T WALK if I never *saw* it blinking DON'T WALK.

This meant that for years I crossed the street in a position in which I could not possibly see any cars coming. If someone had made a turn without paying close attention, they could easily have flattened me. Being as I was not crossing the street in a box shielded from environmentally induced quantum decoherence, nor was my death dependent on the state of a subatomic particle, I would have been dead right off the bat.

(Sorry about the lame geek humor. I'll try to rein that in a bit. Also, I promise there will be no more physics from here on in.)

Eventually, I did learn that one is actually permitted and encouraged to keep crossing when the light blinks DON'T WALK. At this point, I live near Brea, CA where many of the lights feature a little explanation of what to do during each state of the WALK sign, which I find very reassuring.

The point is, I was bright enough and odd enough to derive my street-crossing habits from a *gedanken* experiment from 1935, but was absolutely not able to figure out the correct understanding of how to cross the street.

When I saw that clip from *Rain Man* where Raymond stops dead when the sign blinks DON'T WALK, I was sooooooo happy. Someone, somewhere, was responding appropriately to those goofy blinking lights. It didn't matter that it was a fictional person, it was an example of someone doing the sane thing in an insane world, and it warmed my heart.

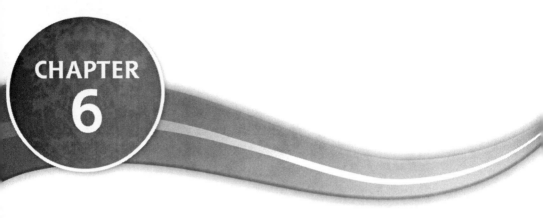

Say What You Need to Say

It can be hard for humans to really say what they mean to say.
Our whole system of communication is based on the idea that our
words don't have to literally match our meaning to be understood. So
much of what we say is interpreted by others through context, tone,
and social understanding that we don't need to be very literal or very
exact. Usually.

When you are teaching a child with an ASD, you really, truly have
to learn to say what you really need to say.

"Normal" ways of teaching common activities and courtesies are hor-
ribly mired in non-literal, even ridiculous, language.

*People on the autism spectrum need their information to come in literal,
user-friendly language.* This includes those children who are Aspergian
"little professors" and understand elaborate metaphors in literature. This
also includes those children who have "more involved" forms of autism
who are used to hearing non-literal language at home, or who have mastered some non-literal phrases.

I'm not in the camp that says you should never use non-literal language, sarcasm, or tongue-in-cheek humor around kids with ASDs.

Those things are a normal part of life, and may even be used to teach, depending on the child and the situation.

However, giving non-literal instructions or directions to people on the spectrum is a great way to get behavior you do not want. It's hard to be "compliant" when you have no idea what your parents and teachers are asking for.

So ask for what you want, rather than asking for something abstract. For example, when I was about eight, I had dinner at the home of my only school friend, and when I asked for the bread to be passed, her mother said, "What's the magic word?" I was puzzled. While I thought she was slightly mad for injecting such a non sequitur into the conversation, I politely replied, "Abracadabra."

This was apparently not the right answer, so she kept asking me for the magic word, and I kept obliging her obvious but mild insanity by coming up with every magic word I could think of: hocus-pocus, bibbity-bobbity-boo, alakazam, Shazam, open sesame ... you get the idea.

Finally, she told me I was supposed to say *please* when asking for something to be passed. This was apparently what she had intended to communicate when asking for the magic word.

What I learned from this event was that (1) my friend's mother was mental and (2) she was not shy about correcting a guest publicly and at length at the table. I decided, however, that there was no point in holding it against her. After all, everyone has some bad behaviors, and hers seemed eccentric but minor.

By the way, this event was one of those that led to my feeling ever more puzzled by the adults around me. I could toss off a perfectly simple reference to Dorothy Parker or the *Aeneid,* and they would act like something was wrong with me, yet they constantly coughed up the most ludicrous sentences and expected me to accept them. Another little brick in that wall of mistrust and confusion that led to my working hard to hide my problems and become invisible whenever I could.

If you want your child to say (or sign) *please*, then tell them so, clearly. Please.

When I was much older, and had gone to the doctor with an earache, I ran into another truly strange phrase commonly used to teach children. He asked if I had been using q-tips to clean inside my ears, and I said, "No, my mother told me never to put anything in my ear."

"... that's smaller than your elbow, right?" he asked, as if he were ending my sentence.

"Um, no," I said, "She just told me not to put stuff in my ear."

He said that many of his patients were familiar with the "smaller than your elbow" phrase. I was astonished. If my mother had ever said such an insane thing to me, I would have spent the day first trying to get my elbow into my ear, and then eventually would have graduated to making a model elbow of clay or wood in order to see how far it would go into my ear. Eventually, the process would have broken down into just putting any object I could find into my ear and then measuring it to compare it to the measurements of my elbow. I doubt I would have stopped before getting something lodged in there.

DON'T SAY IT IF IT AIN'T TRUE

It is usually a good thing to think about what the result of following instructions absolutely literally would mean. Directions you might give to the average person can become dangerous if given to someone on the spectrum—or even someone who isn't quite on the spectrum

My dad does not have an ASD, but he is male and he is an engineer, which puts him only a few percentiles away from Asperger's. Upon becoming a father again while well into his forties, he decided he needed to take better care of his health. He read *Fit or Fat* and some related books and advice, and thus he found, in print, the instruction of a real, actual medical doctor: "You can't eat too little fat." This advice was given as part of instructions for living longer and avoiding heart ailments.

My dad cut his fat intake down to well under 10% of his daily calories. I cannot tell you how dangerous that is. The human body is not able to function well on that little fat input. In the long run, it could compromise one's chances for survival.

Fortunately, my dad is also a smart guy who goes to his doctor when he feels ill—another thing he does to make sure he's around for as much of his kids' lives as possible. His doctor was naturally appalled to find out about the far-too-low-fat diet, and got him to boost his fat intake significantly.

The doctor who wrote that you could not possibly cut down your fat intake too much was using a rule of thumb that most doctors use: assume that the patient will only comply with maybe 80% of your recommendation. Doctors also usually assume that patients will overstate the amount of exercise they do and understate how much coffee, alcohol, and junk food they take in. I'm fairly sure that my doctor doesn't completely understand that when I say I drink four cups of coffee a day, I mean that I always have exactly that number of cups of coffee, by actual count, every morning. Aspies are often like that.

Of course, I would like to point out that when it comes to things like diet and exercise, "normal" people are at least as strange as people with ASDs. When everyone was eating low-fat, an awful lot of people believed they could eat as much of anything "fat free" as they liked, and so would down tubs of Red Vines like they were mother's milk. Then when "low-carb" was everyone's mantra, people believed they were preventing possible heart problems by eating a pile of bacon for lunch and then having a good snack of expensive, calorie-laden, nutrition-free "dietetic" low-carb ice cream.

(Let me say right here that the above last sentence should not be taken to mean that I am anti-bacon. Bacon is good. It's just silly to think of it as "health food.")

Then there was the period where running was the "perfect exercise" to lose weight, and a lot of very heavy people did their knees a lot of damage. Pretty much any observer of our culture could come up with other examples of how normal, perfectly neurologically typical people, will take the current common wisdom on health and diet and take it to silly extremes.

So it is not all that uncommon for humans in general to have difficulty making sense of the life rules they are given. Given that, please be as patient as possible with the child who thinks that using "Shout" laundry stain remover requires actual shouting.

DID YOU REALLY THINK ABOUT IT BEFORE YOU MADE THE RULES?

Rules are often extremely important to people with ASDs, all throughout the autism spectrum. This is part of why Carol Gray's Social Stories™ are so wonderful: they can lay out the rules for specific situations in a pleasant, supportive way. This informative input can greatly help children to understand the situation.

Knowing that rules are important, and that they will usually be followed in a completely literal way, think carefully when making rules, especially written rules. A child with autism will often do exactly what the rules say.

In one instance, I walked into a social skills class for children all along the spectrum, and found there was a list posted of "Our Classroom Rules." One of the rules was (I am not making this up), "We do not hit our friends."

Okay, on the one hand it is important for little Aspies and auties to learn that hitting friends is bad. Sometimes we have difficulty understanding that giving someone a good thump or two can have a negative effect on the friendship.

On the other hand, to a literal minded child, "We do not hit our friends" means exactly that—there is only that partial, very specific restriction on exactly who it is that "we" can hit. We can freely hit our enemies; or people we do not like very much; or people we are usually friends with but do not feel friendly towards today, although then again they might be our friends tomorrow and then we would not be allowed to hit them.

I'm sure the teacher who posted that rule had no idea that she was posting blatant permission for hitting quite a lot of other children. She assumed that all children would understand the non-literal, implied meaning of the rule rather than the actual literal meaning.

What is worse, the actual rules about hitting in grade school are not at all simple. Kids have different levels of hitting, and different levels of fighting. There is such a thing as "play-fighting" where the level of violence is limited to what will not do serious harm; there are also situations where hitting is absolutely de rigueur for the "normal" kids.

For example, there is a stage during which, when boys play tag with no teachers and no girls present (or only a tomboy or two involved), they don't so much tag each other as slug each other. A boy who runs to tell an adult that "they're hitting hard!" is not going to get to play again, and is certain to be labeled a pansy, which is not good when you are eight and just want to get from the classroom to the playground without being clobbered.

I would not suggest that we actually teach our kids to hit; heaven knows that most kids on the spectrum don't have a good estimate of their own strength, and could either wind up gently fanning someone who was seriously beating them up, or else really pummeling some kids who were just goofing around and not fighting seriously.

So I would suggest the simple change of: "We do not hit our friends" to "Do not hit people." And in such a classroom, it might well be a good idea to use Social Stories for each of the rules over the course of the semester.

Mind you, posting rules where they can be clearly seen is great. It gives the children a fighting chance at doing what they need to do. But the rules have to be literally true.

BE AWARE OF POSSIBLE (LITERAL) CHALLENGES

Literal thinking can interfere with learning life skills in other ways as well. Some children on the spectrum (including me) can take certain statements in a literal way such that they see a rule as a literal, personal challenge. This may not always be avoidable, but it happens often enough that I include it here so that if you see it, you might recognize it and be able to correct the problem.

One mistake I've seen several times is that of telling a child he "cannot" do something or "must" do a certain task before beginning another. If you tell a child he "cannot" hang from the chandelier, he may not understand that this just means there is a rule that hanging from chandelier is a punishable offense. He may decide, instead, to determine whether or not you are correct. Those of us with Asperger's can take a particular delight in proving others wrong, and it is hard for a little Aspie to pass up that kind of opportunity.

Similarly, if you tell a little Aspie that he "must" clean up his room before he eats, he may well engage you in a very long argument in which he will explain, repeatedly and in detail, that his ability to consume food is in no way contingent on the state of his room.

It is much safer to simply say, "Clean your room now." Then deal with enforcement and discipline as usual.

While "more involved" (less smart-ass) children may not argue or feel the need to prove you wrong, they may well have a similar reaction. After all, words like "cannot" and "must" aren't very informative, and if they don't come with a little extra information, they may sound pretty silly. Of *course* we can run the water in the bathtub until it overflows—all it takes is a little effort and a washcloth jammed into the overflow outlet. See, Mom, there *is* a way to do it, and aren't you proud that I figured it out all by myself?

In other words, if you tell a child he "cannot" do something, there had better be a reason. Usually the only reason you need is "it's a rule." But it can't hurt to say, "The rule says you can't climb on the roof," which is factual as soon as the rule-maker (you) states it, rather than "You can't," which the autie/Aspie listener may take to be just plain inaccurate on your part.

There is also the directive "Don't climb onto the roof." This avoids any absolutes or confusion. And if the reason is asked for, the first reason given should be "It's a rule." All other reasons are secondary, as other reasons might be argued with.

Yes, I was as likely to think this way as any child. I did not believe that the word *can't* should be used unless it was literally correct. And sometimes I went out of my way to prove that it wasn't.

When I was in third grade, my mother bought me a pair of Toughskins™ jeans. If you are unfamiliar with these, they were an invention of the mid-1970s: jeans designed not to rip or tear. The toughness of the jeans seemed to be based on making them out of some strange amalgam of canvas and plywood.

Those Toughskins™ had a tag on them that said that you couldn't rip through the knees, guaranteed. I begged to wear them as soon as possible, and immediately after dinner I went out into the backyard.

Our backyard jutted out from the house into a bit of a plateau, leading to a short slope, which ended in another little plateau. This provided the perfect venue for my work.

I used the first plateau as a runway to work up some speed, and then threw myself down the hill on my knees, skidding to a stop on the second plateau. Over, and over, and over.

It took twenty-seven run/skid/stop sequences to do it, but I did it! I ran into the house, proud as I could be, yelling, "Mommy, Mommy, I did it!"

Yes, I had gone straight through the knees of my brand-new Toughskins. And I was *thrilled* that I'd done it. A challenge had been issued, in print, and I had risen to it and bested those blasted jeans.

So do be aware, literal thinking can affect how children view concepts like "can't," "must," and "need to." It isn't that you can't ever use those words, but it is good to be aware of potential pitfalls. A word to the wise.

Transmit Information in More than One Way

When your child has trouble processing incoming information, it is a great idea to communicate the same information in multiple ways.

Since my brother and I both developed fairly good receptive language early, a lot of the examples I give from my own life include the use of verbal information—that is, my parents taught us a lot of things by telling us about them. However, talking alone did not work for either of us.

Visual aids and demonstrations are key to teaching any child, even more so for a child with an autism spectrum disorder. Human beings in general are unlikely to learn from just being told; all children are more likely to imitate what their parents actually do than what they say when there is a difference between the two.

Yes, I know that children with ASDs are much less likely to pick up implied information or to imitate others than typical children are. This is usually true when the implied information is new, different, or difficult. We fail to imitate others when we have no interest in their behavior, or we don't see any reason for their behavior. We do a great job of imitating behaviors that are obvious to us, interesting to us, or seem like they are very cool.

The first time I was in a psychiatrist's office, the diagnosis of "Asperger's Syndrome" did not exist. It was 1974, so the idea that autism was part of a spectrum of neurological disorders that included many people with normal testable IQs simply did not exist.

However, the psychiatrist involved did come up with a diagnosis: she said I had an Electra complex, also known as a "father fixation." Even in 1974, this was about as coherent as diagnosing me with a cause of apoplexy and prescribing leeches as a cure, but there was a reason for her idea.

Well before the age of eight, my mannerisms, speech patterns, and smallest actions were modeled on those of my father. Why? Because when I asked why the sky was blue, he explained that the reason the sky looks blue is because of the way the light from the sun is affected and reflected by our atmosphere. When I asked why glasses of cold soda got all wet on the outside, he explained how condensation formed. And when I got a remote control car (it came with a doll called "Baby Go Bye-Bye"), he commandeered it and created obstacle courses for it around the living room.

In short, my dad was an engineer and therefore, to me, the coolest guy on the planet. My mom was concerned with sane, important day-to-day things like getting me to function; my dad was concerned with science—and I was pretty darn sciencey myself.

So, while I failed to imitate my peers in school, had no idea of the "hidden curriculum" or unwritten rules of school and of children's play, and was socially and academically struggling because I simply lacked an understanding of the most basic coping skills for the classroom, I imitated my dad's every mannerism.

Children with autism will pick up all sorts of implied information from whatever sources they are naturally focused on. This means that if you really, really have their attention, they will do what you *do*, not what you *say*. Which means that when you yell, they learn to yell, because you have their attention while you are yelling even if they have no idea what you are yelling about.

WHAT IF WORDS DON'T WORK?

Many children on the spectrum have "poor receptive language." This is a somewhat jargony phrase that just means there are people with ASDs who can't always process or understand what you are telling them in words. Some kids have poor receptive language all of the time; some have a serious deterioration in their ability to understand language when they are stressed.

This means that there are both children and adults on the spectrum who seem to be "non-compliant" but who actually just can't process much in the way of verbal directions. You can't follow instructions that you don't understand.

This is where visual aids are a matter of utmost necessity. There are books, Web sites, and programs out there that can help you develop visual aids. There is a nice set of these in the "Recommended Resources" section at the back of the book, under "Visual Support."

Please, please, please don't hesitate to use whatever visual communication aids you can find that work for your child. Kids who can't understand verbal communication are more likely to retreat mentally, and you need to throw them a rope before they give up on any but the simplest interaction.

And for those who don't absolutely need visual aids for everything, don't dismiss the idea completely. I've described the limitations and abilities my brother and I have; we both have decent receptive language and have for quite a while. But that doesn't mean we can really effectively learn everything that way.

Parents and teachers (and pretty much everybody a child encounters) love to tell children what to do, and then tell them the consequences for not doing it, or the reward for doing it. Hearing this out loud is often not even close to being enough for the child with an autism spectrum disorder.

When I was a kid, my parents had a terrible time getting me to do chores. When my brother was little, and even today, my parents have little trouble getting him to do his scheduled chores. It's really easy. The difference is in the clarity of the rules and in the visual aids. I had none. He had lots. Lucky duck.

MY CHILDHOOD CHORE SCHEDULE

When I was growing up, my parents expressed my chore list in the vaguest possible terms, and those only verbally. My mother would tell me, "It's your turn to do the dishes after dinner." That was it. I was supposed to do the dishes after dinner.

I don't know if you are aware of this, but "after dinner" covers a lot of ground. In fact, if the dishes are those that become dirty during any given dinner period, the time that is defined by the term "after dinner" logically is that which corresponds with the rest of all time until/unless a major disaster causes the utter destruction of said dishes, in which case they will not have to be washed.

So my mom would tell me I had to do the dishes after dinner. There were no particular restrictions on my activities between when dinner ended and washing the dishes began; I could watch TV, read, or do whatever in between. And there was no specific time for doing dishes, and no specific deadline. The only rule I ever noticed was that if I failed to do the dishes before I went to bed, my mom would have a giant hairy cat fit in my direction.

This did not work well. My mom was constantly annoyed by how long I took to do the dishes, and I was constantly annoyed by the fact that she kept asking me when I intended to do them. The answer was obvious: I was going to put off doing the dishes as long as possible. After all, this meant that the little criticisms of how I did dishes would be put off as long as possible, which meant she would have less time to tell me what I had done wrong if I just waited.

As for the rest of my chores, the only schedule I knew about took place once or twice a year. My sister and I would do less and less around the house over time, my mom would get more and more frazzled and frustrated about it, and finally she would tell Dad how much of too much of us not helping she had had.

Then Dad would sit Catherine and me down for a talk. He would explain that Mom and he had many responsibilities, and that we should also take some responsibility for the household, and that this meant we should help a lot more around the house. This talk was heavy on why we *ought* to do more but did not include any specific schedules, lists, or chore charts.

So Cath and I would start doing things around the house. However, we had no idea what we were really supposed to be doing, so we'd always wind up getting a short, sharp talk about what we *ought* to be doing instead of what we already had done, or perhaps a similar little talk on how we had not done the chore properly anyway. Since this was never in the form of a schedule, but only in the form of being given another chore or being asked to redo a chore differently at that moment, we had no idea of what chores we were to do from day to day or week to week.

Eventually, we'd get frustrated by our own inability to figure out the right pattern of chores, so we'd gradually stop doing one chore after another, and then we'd be doing almost nothing for months, and then Mom would get upset that we weren't helping around the house, and then Dad would give us another lecture, and we were off and running again.

You can see that this would be a difficult thing for any child to figure out, but for me, an Aspie, it was crazy. My sister always seemed to be able to do at least a bit of the right thing, enough so that my parents would enumerate her activities to me as examples of what I should be doing, but I could never find that place where I was doing stuff right on a regular basis.

The less concrete the instructions given, the less any child, anywhere on the spectrum, learns. It didn't matter that I could read, or that I'd aced algebra. None of those "smarts" mattered when it came to the tasks of day-to-day living.

WHAT I WANTED

Once, I slept over at a friend's house (both friends and sleepovers were rarities for me), and on Saturday morning, she and her sister got out their chore chart and started doing their chores. Each chore was listed on the day it was done, with a special separate section for Saturday morning that included the amount each chore was worth written next to it. Hence, their allowances tied into the chore chart: fail to vacuum the house, that's $1.00 off right there.

I was enchanted by this. It seemed so cool; the fact was, this was the coolest friend I'd ever managed to have, so anything she did was cool to me.

When I got home, I accosted my father and suggested we have the same kind of system: a chore chart tied in to our allowances that would be posted where it was readily visible.

He turned me down. I haven't the foggiest idea why, but he didn't like the idea. It sort of seemed that he felt we shouldn't be limited by a written list, since it was impossible to be sure what would need doing when. He wanted to keep the verbal notification system, where he and Mom would give us information about what kinds of things needed doing and a general idea of how frequently different chores had to be done.

My parents are brilliant, wonderful people whom I love dearly. This book is full of examples of how they taught me to function by teaching me the life skills I needed to survive and, eventually, thrive in the world. But they blew it on the chore thing.

And they were constantly frustrated by the problem of getting me to do chores, getting me to do chores on time, and getting me to do chores correctly. It was an endless problem for them.

WHAT MY BROTHER GOT

When my brother Jimmy was born, my dad told me, "We're not going to make the same mistakes with Jimmy that we made with you and Catherine. We're going to make a whole new set of mistakes." You've gotta love an honest man.

Jimmy did get some great parents who my sister and I had thoroughly broken in for him. He also got a diagnosis of PDD:NOS when he was four. My dad called me and told me how thrilled he was that they finally knew what was going on with Jimmy, so they could find out how to help him. It was a red-letter day all around.

Having an accurate diagnosis of an autism spectrum disorder is a great thing. It opens the door to learning, surviving, and thriving at the best rate possible. It opens the door to help and support. (And yes, it also means going from being "regular parents" straight into a crash course in becoming the Navy Seals of the parenting world.)

It also meant that my parents were able to find lots of good advice and guidance through reading and through talking to teachers, OTs, and speech pathologists. And what they were told was that, while Jimmy could talk, and had a good ability to understand what people were saying a lot of the time, he needed clear visual structure and support to get through the day.

One of the things this meant was a chore chart. He had to have a clear visual chart with pictures of the things he needed to do. He needed to be able to see his accomplishments being marked off as he got through each chore, activity, or responsibility. He needed to see it as well as hear it, and it needed to all be there, on the fridge, where he could consult it, ponder it, or just check it out any time he wanted.

Obviously, the charts had to start with simple things he needed to do: Wash up. Brush teeth. Put toys in toy box. All things that could be marked off easily.

Less obviously, the charts had to include anything he could earn by doing chores (and anything he could lose by not doing them). Fifteen minutes of computer time needed to be visually represented so he could have a clear set of fifteen-minute chunks of time that could be added to or taken away.

If you use these kinds of supports, it gives children anywhere along the spectrum a crystal-clear idea of what is expected. Using visual supports that include both visual schedules or "to-do" charts AND lists of what can be earned or lost can give your child a chance at learning about cause and effect visually.

My brother was far, far quicker to do his chores than I had ever been. It wasn't because I was an "unmotivated" (lazy), "underachieving" (lazy), and "distractible" (lazy) child the way my report cards had always said. It was because he had really, really clear requirements and expectations set up for him, so he knew what the heck he was supposed to do and when he was supposed to do it.

Trust me, if I'd had a chart on the fridge that showed that I had to "do the dishes" on certain nights, with a note that "dishes must be done before any television or reading," my mom would not have had one-tenth the trouble she had. If I'd had a chart showing that I had to vacuum my room weekly, scrub the tub every other week, and dust monthly to get my allowance, I'd have gotten the chores done. And yes, maybe there would have been grumbling, balking, or just crabbiness involved, but a clear set of expectations and consequences would have gone very, very far in getting me motivated.

And having VISUAL REMINDERS is non-optional, even for the most verbal kids. You can say, "Make your bed every morning" a thousand times, and it won't mean as much as a clear list with a little icon of a made bed to check off each day.

This isn't a book on creating and using visual aids. There are people who have created great resources on that (some are listed in the "Recommended Resources" section at the back of this book). But I'd be remiss if I didn't include the information that you need to seriously look into using simple visual aids.

Visual aids don't hurt non-autistic kids either, by the way. Having visual aids in the classroom can help everybody. Having visual aids in the home can promote clear communication between parents and children. You will not hurt any other kids who happen to be present by having visual aids as part of your parenting or teaching tool kit.

Information in Translation:
Speak the Language Your Child Understands

A major issue in teaching life skills to children on the autism spectrum is that it is often tricky to communicate well with people on the spectrum at all. Mind you, "normal" children can be pretty hard to communicate with too, being as they are born with only two main modes of communication: crying and emitting various bodily fluids.

Eventually, the "normal" children do learn to talk, although you never really know how much they understand. Eventually, most kids on the spectrum learn to talk, or to use PECS, or to sign, or to type, or something useful like that. But it can still be difficult to really communicate.

It is key to remember that communicating with humans is not just about things like IQ and the number of words they know. If it were that simple, we'd be able to make nice, friendly charts that listed the correct instructions to give to any child based on those numbers.

Unfortunately (and fortunately) human beings are more complicated than that, and children with ASDs are very, very human.

It isn't just a matter of knowing that a child has "good receptive language" or can use 572 different Picture Exchange Communication System (PECS) cards. Paying attention to the reactions you get from your child when you use different types of communication, including different types of verbal communication, is very important.

USING WORDS: SOMETIMES LESS IS MORE

I get to observe a lot of classes, and it's pretty fun, mainly because I am not the person who is trying to convince a room full of children that they really want to glue macaroni onto an industrial thread spool to make a "Christmas tree" or "Hanukah cone" or whatever. But this class observation was different. It was really, really hilarious. Potentially disastrous, but hilarious.

I had been asked to observe a teacher's class because the teacher, whom we will call "Miss Smith," was really struggling to get even the most minimal compliance from the children. She was frustrated, confused, and didn't know what to do—and the children pretty much felt the same.

Miss Smith had been given, for her very first assignment as a new teacher, a class of nine children, four of whom were nonverbal children with autism, two of whom had Down's Syndrome, and the rest of whom had various developmental disabilities. Miss Smith's entire previous classroom experience had been student-teaching a class of typical fifth graders.

While this situation would be an ideal set-up for an inspiring movie about a young, inexperienced teacher using her moxie, spunk, and sheer "heart" to reach a classroom full of kids others had believed hopeless, in real life it was a mess. Miss Smith had therefore very sensibly called everyone she could think of who might be able to help her teach these kids, and through one of her contacts I had been drafted into a team of observers who were there to figure out how to make the school year work.

There were two aides in the classroom; Aide HappyChick, who had quite a bit of training and experience working with disabled kids, and Aide GrumpsaLot, who had no such experience and training. Yes, the teacher who had not ever taught a disabled child was given a brand-new aide who really, really didn't seem to like kids much. Sometimes even good school districts get bad karma.

Shortly after I arrived with the rest of the team, it was time for the children to "rotate" activities. Each of the three little groups of children was supposed to go to the next table, where an educational activity would take place. Aide HappyChick had to leave the room momentarily, so the rotation was to be accomplished with two adults supervising.

It looked like the class was actually going to quietly proceed to their next task when one child, Edgar, decided he wanted to run around the room repeatedly. Edgar was a fairly bright young autistic boy with no ability to speak.

So there's Edgar, having the time of his life running up and down one side of the classroom, occasionally stopping, looking around like a hyperactive meerkat, and then running again. He's happy, he's active, but he sure isn't going to his station to do his next task.

Miss Smith took immediate action. In a rather pleading voice she started explaining the problem to Edgar at quite a clip: "Edgar, you have a choice of what to do now and a good choice would be to sit down at your station. If you run around and up and down, we can't start our next activity, and I need you to sit down or everyone else has to wait for you. You're making a bad choice to keep running, and I need you to make a good choice so we can all stay on schedule and be on time for recess...."

She didn't stop talking, she just kept reiterating all of the reasons it would be a "better choice" for Edgar to sit down.

Meanwhile, Aide GrumpsaLot decided she'd need to grab Edgar and darn well make him sit down. This meant that she started chasing Edgar, much to his delight. The fact that she had very short legs and was rather out of shape meant that Edgar could easily outmaneuver her, and he would allow her to almost catch him and then dart away at the last moment. She was chasing him—it was a cool game—life was fun!

Oh, and Aide GrumpsaLot was also trying to verbally control Edgar by saying, "You've got to sit down now, stop running away from me, you aren't supposed to run away, you're supposed to sit down now."

At one point, after Edgar had escaped her grasp for perhaps the twentieth time, Aide GrumpsaLot put her hands on her hips, glowered at Edgar, and said, "Enough is enough already!"

I was watching all of this quite attentively, thinking to myself, "I will not laugh, I will not laugh, I will not laugh, I will not laugh." I know I should have been thinking about how to help Miss Smith learn to handle things better, but it was so darn hilarious. My demeanor was not helped by the fact that Aide Grumpsalot had a really, really orange spray tan, which made it all look even funnier.

Then Aide HappyChick walked in. Assessing the situation in roughly half a second, she walked over to the next activity table, pulled out a chair and said, "Edgar, sit here."

And without hesitation, Edgar did.

Edgar was not a difficult, obstreperous, "non-compliant" child—well, not at that moment. He was bright enough and energetic enough that I'm sure he wasn't always perfect.

However, right then, Edgar happened to be a person who was completely happy to do exactly as he was asked. Not only that, he did his next activity—tracing his name— quickly and well.

Edgar knew the meanings of a lot of words. He even knew what "good," "bad," and even "choice" meant. What Edgar could not do is understand a long series of non-literal instructions that had nothing to do with what either Miss Smith or Aide Grumpsalot actually wanted.

Miss Smith told him, "You have a choice." She didn't actually mean it. As long as he was being told he had a choice, why on earth would he not choose to run around and play?

Of course, there is every chance that Edgar did not understand a word of what Miss Smith was saying. She was using a huge flurry of non-literal language. Huge flurries of language do not make sense to most kids when they are running around and playing—how the heck would a nonverbal first grader with autism possibly figure out what all of her "good choice" vs. "bad choice" jargon actually meant?

Aide Grumpsalot didn't help by chasing Edgar around. Instead of going where he needed to go, she was, as far as he could tell, playing with him. She made stern faces at him and put her hands on her hips—which meant absolutely nothing to a child who could not read faces or body language, and who was running away from (not even facing) her anyway.

The thing that nearly made me laugh despite myself was when Aide Grumpsalot said, with such firmness and finality, "Enough is enough!" How was Edgar to guess that the desired/expected response to "enough is enough" was to stop running and sit in a particular seat at a particular table?

Since when do all young children, even typical children, know what the very non-literal phrase "enough is enough" means? It's not an obvious meaning.

There are, absolutely, times when children (all children) run around and play when they are not supposed to. There are times when children disobey direct instructions, even if those instructions are clear. There are times when children just plain misbehave. Heck, if a parent tells me that since they put their child on three medications he never misbehaves, I ask what on earth they are drugging him with to cause such strange behavior!

Despite all of the above caveats, a lot of children, including a lot of children on the autism spectrum, are pretty willing to be cooperative and helpful quite a bit of the time. They might not like going to school or learning new life skills, but they will at least sometimes cooperate and learn—if they are not too tired or hungry and have adequate breaks for play and rest.

Edgar was actually really good at following instructions, as long as someone actually gave him real instructions that made sense to him.

Just so you know: the observing team included people who worked with children with autism in that school district. We immediately worked out a plan to teach the teacher and get a different aide and a second teacher in there.

While my part of giving feedback, suggestions, and instructions was soon over, the two district staffers continued on to put together a whole plan that got those kids and that teacher working and learning together. It turned out okay, although I believe someone caught all blazes for the mix-up that had resulted in the assignment of Aide Grumpsalot and that teacher to that class.

SO WHAT DOES THIS MEAN TO ME (YOU)?

What this means is that you are going to have to do some detective work if/when your child doesn't respond to or cooperate with your attempts to teach life skills.

Some children, like Edgar, can follow one short, clear instruction at almost any time, but get completely lost if they are given long, involved, or detailed instructions.

Some children find it almost impossible to follow verbal directions without some kind of visual aid. A visual aid can be as simple as demonstrating what you want the child to do, or as complex as editing together a video of classmates doing a task for the child to watch and re-watch (and re-watch, and re-watch).

Don't worry; if your child cannot follow you when you act out a task or show him what you want him to try to do, it doesn't mean you have to immediately make an elaborate movie montage. There are plenty of things in between. Here are a few tips.

The first attempt to teach a life skill should most likely be simply walking through the situation with the child and briefly telling and showing him what you want to do. Don't make up elaborate icons,

Social Stories, or PowerPoint presentations (yes, I knew a dad who did that) until you try very basic ways of giving instructions.

If nothing else, making that first basic attempt is likely to give you an idea of what the child thinks is appropriate to do, and if they have any understanding of the activity.

When teaching anything, remember your child is an individual. A lot of children, especially young children, on the autism spectrum need really short, straightforward instructions, but there will be the occasional hyper-verbal Aspie like me who prefers long, elaborate, detailed explanations. Once you get a handle one what floats your particular child's boat, milk that for all it's worth.

(Ha! I just pictured a milk boat. The sails are white with black spots.)

Remember that human beings, including children, vary through the day. Hey, I love those elaborate verbal instructions and discussions in the morning, but around 7:00 P.M. I can't handle anything more elaborate than, "You want a cup of decaf, honey?" Fortunately, my husband figured out early that I like to watch Science Channel specials on string theory during the daytime but prefer to re-watch my favorite MST3K episodes (that I've already watched several dozen times) in the early evening. It's my "down time."

This last boils down to: don't try to get your child to be learning, learning, learning 24/7. Children really do need play and rest to digest and process all the information they get in a day.

When giving verbal instructions, in most cases, fewer words are better. Try keeping it short, simple, and straightforward.

Instead of, "I need you to march upstairs and straighten up that room right now mister, if you know what's good for you," try one of these (according to your child's age and understanding):

- "Clean your room starting at one this afternoon."
- "Clean your room now."
- "Put your toys in the toy box."

- "Toys in toy box." (Then, after that is done) "Clothes in hamper." (And so forth.)
- A nonverbal demonstration.
- Or you could just sing that darn Barney song about putting toys away.

Your Aspie high school student will not appreciate it if you sing the Barney song to get him to clean his room, but may well clean up if you explain that you will keep singing it until he does.

When giving any kind of instructions, do not expect your child to follow a long string of instructions given all at once. Give one or two instructions at a time. Once your child is literate, you can give him a written list to go with the instructions, but you probably will still need to give him that toehold of one or two to start with.

A pre-literate child can use a visual list with simple pictures in sequence. Think stick figures or icons that you grab off of the Internet.

You can use a visual schedule to help get through the day and also to get your child used to using icons to represent instructions and activities. A visual schedule is generally made of two basic parts: a strip of Velcro™ on some solid card stock, and a set of cut-out pictures (icons) that represent various activities, also glued to solid card stock, with Velcro on the back.

To make the visual schedule work, you line up the activities for the day on the daily schedule strip of Velcro, and then have the child remove each activity's icon once it is done. Having an envelope labeled "Done" for them to put the icons in is a nice touch.

If you haven't got time for a visual schedule, writing down a schedule on paper with stick-figure illustrations is good too. Use a pencil so that the schedule can be changed.

Do not be afraid to use exaggerated movements, vocalizations, and enactments of the behavior, task, or skill you are trying to teach. For those on the spectrum who can only "get" really, really big expressions and really super-clear speech, it's a very big and very necessary help. For those of us who don't necessarily need all of that just to get the gist of what is going on, exaggeration, even to the point of incredible silliness, will help us to remember your point.

Example of that last: in junior high school, we had a substitute teacher while we were going over prepositions. Instead of using the little sentence our regular teacher used, "The mouse ran [fill in the blank] the box," she emptied the trash can, put it in the front of the room, and acted out the prepositions for us, as in, "The teacher stood in the trash can," "the teacher ran around the trash can," "the teacher jumped into the trash can."

All I remember of my regular English teacher is that she had thighs like a speed skater and embarrassed me in front of the class fairly often. But I remember that substitute teacher differently.

So don't be afraid to make a gosh-darn fool of yourself. Not only can it help your child learn, but in the process you may well make yourself more 'and more "embarrassment proof." Once you've jumped into a whole lot of trashcans, having a child who lies on the floor and screams in the department store is hardly embarrassing at all.

Repetition and Persistence

USE REPETITION TO TEACH

Most people with autism, Asperger's, high-functioning autism, or pervasive developmental disabilities have some learning traits in common. One of the most important and useful is that *we learn by repetition very well.*

The more often something is taught in a clear, relevant way, the better it is integrated into memory and readily retrievable for practical use. That means if we get taught the same thing a lot of times in multiple situations to which the information is relevant, we have a really good chance of remembering and using that information.

This is especially true because we don't generalize very well. Repeating the same information (in words, pictures, or song) in different situations where it applies can help us bridge that gap of generalization.

Repeating information in a context that is not related to the real-world need for that information can be ineffective. For example, there are plenty of teachers who believe that having posters and worksheets showing stop signs allows them to teach children with autism what a stop sign is for.

However, teaching a child with autism that a red octagon that says STOP on a poster in the classroom means to "stop" gives that child the knowledge that posters in classrooms with stop signs on them mean "stop." Or that if the teacher asks what the poster means, saying, signing, or pointing to "stop" will make the teacher happy.

This kind of information does generalize for most typical children and even some children with ASDs. But it's far, far more effective to point out stop signs in the real world, so that the child finds out what the signs mean in many different places.

Traffic signs and signals are so important that practice in the real world is vital. There are plenty of young kids on the spectrum who will stop at all the stop signs on the route to school, but will completely ignore stop signs elsewhere because the knowledge was never generalized.

Fortunately, repetition in different situations is a very effective teaching tool that can overcome this sort of problem. This even worked when my mom was teaching me about money.

Money is often a very hard thing for people with ASDs to understand. It is a weird, abstract concept. One of the worst problems that adults on the spectrum can have is serious debt from using credit cards, debit cards, and checking accounts unrealistically.

Yes, there are people with ASDs who have told their families, in all seriousness, "I can't be out of money, I still have checks left."

For those who are unable to be independent, the difficulty of understanding money can be a serious problem as well. Meltdowns, rages, and serious depression can result when an adult doesn't understand that his or her family and caregivers have to put realistic limitations on buying video games, eating out, or other preferred activities.

I have just as much trouble with the abstract quality of the whole money concept as anyone—hey, we've all agreed that these little green pieces of paper are worth something, but only if they are printed by the right people, and only in the right places. And if you travel, the little pieces of paper have to be printed by somebody else, and have to be a different color, or many colors, and have the right numbers on them, and—well, the whole thing is very, very strange.

So how did my mom debt-proof me? During my early childhood, *every single time* she used a credit card in front of me, she reminded me that, "We only use credit cards so that we don't have to carry a large amount of cash. You can never use a credit card to spend any more than you actually have available in the bank, and you must always pay your whole credit card bill every month."

I had good receptive language, so hearing this information conveyed in words worked well for me. The thing that really made it work, though, was the combination of frequent repetition in places that the advice was immediately connected to. The rules about credit cards were repeated in various stores while we were buying things, so that those rules were forever associated with shopping and with all stores in general.

Obviously, you have to choose the topics and type of teaching with your child in mind. Verbal repetition, repeated use of visual aids, or setting vital information to familiar tunes are all great approaches, so use the one(s) that work for your child. And don't be afraid to mix it up; a child with great language skills may respond really well to visual aids. A child who doesn't speak may hear and remember more than you think. And most humans at all levels of abilities remember things set to music incredibly well.

REPETITION WITH VARIATION

When a child (or adult) seems to just not "get" something, repetition in the real-life situation can help, but adding *variation* to the mix gives you a really good chance of getting through.

Sometimes you may find yourself repeating the same rules, concepts, or instructions over and over, trying to elicit a behavior at the appropriate time in real-life situations in which the child seems able to understand what you are communicating—and yet, the same problem recurs. The same behavior you are trying to head off keeps happening, or the behavior you do want keeps not happening.

In cases like this, varying the *way* you communicate and repeatedly changing *your* approach to coaching your child can give him a decent chance of "getting it."

Of course, sometimes other issues are involved: sensory problems, fine-motor issues, or just plain too much input, can stop a child dead or propel him pell-mell into a "behavioral issue." But using repetition with variation can at least give him a chance at learning what is expected—and maybe even give him a chance to respond in a way that will help you understand him.

My parents had a running situation like this with my brother several years ago. Jimmy was (and is) gregarious and outgoing. He loves to meet people, he loves to talk with new people, and he loves kids.

This all added up to Jimmy, then a teenager over six feet tall, going up to small children at every opportunity, quickly introducing himself, and immediately launching into questions.

"Hi, my name is Jimmy. Do you like Thomas the Tank Engine? I have five Thomas the Tank Engines and five Percys and three Gordons. How many Thomas the Tank Engine toys do you have? Do you have a Buzz Lightyear?" And so on and so forth.

The stunned three-year-olds who were the recipients of these sudden inquests would often be more than a little freaked out. It was rather like a strange giant had just walked over and started talking excitedly. There was nothing negative about Jimmy's appearance, attitude, or intentions, but it was rather overwhelming for small children. Plus, it could kind of weird out their parents.

My parents took Jimmy aside after each of these encounters and explained to him that he couldn't just go up to children and start talking and asking them questions. He didn't see any reason why he shouldn't. After all, it had been just the kind of behavior everyone had encouraged him in for years. When he was a young child, his teachers would have praised him for being outgoing, verbally adept, and friendly in this way.

It seemed that no matter how my parents put it, Jimmy could not understand that what was really great and praiseworthy behavior when he was small was now off-limits. They tried every different approach they could find, but he still kept unnerving small children in this way. He was just too darn good at learning the lesson of being friendly and outgoing.

At some point, my folks tried a new approach. They talked to Jimmy about how it was very important for children to learn not to talk to strangers, which he, of course, agreed with. They then pointed out that when he approached children this way, he was a stranger to them.

Finally, they explained, it was very important that he *help* these children to learn not to talk to strangers by *not* talking to them unless their parents gave him permission to talk to them. After all, if the parents introduced him, he was not a stranger. But if the parents did not introduce him, he was teaching those young children to break an important rule.

After soooo many repetitions and variations, this is the one that got through. It wasn't through yelling, or punishing, or "being more firm" that my parents got an effective result, but through varying their approach while repeating the same basic message until they found a way of communicating that particular message that got through.

PERSISTENCE, PATIENCE, AND FLEXIBILITY

What any child can learn at a given time varies, and what parents can teach varies. What is important is that you don't give up on teaching your child just because you haven't figured out how to teach one particular lesson yet.

Patience and flexibility are important. When my brother Jimmy and nephew Peter were five and four years old respectively, my father started taking them to McDonald's for lunch every Friday on his lunch hour. He regarded this as being far cheaper than the therapy my mom would have needed if she didn't get a break from taking care of one child with autism and one who was both gifted and creative.

One week, Dad decided that it was time for the boys to learn to order their own food. No one had ever explained to him that a five-year-old with autism cannot order his own lunch. Being as my dad is an engineer, it probably wouldn't have changed things if someone had explained the limitations of children with autism to him.

When I asked him about it, Dad told me that he had taken the boys to McDonald's, and explained to them that they would be ordering for themselves that day. He coached them, and let Peter, who had more fluent speech and interaction skills, go first.

Peter got through it without much trouble, and then it was Jimmy's turn.

Do you ever watch *Mythbusters*? Apparently my brother's attempt to order and pay for his own meal resulted in an explosion rivaling that of the entire cement truck they obliterated in Season Three.

Like many of us on the spectrum, my brother did not handle it well when his order was not immediately understood and given to him perfectly. For him, misunderstanding his order the first time it was given, giving him the wrong sauce for his chicken nuggets or a failure to provide sufficient ketchup was a *major error requiring an immediate and total meltdown.*

In fact, Jimmy would begin to get distressed if the counter clerk asked the wrong question. If he started out by ordering a happy meal, and the clerk said, "Would you like orange juice to drink?" and Jimmy did *not* want orange juice, then Jimmy would begin to get distressed. The response to a *wrong question* like this from the clerk could easily be a very long, loud, "Noooooooo!" spread out over multiple pitches. The obvious stupidity and just sheer meanness of a clerk who suggested things he didn't want upset Jimmy quite a bit.

Woe betide the clerk who absent-mindedly asked if he wanted fries with that. (Fries came automatically in the kids' meals at the time. A clerk who forgot that would really stress Jimmy out.)

So, that day my brother learned part of how to order his own food—he got started on it fairly okay. And my dad learned that being able to say the correct words and hand over a five-dollar bill was not enough for Jimmy to handle this transaction smoothly.

I asked Dad what he did about it when this experiment didn't work. He said, "Well, the first fifteen or so times Jimmy ordered his own meal were pretty rough, but after that he started to get it."

See, engineers not only do not understand the limitations of children with autism, they also don't understand when they are licked. Sometimes this is a serious problem; in this case, it was a serious advantage.

What my dad wound up doing was trying, once a week, to have Jimmy order his kids' meal. I hesitate to call it a "happy meal" under the circumstances.

Each week involved my dad coaching Jimmy on the rules for ordering. This meant my dad had to find out the rules for ordering, which are very different for a child with autism. For example, one of the rules that most people on the aut-spec need to be taught is "If your order is incorrect when it is given to you, tell the counter person so in a polite, calm way."

This is an important rule, because the natural response to getting handed an incorrectly prepared hamburger is, for many of us in the spectrum, one involving a severe reprimand for that counter person, which may well detail the concept that he is so stupid it is amazing that his brain is able to regulate his breathing and heart rate well enough for him to remain conscious.

Or, we might just use words like dummy, doody-head, and booger-brain. Same problem, different window-dressing.

So, week after week, my dad coached Jimmy on how to order in a counter-service restaurant. And week after week, my dad was able to observe and figure out more and more about what information and support Jimmy needed to be successful in his task.

This was not a tidy process. It was not done with a clipboard and "behavioral issues" checklist. It was just a dad determined that his kid would be able to do this for himself.

It also helped, a lot, that Peter could place his order first. Not only did ordering first mean that Pete could get his food before the whole thing went to heck, but also it meant that Jimmy had someone close to his age and size who was demonstrating the procedure for him. Never underestimate the power of kids teaching other kids.

Notice that in the above example, this was a once-a-week thing. When dealing with really difficult tasks that involve a lot of frustration for the person with an ASD, it's sometimes better not to pile up a lot of forced practice all at once. A child who has not recovered from the stress of the previous attempt is not going to be in receptive-learning mode.

Also, a child who is handed a huge amount of frustration every day is not going to thrive. If a child struggles to buy milk at school every lunchtime, this means that just getting one of the basic necessities of life comes with a big slice of FAIL every day. Get that kid a thermos for milk so he can have lunch in peace.

THIS EXAMPLE BERATED

When I've used this example in talks, occasionally I've been chided by a parent or teacher who tells me it is a *terrible* example, because children shouldn't be learning to order fast food when it is so bad for them.

Reality check: one fast food meal a week is not going to hurt most kids—at least, it won't hurt those whose digestion is in good order. It is not a bad thing at all for kids to learn that, while these kinds of foods can be fun, once a week is plenty.

Or, as Cookie Monster is now wont to say, "Cookies are a sometimes food."

More importantly, learning life skills is about being able to function in the world as it exists. When a bunch of teens, such as the high school youth group, computer club, or AV club hangs out together, they tend to wind up at places like McD's, DQ, and other purveyors of cheap, greasy food.

There are a lot of chess clubs, robot-building clubs, volunteer groups, temples, churches, and other institutions where a kid with autism or Asperger's could hang out with other kids, which is a great way to get social.

However, when the kids all go to that Cheapie McGreasalot restaurant afterwards, the autistic kid will fit in a lot better if he can either order for himself or just get a water for himself.

For the high-functioning kid, doing this for him/herself is the minimum necessary ability to be seen as okay. For the lower-functioning kids, being able to do this is a reminder to the others that hey, this is a person, not someone who is just being led around by a "handler."

For the child who is on a restricted diet, knowing what to order in places where acceptable foods are rare is a good thing, and something that can only be learned through practice. The "safe" food may be orange juice, a salad, or even just a cup for water, but if you can get it for yourself, you are more part of the gang than if you can't.

Opportunities to Teach, Opportunities for Success

OPPORTUNITIES ARE EVERYWHERE

Children with ASDs learn life skills best when (1) the "lessons" are generalized by being re-taught in a variety of environments (stop signs in many places, proper use of credit cards in many stores); (2) the lessons are repeated many times; and (3) the lessons are taught in real-life situations where the information is meaningful (learn to ask for the key to the restroom at a service station).

Fortunately for all of us, opportunities to do just these things are everywhere. Using those opportunities as they come up is better than a formal curriculum for trying to teach the many little bits of information that form life skills. Certainly there are skills that you have to plan to work on, but using events in the real world, as they happen, can provide great benefits.

Grocery shopping is a great chance to teach a child the important real-life skills that are touched on only slightly in school. Finding various items based on verbal or visual prompts from you at the grocery store can help your child generalize concepts like colors and shapes.

"Point to some red apples" is a pretty basic instruction for many small children, but it requires the generalization of the color red to mean one of the many shades of red found in nature; it also requires understanding that not all apples look like the apples on the alphabet chart at school.

Grocery stores also provide a great real-life visual aid: weekly ads full of brightly colored pictures. Matching the items in the ad to the items in the store is a great game, and additionally teaches the very important skill of focusing on finding a few specific things in a large group of many distracting things.

By the way, don't think this is a trivial skill. I've had to send my husband to the store for tampons when I was ill, and I had to provide him with the front of the empty box that had just run out, because it is really, really hard to look at that wall of competing products and pick out the one that matches. Just doing it by the product name when there are so many distracters is an advanced skill.

As children learn concepts like greater-than/less-than in school, then you can bring in the concept of figuring out which item at the store is least expensive. With some kids you can even include the idea of stocking up when something is on a really good sale.

These are important things. It is of little use to be able to memorize many numbers if you can't tell whether the sale price on an item you use a lot of is a good price or not.

RECOGNIZING VITAL PEOPLE AND THINGS

When I was a kid, any time we were on a car trip and my dad saw someone who'd been pulled over by the police, it was the trigger for one of Dad's lectures on behavior.

Yes, pretty much every time we saw someone stopped for speeding, my dad would say something like, "Do you see that police car? Remember, if you are ever driving and you see a police car behind you, it is important to pull over carefully, as quickly as you safely can, and to be very, very polite when the police officer speaks to you."

Dad would often go on about how you had to be polite to police officers and not get angry or yell, and how you would most likely have to hand them your driver's license and car registration, and how you should wait politely and patiently for the officer to tell you when you were permitted to leave.

A lot of people would see no reason to lecture a four-year-old on the topic of proper behavior during a traffic stop, but my dad was very keen on us learning good manners, and he went on with these little lectures for years on end, car trip after car trip.

Those lectures weren't very long, nor were they very complicated, but they mattered a lot. For one thing, I learned to generalize the concept of a police officer and of a police car, since it was always different officers and cars.

We expect children to recognize any police officer just from pictures in books and on TV shows, but it's actually a difficult concept. Police officers vary in gender, race, height, and build. Uniforms vary a great deal from place to place as well. Parents work hard to teach children that, if they are lost, they should approach any police officer they see. However, that only works if you can recognize an officer regardless of your surroundings.

What's more, Dad talked about how no matter what you did or didn't do, you will have the best chance of things going well if you are polite, honest, and say as little as possible. This is a big concept, and a vital one. Politeness, honesty, and letting other people talk and ask questions—and knowing when to keep one's mouth shut—are all good ways to improve the chances of a positive interaction.

There are, of course, many children who would be overwhelmed by the amount of verbal information that my dad shared with me. These same children would benefit a lot from that ability to generalize the concept of a police officer and of a police car.

If "that is a police car" is the most verbal information your child can parse, then that is the amount you give him or her. If you can coach your child to point out things like police officers to you while you are driving, then you make spotting important things into a game that makes scanning the real world interesting. Not more interesting than say, a toy train, but at least a little bit of fun.

There are so many people and things we walk or drive by every day that are useful to generalize. Schools, shops, churches, ATMs and post offices are some of the things that we need to be able to pick out, either to use them or to identify them as landmarks. These can all vary a great deal in appearance and it can take a lot of practice to readily spot them.

SET YOUR CHILD UP FOR INCREMENTAL SUCCESSES

While opportunities for learning are everywhere, opportunities for the ASD child to succeed may not be. We tend to learn complex tasks in small, even tiny, pieces, so it is often vital to set things up so that fitting a few small pieces of a task together gets us some positive feedback or an obvious sign of success.

Yes, we as humans do all need to learn to deal with frustrations and errors, but most kids with ASDs get more than their share of these.

Too little success and too much frustration will add up to learned helplessness. Too little experience overcoming frustration and other obstacles will lead to a total lack of frustration tolerance. Figuring out ways to balance this is a tough job for parents, but it can be done.

Unfortunately, some parents work hard to set things up so their child is never frustrated or thwarted by life. This creates a whole new world of hurt. But creating frustrations so great that the child gives up is no better.

When teaching your child to participate in shopping or to perform simple transactions, set the child up to succeed some of the time. Make sure your child gets to experience successful simple transactions with the outside world.

That means providing "starter" tasks within that child's abilities. When getting a child to help find things at the grocery store, at first you ask him to find things that you can clearly see nearby that are at the child's eye level. Don't start by asking him to find things that may or may not be in stock!

If a child is using PECS or some other form of nonverbal communication, you may have to communicate with store personnel ahead of time to get the best level of cooperation for your child. Of course, if this is impossible, it may be better to risk a failure to communicate than to let your child continue to be "invisible" in such situations.

It is really hard for kids and other humans with ASDs to be set up for failure, as we often are. Teachers and parents unknowingly set up horrible, frustrating situations where failure is inevitable, which leads to that previously mentioned situation: "learned helplessness." That means learning to give up before you even get started.

Let me give you an example. This is a situation that happens in various forms terribly often:

A very helpful, dedicated teacher I know has a girl in her class with high-functioning autism. I'll call the girl "Frederica." Frederica is intellectually bright but struggles with speech, with social situations, and with panic attacks.

This genuinely nice, intelligent teacher decided to give Frederica more motivation so the girl would stop "melting down" in class and learn not to yell at classmates on the playground.

This gift of motivation came in the form of a Wolverine action figure. The teacher knew darn well that Frederica would cheerfully give her left arm for a Wolverine action figure, so she went above and beyond and searched several different stores until she found one.

So now Frederica knows that there is a Wolverine action figure in her teacher's desk drawer—she's seen it, as the teacher showed it to her while explaining that if little Frederica could go just one day without any form of misbehavior, the action figure would be hers.

AAAAACK! Can you see what is wrong with this picture? I sure can. Every day, Frederica comes in to school knowing that if she can be calm, correct her mistakes without getting upset, and not yell at other children on the playground, she will get something she desperately longs for.

And every day, little Frederica is faced with bullying and teasing on the playground, often about her speech difficulties. Every day, Frederica has to function in an "open" classroom where it is common for children to work on various tasks in small groups, so the sound level and sheer amount of activity make her want to cry.

Frederica's "behavioral" issues don't stem from lack of motivation: they stem from social and sensory issues that are immune to even the most determined little girl's willpower.

And every time Frederica gets upset, she remembers that when she can't take it any more and bursts out screaming or crying, she has lost yet another day's chance at that precious Wolverine figure. To a little girl with her heart set on her favorite of the X-Men, that feels like a tragedy—one she is helpless to prevent.

Frederica has been set up to fail, without anyone meaning to do anything but help her. She is trying to learn a complex set of tasks that include developing the ability to speak clearly, understanding (or at least coping with) playground interactions, keeping calm when she is bullied (very difficult, sometimes impossible for children), surviving sensory issues with minimal support, and just plain getting through the day.

When a child is expected to do all of these things well at the same time over an extended period—a whole day!—before she can get a reward, she is truly set up to fail. If there is no positive motivation or help for incremental learning and small successes, she has little reason to feel that it is even worth trying.

After years of misguided "motivation" from various sources, many kids with ASDs just give up. Why try if your best efforts get the same result as no effort at all?

THE PARENTAL CHALLENGE

This means there is a *major* challenge for parents (and teachers, and OTs, etc.) who are trying to teach life skills. How do you teach a child to do new and different things without setting up too many situations where the child feels overwhelmed by failure?

There isn't a formula for this. I'll give you some hints and examples throughout the book, but the most important thing is that one of the roles parents need to play is that of scientific observer. Observing your child's successes and failures as thoughtfully as you can in order to gather data is a hugely beneficial habit to cultivate.

No, you won't be able to correctly observe and interpret your child's behavior all of the time. Sometimes parenting consists mainly of getting your child to school on time with all of your and their limbs intact.

And yes, it is hard to calmly observe and interpret the behavior of a child who is in the process of, say, trying to give the dog a bath with lighter fluid. There are plenty of times when parents have to be in all-out Emergency Coping Mode.

But maybe, just maybe, you can take a deep breath later and try to parse what led to the problem in the first place—sometime after you dash to the hardware store to buy a locking cabinet for household flammables.

AN EXAMPLE OF SETTING UP
A CHILD FOR SUCCESS

Sometimes setting up a child for success is as simple as bringing that child's interests in the equation.

Human beings in general learn faster and retain more if they are studying a subject they are interested in. It's just a human trait; you can't magically apply the same level of study to a subject you aren't interested in.

One boy was having a terrible time doing his math worksheets at school. He had an aide who would direct him to do each problem, one at a time, and redirect his attention back to the worksheet when his attention wandered—which means she might have to prompt him two or three times per problem.

Obviously, this boy was lacking a very important skill: simply not being able to do a worksheet on his own meant that his "normal" IQ and aptitude scores weren't worth much. Every kid in his class had long since noticed that he needed an aide to prompt him all day, so not only was he compromised academically, but socially as well.

The teacher involved tried a variety of motivating techniques, all of which involved external rewards. Finally, she hit upon a good one: she photocopied pictures of Bakugan characters onto sheets of copy paper, which she then used to print up each of his worksheets.

With a Bakugan right in front of him, this boy became totally focused on his worksheets. He needed no prompting because the task itself involved something motivating to him.

This child has been set up to succeed. Once he develops some academic confidence from doing many worksheets, the Bakugan on the worksheets can be phased out and instead the boy could be allowed to keep a Bakugan keychain in his pocket to keep his spirits up.

A MORE COMPLEX EXAMPLE

But what about life skills outside the classroom? There's no way a parent can embed Bakugan, Pokemon, or whatever the heck it is this week, in every day-to-day life task.

One method is to keep careful track of how far along your child is in accomplishing a certain type of task, such as shopping. Subtasks of shopping include things like knowing which stores have certain items, being able to find out the cost of an item, being able to determine if an item costs more or less money than is available, chosing among several items, finding items in the store, interacting with a salesperson, paying for an item, counting change, and exchanging pleasantries with salespeople. By knowing which subtasks the child can do, you can set them up for success, eventually providing many more successful experiences than failures. The chance to succeed, and the sense of self-efficacy the child is building up, become intrinsic motivators in that task or set of tasks.

An example should make that clearer.

My mom has been working on shopping skills with my brother Jimmy since he was very small. Having him find certain items at the store gave way eventually to having him determine which of two items was less expensive, which led to determining which of several items could be had for less than, say, ten dollars.

He was about fourteen when my mom realized he was ready to put several of those shopping skills together at once. So one week, she put shopping for new boots on his schedule. She got him off to school on the appointed day with a reminder that after school they were going boot shopping.

Mom then got herself together and went boot shopping—all by herself, on her own not-so-free time. She hunted through the boot selection at several stores until she found one that had a few different pairs of boots that were within the right price range and were similar to boots that Jimmy already liked. She found that they were available in a good range of sizes.

Then she went home without buying any boots at all. She went about her busy day until the end of Jimmy's school day. Then she took him to the store that she already knew had several pairs of boots for him to choose from. She told him exactly what he could spend, took him to the shoe department, and turned him loose.

After a good nine years of coaching at shopping skills, Jimmy was up to the task. He took a while to decide which boots he liked best, chose a pair within his budget, and bought them.

Yes, it would have been simpler for my mom to just take him boot shopping after school without taking time to do reconnaissance. It would have been simpler still for her to buy the boots herself.

But if she hadn't done her boot reconnaissance run, she might have wound up taking Jimmy to store after store, while he became more and more frustrated by not finding anything, and more and more overwhelmed by all the sensory problems that go with shopping: fluorescent lights, smells from newly manufactured clothing, and the general cacophony of sights and sounds that are part of the average shopping experience.

And if she'd simply bought the boots herself, Jimmy wouldn't get any experience in doing his own shopping. He wouldn't have any understanding of the difficulty of picking out specific items, or of working within a budget, or of the interactions required when making a purchase.

There are people with autism or Asperger's who are well into adulthood who have never had to buy themselves so much as a pair of socks. Some folks with ASDs have such overwhelming disabilities that it just isn't possible, but many times it's because parents and caretakers have taken the seemingly easy path of just doing it themselves, time after time, every time.

It's pretty rough to be caring for your forty-year-old with autism and having to deal with his meltdown when you can no longer find his old brand of socks, t-shirts, or whatever.

A person who has no experience of shopping just doesn't understand that you can't buy what isn't there. Once a person learns that stores don't always have what you think they have, they may well be able to move on to the next level: hunting down a new brand or making do with the old ones.

Similarly, I often have parents ask me if their child with high-functioning autism or Asperger's will ever date, or have a girl/boyfriend, or marry. There's no way for me to be able to tell them for sure. However, I can say that if, when a girl says to your son, "Hey, I like your shirt" he replies, "Thanks, my mom picked it out for me," then the answer is NO, he is not going to get very far with girls.

By the way, bad manners are another area where I can give you a nearly guaranteed negative outcome. If your son doesn't understand how to be polite to food servers, movie ushers, and other folks in general, his chances of successful dating or marriage will plummet. Yelling at the waiter over something minor is a great way to get one's date to fake an "emergency" that she must attend to—or to simply go to the ladies' room and never come back.

Back to the boot-shopping example. My mom took my brother boot shopping in the most difficult way possible, so that she had to invest time and effort that she could have saved by using an "easier" method—but any easier way of dealing with the situation would have created much, much more work later.

Unfortunately, raising kids is a "pay me now or pay me later" situation. It's a lot like credit card debt—you can do the "easy" thing and spend a lot of money on your credit card without worrying about a budget, but then you wind up paying huge amounts of interest over long years, while your credit rating takes hit after hit.

The alternative to horrible credit card debt is to set the best budget you can, work as hard as you can, and avoid debt so that the future won't be harder than today. The alternative to doing everything for your child so as to avoid the difficulty of teaching them is to find ways to set them up to succeed at simple tasks, then increasingly harder ones, so that they develop the greatest amount of self-sufficiency that can be managed.

Tap into Your Child's Interests

AN OBSESSION IS AN OPPORTUNITY!

There are many ways to use special interests (sometimes called "autistic obsessions") to teach life skills. Every special interest is a great opportunity.

Please note: I am not speaking here about the kinds of behaviors associated with obsessive-compulsive disorder, even though OCD does occur in some children with ASDs. That is a completely different field, and beyond the scope of this book.

Here I am talking about the very intense interests that both children and adults on the autism spectrum often develop. These can range from Thomas the Tank Engine to escalators to astronomy to fingerprints.

Parents and educators alike sometimes try to stop or limit these interests. While it is necessary to create appropriate rules, boundaries, and limitations (thank you Cesar Millan) to prevent an interest from becoming a serious problem, trying to get rid of a special interest is like trying to break up Romeo and Juliet. You just wind up causing a lot of pain and making yourself into your child's enemy.

In a later chapter, I will detail how understanding appropriate boundaries for special interests is an important life skill for children on the spectrum to learn, but for now let's just talk about the vital ways in which these interests can enhance learning, especially life skills learning!

USE YOUR CHILD'S INTERESTS FOR MOTIVATION

As my mother has often said, getting a child with an ASD to do what you want is often like pushing a rope—doomed to fail. Even more than other folks, those of us with ASDs often have many areas where we are *self-motivated* rather than *other-motivated.*

So, how can you get your child, or any child, motivated to learn a specific life skill? Fortunately, the method of setting a child up for success by using his or her favorite interests is not just good for your child's sense of self-efficacy. It's also a great way to create motivation where there is none.

You may want your child to learn a truly basic life skill such as engaging in parallel play, but the average child with autism may see no reason whatsoever to sit with other children doing the same activity they are doing.

This is where you can observe your child's special interests, see what draws his attention, and then sneak it into whatever activity you are trying to draw him in to.

One evening I gave a presentation on this topic at a parents' support-group meeting—a roomful of mothers who were all experts on their own children, but who still struggled to break through the social and emotional barriers of autism.

So I came in with my little presentation and talked about how to use any topic a child was interested in to good advantage. I talked about using Thomas the Tank Engine to motivate children to wait their turn (it is super-important for trains to wait their turn to leave the siding for the main track). I came up with all kinds of what I thought were super-spiffy examples of using a child's most obsessive interest to get that child to do important things like standing in line, taking a bath, and other mundane tasks.

I was pretty contented with my talk, and felt I'd done a good job. Then, perhaps a month and a half later, I got an email from a mom who completely blew me out of the water.

She had listened to my talk and even reread the handout when she got home. Her little three-year-old son, "Egon," was not doing so well in his special-support nursery school. He would not engage in any kind of parallel play, and he would not, not, not look at people's faces when they spoke.

But Egon had another quirk as well. While he was thoroughly non-verbal and seemed to have fairly poor receptive language, he loooooooved numbers. He loved to watch children's shows with numbers. When numbers were featured on *Sesame Street*, he would bounce and flap with excitement. He loved The Count.

More than anything, Egon loved to look at numbers and to hear people say numbers out loud. So his mom developed a plan and got his teachers in on it.

Instead of just trying to get him to sit with the other children during finger-painting, they showed him a piece of paper with a number drawn on it and how the finger-paints could be used to trace the number.

Egon was hooked. It had never occurred to him that arts and crafts could be about numbers, but soon he was eager to join the other little ones for finger-painting, crayoning, or another other form of activity that could be done in such a way that it could include paper that his teachers had written numbers on. And after a little while, he started just enjoying the activities regardless of whether numbers were involved.

But wait—there's more. Egon's mother also went to the trouble of cutting out numbers from construction paper so that she could hold a number up next to her face. The second little Egon looked up and (generally accidentally) made eye contact with her, she would *say the name of the number*.

Again, this mom got the nursery school teachers in on the act. Pretty soon Egon was comfortable looking at faces regardless of whether a number was involved or not; he just needed a way to learn that looking at faces and making eye contact were not such bad things after all.

My talk had some decent little ideas in it, but nothing as awesome and cool as what this creative mom had come up with on her own. She was the expert on her own child, and had come up with something truly awesome.

Not only that, but she had done the opposite of the standard way children with autism are "taught" to make eye contact. Usually, these poor kids are being told, over and over, "look me in the eye" or having their heads physically pushed into making eye contact.

Just so you know, those of us on the spectrum can find eye contact to be anything from oddly unsettling to super-painful. The more we get scolded for not making eye contact, the more we are forced to look teachers and parents in the eye, the more we associate eye contact with hostility, punishment, and deep crankiness.

Egon's mom made sure that looking at other people's eyes meant was linked to pure happiness for him. Every time a teacher practiced this with him, he was learning that eye contact was a way for him to win a fun game—instead of being inadvertently trained to feel that eye contact was yet another irrational and hostile demand of a difficult and enigmatic world.

IT WORKED FOR ME TOO!

Little Egon is far from being the only child who has benefited from a mother with an interest in his special interest. My parents did a great job of exploiting my obsessions and turning them into learning opportunities.

From the age at which I first was able to go to the library with my parents to get some picture books, they showed me that the library was a great place to find cool stuff about whatever my current interest was.

At first, they did the work. When I was interested in cats, they found me books with pictures of cats. When I was fascinated by Snoopy, they found me books of *Peanuts* cartoons.

As I got older, my dad took the time to show me how to use a card catalog to find things relevant to my interests. You don't need to be able to read to find the drawer of the card catalog that starts with "Ca" for "cat."

(For those of you who don't know what a card catalog is, it was the way books were cataloged in libraries for untold decades before the Information Age. The cards were kept in long drawers chiseled from stone with primitive tools—or at least, they weighed as much as stones carved with primitive tools.)

Eventually Dad helped me work my way up to finding books on my own. He showed me how the card catalog indexed books by title, author, and subject, and how to use the Dewey Decimal system not just to find specific books, but to find shelves of books related to various general topics.

As I got older, when I was ten or eleven, he showed me how to use the *Reader's Guide to Periodical Literature* and similar references to find out what articles existed on different topics, and to find out whether a given book existed and where it might be found if it was not in our library.

In other words, my dad used all of my various obsessive interests to show me how to use a library to do research.

I wound up being way ahead of a lot of kids when it came to finding books and articles when I needed to write a report for school, and because I was well trained in the general concepts involved in library research, I was able to pick up new reference tools easily.

It is really, really helpful to enter junior high, high school, and college ahead of the game in the area of finding facts and useful data.

Today, there are different rules for research. For example, even the brightest Aspie will not figure out for him- or herself that when hunting for data on the Internet, it is vital to be alert to the level of BS on a given site.

Another thing that obsessive children need to be taught is that the number of people who support an idea or explanation on the Internet is not a good guide to how truthful or important it is.

In other words, there is just as much for children to learn about finding information in the Information Age as there was when I was a child, living in a cave and unable to find out if a book was still in print without saddling up my woolly mammoth and riding it to the library to look it up in *Books In Print*.

By tying research to whatever I was really fascinated by, my dad got me to *want* to learn to do research and to *practice* the process of researching a given topic over and over again.

BRITISH ACTOR SYNDROME

One trick my mother frequently used to tie my current interest into something she wanted me to pay attention to was the use of her very high awareness of what I call "British Actor Syndrome."

For those of you who are not aware, British actors are the Border Collies of the entertainment world. They like to work, and seemingly will take on as many jobs as they can get. The do not have any prejudice against specific fields, and if the work is available the will go happily from TV to movies to theater, from genre pics to cheesy special effects pictures to serious art films.

Chances of an American sit-com actress or action-movie actor repeatedly going back and forth between their usual genre and, say, Shakespeare, sitcoms, and radio plays—highly variable, and never a sure thing. Chances that a Brit will do the same are about 99.999%.

This means that if your child's special interest in some way involves a movie or TV show, and you want to get your child interested in something outside of his or her special interest, you'd better darn well check out the Internet Movie Database (IMDB.com) and find out what any British actors involved have been up to.

This is a great way to expand your child's interests "sideways" into other fields. Even when the actors involved don't have any "serious" or "educational" films on their resumes, they are bound to have done *something* outside of your child's narrow field of vision. That can be key to expanding your child's inner world.

Take Harry Potter, for example. I just love Harry Potter. And when the first HP movie came out, I was quick to look up the resumes of the various actors online.

I am not a socially minded person. I tend to avoid the kinds of movies that address real human social behaviors. In fact, given my general tastes, it is very unlikely that I would voluntarily go to see a movie that doesn't involve explosions, vampires, starships, exploding vampires on starships, or the like.

After the first Harry Potter film came out, I actually went and saw a movie called *Gosford Park* in the theater. No, really.

You see, Maggie Smith plays Professor McGonagall in the Harry Potter movies, and she was also in this *Gosford Park* thing. The movie had a lot to do with how people do and don't connect in social ways, the differences and similarities of life across class boundaries, and how people deal with serious sorrows.

It was also directed by this fellow named Robert Altman who, I read in the reviews, directs actors to evince behaviors that are closer to natural human behavior that one typically sees in a movie—for example, in real life, people often converse in a very untidy way that involves talking over each other.

So, because I was in the thrall of the Harry Potter mystique, I tracked down this film online, read a zillion reviews of it so I would know what the heck was going on, and dragged my sorry self into a theater to watch it. I got to see a film that had somewhat ordinary interactions in it, with ordinary people reacting to a murder instead of dramatic genre characters reacting to a murder.

Yeah, somebody gets killed in the film. Sorry. Retroactive spoiler alert.

My point is *not* that every child with an ASD is going to be able to consciously observe different kinds of films and examine the differences between real-life behavior and different film behaviors. I'm just weird and obsessive that way.

The point is that when you tap into British Actor Syndrome you have a chance to broaden your child's horizons. Making meaningful connections across categories is not something that comes naturally to most people with autism, but it really helps the brain to deal with the real world, where we often have to make connections of ideas, activities, and behaviors across different people, places, or situations.

Special interests don't have to be narrow interests, nor do they have to promote a narrowing of the mind.

Remember, all children learn best when the subjects of their interest are involved. All children are more motivated when things they like are the topic at hand. Children on the autism spectrum are even *more* likely to embrace behaviors and skills that can be tied to their favorite interest.

Attitudes That Win (and One That Doesn't)

When it comes to raising and teaching a child with an autism spectrum disorder, the most powerful, effective, and important teachers that child will ever have are his or her parents!

When parents take the supposedly easy path and avoid spending large amounts of time interacting with, drawing out, and providing structure and discipline for children, those parents tend to be exhausted and extremely frustrated, and to constantly feel that they are in a hopeless situation.

(Yes, I know there are parents for whom every hour of the day is needed to earn a wage and to provide for their children's basic needs. But some others do seem to have a fear of being the grown-up who does the parental thing.)

When parents take the supposedly difficult path and spend large amounts of time and energy engaging their child, "wooing" their child, and providing plenty of structure and discipline for their child, those parents also tend to get pretty exhausted—but not quite as exhausted as those who don't. And while these parents still get frustrated, the frustration—and the hopelessness—is not as constant or as intense as the frustration and hopeless feelings of parents who have "checked out."

In other words, parenting is an amazingly tough job, and it will be overwhelming and exhausting even when done right, but as Tom Lehrer has said, "What you get out of it depends on what you put into it."

Note to parents—the above is *not* being said here to scare you or "guilt" you. The above is here because it is all true. I've got a passel of parents on my "reality check" squad to back me up here.

I want the parents who are working sooooo hard but still have frustrations and wind up exhausted to know that it is okay to work hard and not have everything fall into place all (or even much) of the time. Getting to "good" is hard work; please don't guilt yourself for imperfect results.

Also, it is important to bring these things up for the sake of those stressed-out people who feel like "I don't play one-on-one with my child, or post rules, but I'm already exhausted. How can I possibly add this life-skills thing and not drop dead?"

When parents avoid scheduling one-on-one time with each child, when parents feel that the child (or children) are all constantly interrupting and demanding attention, when parents feel that it is just too much work to create the rules, structure, and communication that are all necessary to teaching a child with autism to face the world, well, those parents are missing something important.

What is so vitally important is that working hard at parenting really pays off, and backing off or "slacking off" due to fear or due to anything else is a false way out.

Children, all children, have a strong tendency to thrive on structure and a greater chance to thrive when they are taught life skills.

I wish there was a way to make it all easy, but all of the parents I've observed who have thrown up their hands and said, "I just don't know what to do, it's no use!" wind up with truly disastrous outcomes.

Persistence, structure, and the act of stepping up to be the adult in the situation—these matter. They simply can't be omitted from the process of teaching life skills, or from daily life in general when you have a child with autism or Asperger's.

It is a pain in the neck to have to figure out how to create visuals that work for your child. It is a pain in the neck to let the child do things for him- or herself when it would be faster, easier, neater, tidier, and would just plain get done better if you did them yourself.

It is a real pain in the neck and a lot of effort when you have to stand your ground with a child who could out-stubborn a mule and doesn't want to learn to do something as simple as wiping his own bottom or sitting at the dinner table.

But it can be done. And the only thing harder than doing it is not doing it. The price paid for not teaching, not out-stubborning your stubborn child, and not being the calm, firm, tougher-than-nails parent is a through-the-roof high price.

AN ASIDE TO ALL WHO ARE
THINKING JUDGMENTAL THOUGHTS

This is a vital note to any non-parents reading this, including but not limited to teachers, grandparents, and friends of the parents of children with ASDs.

Just because you don't see the results or behaviors that you believe you "should" see in the child if the parents are doing their job "right," don't assume that those parents aren't working their consarned asses off.

If a child with any ASD is showing up for school fed and clothed and more or less on time, the parents are working very hard indeed.

If the parents can successfully disengage and calm a child who is having a meltdown at your home, they are doing an insanely great job. If the best they can do is to remove the child, they are still doing a truly remarkable job.

If you don't live with that child in that situation, you just don't know.

Besides, judgment isn't helpful. Whether it's declarations of how things *should* be done or any other kind of looking-down-the-nose at these parents, it just doesn't help. Even if you know a parent somewhere out there who has truly checked out and is truly not doing the minimum, a hostile or judgmental intervention will not change that.

Hope, and the belief that trying is worth it, can change people. Judgment and the belief that they are bad can make people stay the same. I'm just saying.

We now return you to your regularly scheduled chapter.

YES, MOMS AND DADS, YOU CAN!

Parents, when it comes to being that vitally important person who can teach, lead, and support a child, just like Rosie the Riveter, you can do it!

My mom did it, magnificent creature that she is. She didn't have a degree in education or child development—her degree is in business management. My dad did it, brilliant man that he is. He didn't have even the slightest clue about educating children or child development.

What they did have is the belief that they were responsible for being the parents. They had a firm, unshakable belief that it was their job to be the authority figures, the pack leaders, and they were willing to do what it took to bear that out.

If you don't have the understanding that you are the parents, the pack leaders, the people in charge, well, that's something you may need to fake. Since you are actually in charge, just remember to fake the belief that you are such—for as long as it takes for you to really learn to believe it.

All men and women are indeed created equal, but five-year-olds do not get the same say or authority as Mom and Dad. Remember that when you are dealing with a five-year-old who has decided to run the household.

HOW THEY DID IT

My parents were the authorities, and my mom knew how to make that stick.

For one thing, she controlled every non-necessity that we kids had access to. Candy, cookies, toys, radios, and the TV were under her control, not ours. When the VCR, the home computer, and later on the DVD player and DVR came in, she was in charge of those too.

Vitally, she did not ever let one of us win a battle over discipline. If we were supposed to go without dessert because we had legitimately done something for which that was the punishment, we could not wheedle, beg, or apologize our way out of that.

It was fairly recently that I saw on TV an example of the kind of fortitude my mom showed. It was a beautiful example to me, because it was typical of the kind of problem that can arise with a child on the spectrum.

It was on the show *Supernanny*. Admittedly, this show is not perfect; they usually cut the show together to make it look like the process of getting order and discipline going takes only a few days. You know darn well it takes weeks to shoot an episode of that show, 'cuz those things don't happen in three days.

However, this example was so perfect, and the principles on the show are so good, I just have to use it.

A simple situation: a little boy has acted up, and he is being put in time out (or, as it is also called, "the naughty spot"). He has to sit there for six minutes.

Mom puts little boy in time out. Boy gets up and starts running around. Supernanny tells the mom to put him back on the spot, without reacting to him, talking to him, or making eye contact.

Mom puts little boy back on spot. Boy gets up and starts running around. Supernanny tells the mom to put him back on the spot, without reacting to him, talking to him, or making eye contact.

Mom puts little boy back on spot. Boy gets up and starts running around. Supernanny tells the mom to put him back on the spot, without reacting to him, talking to him, or making eye contact.

No, that's not a printing error. The same thing kept happening, over and over. The boy in this case got up and ran away from time out *one hundred and twenty times.*

And every single time, the mom calmly, without yelling or talking, got him and put him back in time out. Over, and over, and over.

And finally, finally, the one-hundred-and-twenty-first time he was put into time out, he sat there for six continuous minutes. Then mom came over, had him say "sorry," gave him a hug and a kiss, and let him rejoin the world.

That's what it takes. It takes the ability to simply out-stubborn a child without yelling, screaming, gesticulating, or otherwise making things worse.

My mom was like that. I don't have a particular memory of her having to do that, but I do know that she got me off to school pretty much every darn morning for years when I made it nearly impossible to do so. Day after day, she dragged me through the getting-ready-for-school process.

And when high school came, I joined the choir, had to catch an early bus, and got myself up and out the door in the morning. It may have taken hundreds of days of getting me through the process, but she taught me, and I learned it.

Of course, I didn't learn until years later that once I was out the door, she would often scream, stomp, and slam a few cabinets. She only did it when there was no one to observe her, but that's what it took.

She never showed me any weakness in her determination to teach me to be a person. She just kept going.

WHAT DOESN'T WORK

The title of this chapter includes one attitude that doesn't work. It's an important one.

The book is about teaching life skills in the hopes of helping some people with ASDs to develop their best possible level of independence. Sometimes that level is of being able to do some tasks for themselves while living with family or in another supervised situation. Sometimes that level is complete independence at age of eighteen or so. More often it falls in between.

The attitude that I have seen work, and work well, can be stated as, "My job is to help this child become an adult who is as independent and self-directed as possible."

There is an attitude that seems similar to some parents, but it isn't. This problem attitude can be stated as, "My child will be happier if he is able to make decisions and choose his activities independently, starting as early as possible. If he resists my guidance, I will just back off."

Real adult independence doesn't come from letting a child be self-directed all darn day long. Even the largest (or smallest) amount of potential independence can be destroyed by overindulging a child. Letting a child be in charge of his own life promotes a prolonged, perhaps infinite, childhood.

PROMOTE ADULT INDEPENDENCE, NOT PERPETUAL CHILDHOOD

Yes, sometimes parents do make this error during the process of teaching a child life skills for independence. Letting a child do all sorts of things without supervision, boundaries, or rules, doesn't actually help the child develop life skills. The world we live in just doesn't work that way.

I've taken many, many questions during my Life Skills talks, some of them from very emotional parents struggling with very severe problems. But somehow none were ever as upset as one parent who was sure she was doing the right thing.

"Emma" was a young mother of an eight-year-old boy with autism, "Otho." She had been at loggerheads with the OTs and speech pathologists working with Otho for some time, and she was upset.

Nearly in tears, Emma told me how she had tried very hard to promote Otho's independence, but the therapists who worked with him were constantly telling her not to. For example, she let Otho set his own bedtime, choose his own TV shows, and she had even set up the kitchen pantry so that Otho could easily grab any of his favorite snacks at any time, completely independently—yet these supposed experts were telling her that she needed to do things differently.

Emma was very upset when she spoke to me. Obviously, she felt like she was under siege from therapists who were telling her that everything she was doing was wrong.

I don't know if she heard my answer. I tried to be very gentle, but the fact is, everything she was doing really *was* wrong.

Letting an eight-year-old choose his own bedtime and eat whatever he wanted whenever he wanted was not helping him become independent. In fact, he was developing bad habits that would hurt him no matter whether he grew up "severely autistic" or "cured." He wasn't independent; he was just getting more and more spoiled.

But the mistake his mother made was completely logical. Otho was, in a very literal sense, independent in his choices. His mother's interpretation of "independence" was so literal, I wondered if she might be on the spectrum, like me.

In the real world, what we eat and when we eat has a huge bearing on how well we function. Likewise, in the real world, our sleep habits and leisure activities (like watching TV) can have a huge impact on our well-being.

Poor Emma wanted so badly for Otho to be "independent" when he grew up, but she didn't understand that what an eight-year-old (or any child) needs is to be taught good habits and to have realistic boundaries. No child, with or without autism, can make all of those choices independently and learn to make good choices and develop useful habits.

A child who chooses his own bedtime can easily grow into a teen or adult who never gets enough sleep, even under the best of circumstances.

A child who has no need to join the family at the table will have serious trouble in a world where socializing often centers around food. Table manners, interacting with others over a meal, and just being able to eat in the presence of others at an appointed time is a vital skill—how else to join the gang at work for lunch, or to have dinner with a friend?

Even at a job where coworkers seldom eat together, the office worker who stows tons of snacks in file drawers and munches all day can annoy everyone in the office, undermining social and business relationships. Whether a fellow is a manager or an intern, he is not going to earn any points by nipping off for a candy bar any time he feels like it.

There are no jobs for people who learn to be "independent" the way little Otho did—not to mention the fact that his poor nutrition and lack of sleep were both definitely affecting his schoolwork. Eventually those same traits would affect his employability, date-ability, and even the ability of others to stand him at all.

And his choices of TV shows included some that were chock-full of "imitable behaviors" that he emulated on the playground. Cussing and verbally harassing his schoolmates was not working in his favor. It's hard to develop life skills when you spend a lot of time in the nurse's office with an icepack on a fresh black eye.

PARENT POWER!

So there it is. Parental attitude and involvement are vitally important. Where you choose to stand, as a parent, can be the difference between independence and permanent, childlike dependence for your child. Scares the heck out of most people. Life is like that.

Specific Life Skills

Intro to the Specific Skills

This section is a guide to teaching some specific life skills and some specific areas of life skills. I'll cover teaching chores in general, teaching punctuality, and a few other primary areas that children need to learn to be able to function at home, at school, and eventually in a work situation.

This is definitely not a complete listing of skills to teach, or of ways to teach skills. Even if I wrote volumes and volumes of instructions, ideas, and support for teaching many, many more specific skills, I would still not be able to guess what your child needs to learn right now, nor which means of teaching would work best for him or her.

What this section does provide is some important information about areas to focus on in order to teach skills that will begin (or continue) the important work of preparing your child for life—and for eventual possible employment. You may not be sure that your child will ever be employable or even has the ability to reach that goal in this lifetime, but you can give your child a fair chance at learning the kind of under-lying skills that promote employability.

You won't ever know if your child might have developed employment skills if you never start work on the skills that promote good work habits. Chores promote working as part of a team or group with a common goal; punctuality and manners make it possible to get and hang on to a job. These are really key to functioning.

The skills discussed in these next chapters don't merely promote employability, but also *livability*—which in this case means "being able to live with others without making life unnecessarily difficult and unpleasant for the people one lives with."

CONCEPTS AND SKILLS

While the number of skills I can cover is limited, the examples and types of skills covered are chosen so as to give you, dear reader, the chance to learn overarching ideas, concepts, and ways of approaching problems that will work in many situations and for many other skills.

The examples and advice given are like examples and hints given in a math or science class. The teacher will not do the exact problems you will need to do for the exam or lab, but will go over enough different kinds of problems to prepare you to solve problems on your own.

So the section on giving clear and literal instructions for household chores applies to other situations, like giving clear and literal instructions for putting on clothes or studying vector calculus.

This section is not meant to teach you every little thing you will need to teach or do. It is meant to provide good ideas about what kinds of things you need to teach, and to feed your brain with useful information that you can apply yourself.

I really, really hope this section will make it clear that the time to begin teaching these things is now, and that your child's disabilities or differences are definitely *not* a reason to wait to teach basic life skills.

Let me put it this way: I get asked questions about how to teach life skills at conferences around the US all of the time. Some questions are pretty straightforward, like, "How do I encourage teens and adults with ASDs to be their own advocates?"

Some questions, however, hint at how severe the results of lack of life skills training can be. For example, I have been asked (I swear I am not making this one up), "What books would you recommend I give as gifts to a family where the teenage son has Asperger's, has graduated from high school, but is not able to bathe himself or even do any basic self-care?"

Or, another favorite: "My daughter is eighteen years old and has Asperger's. She is starting college this fall. When should I start talking to her about sex and dating?"

I consider it to be a proof of my great internal strength and inestimable tact that in both of those (and many other) cases I did *not* recommend getting on eBay to buy a DeLorean and a flux capacitor.

(That's another bit of geek humor. A Delorean and a flux capacitor are key parts of the time machine in the *Back to the Future* movies. Nerdiness? Why, yes, I'm soaking in it.)

EVERY LITTLE THING

While I cannot give you instructions for teaching every single life skill, it is vital that you watch your child, and look for what it is that he or she can and cannot do. You do have to make sure your child learns every little thing he or she truly needs to.

Yes, once again, a parent is like a scientist who must observe and think about what that child can and can't do. You can't be in "scientist mode" every single second, but you can watch and observe and think enough to learn what is missing.

My mom realized very early on that I had a tremendous tendency to let the adults take care of me, a habit of holding back and failing to do minor things for myself, and a near-pathological avoidance of doing the many little practical things that most of us do for ourselves every day.

She also noticed that I was eager to join in adult conversations and tried to function more as the classic Aspergian "little professor" than as a child. She didn't know the word Asperger's, she didn't know about that classic pattern of difficulty in picking up day-to-day skills, but she did know something was "off." A pro might have called me an "FLK"—funny lookin' kid. My mom simply decided that she'd better get into gear and train me ASAP.

Because of my supposed "brilliance" (ha!) my dad's folks were very upset that my mom wasn't working with me on things like learning to read early. After all, I had a cousin who was reading at three, so surely I could get the same jump on life that way.

Mom soldiered on with more practical training. She knew that the time spent using some special "early reading" program would be time stolen from basic developmental needs that I was already weaker on than the average kid. She did not mess around.

She was not interested in bragging rights. She was too busy raising her kids.

With my brother, the story was a little different: he was diagnosed with PDD:NOS when he was four (the diagnosis was later changed to autism) and my mom and dad were able to get good support for him. He had speech therapy to enhance his ability to communicate verbally, occupational therapy to help with his fine-motor skills and sensory issues, and was in a modified classroom setting.

Teachers and others spent a lot of time with my parents on developing Jimmy's academic skills. But my parents made a very conscious decision to favor practical life skills over academics.

In both cases, my mother was smart enough and stubborn enough to realize that all those little things that people need to do for themselves all day long are more important than the kinds of academic training and pushing ahead that many of the people around them valued so highly.

My parents feel strongly that the main goal of parenting is to produce adults who can take care of themselves and be independent to the greatest degree possible. Life skills, after all, are work skills. Independence, even limited independence, does not come from reading at a third-grade level before or during third grade. Reading is great and useful, but the clock is ticking much faster on the interval in which the skills detailed here can be taught.

Is reviewing and detailing the above repetitively redundant? After all, I dealt with some of this in the first and second sections of this book.

Repetition and details are important here because we live in a world that often emphasizes the opposite view. People become super-obsessive about what grade level their child is reading at, doing math at, spelling at, writing at, while forgetting all about the real-life skills that are so vital.

So there will be repetition of concepts that are so important that they have to be addressed and tackled a number of ways, such as the next one.

CURED? FIXED? HOW ABOUT FUNCTIONAL?

A lot of people with autism are, eventually, considered to be recovered or cured. A lot of others aren't.

Temple is the most famous "recovered autistic," and she still has lots and lots of the traits associated with autism or Asperger's. Even if your child gets to the PhD level, that doesn't mean that the autism will be completely erased.

Meanwhile, people on the autism spectrum most often retain their difficulty in developing life skills throughout their lives. For example, a child who started out with a "classically autistic" label may well learn to talk, to behave reasonably in school, and then go on to college, but lack the ability to intuitively pick up a lot of the life skills that are needed for college in the way that the other freshmen do.

The autism world is rife with stories about college students on the spectrum who don't know how to get fed on campus and so eat only what they can get from vending machines, or who have never done laundry and wind up re-wearing dirty clothes all semester. There are even kids who retreat to their dorm room and by the end of the semester no longer leave it except to use the bathroom.

From that, you can guess what it is like for teens and adults with autism who are seeking employment. If you are twenty and have never learned to handle issues such as appropriate dress, being polite, or asking for simple accommodations by yourself, you are in trouble in the workplace.

My brother and I have the advantage over many people on the spectrum who are smarter, less disabled, or come from richer families. We can take care of ourselves, behave appropriately in most (not necessarily all) work situations, and we can earn money.

I'm not cured. He's not cured. Guess what? In the real world, the difference that matters is not the difference between "cured" and "not cured" but between being *functional* and *not functional*.

If your child was suddenly cured the day he or she turned eighteen, what set of life skills would your child have? After all, being cured doesn't change how much you've been taught, or the life you've experienced.

And what if your child was never cured? How much can he or she do for him- or herself? Can she pick out her own clothes? Can he indicate what he wants to someone who hasn't lived with him since he was born? Every little thing helps.

Okay, enough with the redundancy. I think. Let's move on to what kind of life skills to teach.

Chores and More

THE FAMILY IS A TEAM

One of the more difficult skills for people on the spectrum to learn is to work as part of a team or group. This is a skill that needs to be taught very gently and gradually. Just signing up a kid for little league or soccer and figuring he'll learn teamwork that way really, really doesn't work in most cases. Do not do that.

The first team any of us gets a chance to be part of is the family we live with. Whether this is a two-person team or a marauding horde, it's the first time we get the chance to join in and help do things that benefit us as individuals by benefiting the group.

That last is important. The point of teamwork is not just some abstract thing. Working in groups benefits us as individuals who are members of that group. If your child's cognitive level allows for it, please teach them that—if you belong to a group, and you do something that benefits the group, it also benefits *you* personally.

But the philosophy of teamwork aside, it is important for all children to go through the concrete tasks involved in being a contributing member of the family—chores.

Children on the autism spectrum often miss out on a vital privilege that most "normal" kids get to have—doing regular chores. That's right, I said *privilege*. Doing chores is something that kids may not like much, but it is the first means they have of helping themselves and the group, and it is great training for the world. Like getting to vote, or blue-collar work, it is an often-undervalued life bonus that helps everybody.

You might think of chores as a pretty limited set of things: vacuuming, taking the trash out, making beds, and setting the table. But in reality, any little thing a child can do that contributes to the whole is a valuable opportunity to assign that child a chore.

No, I do not believe in overworking kids, nor in trying to make them do things beyond their abilities. But I do believe in pushing them to develop their abilities in the area of household tasks.

And developing those abilities means that you may well have to tolerate your child helping you in non-helpful ways at first. Remember that scary little girl from the old Shake'n'Bake® commercials? The one who proudly bragged, "And ah hayelped?" (Translates as "And I helped.")

That little girl was representative of all of the little kids who "help" in the kitchen or garage by being carefully guided to make a tiny contribution to the process of feeding the family or caring for the car. It takes much more effort to coach a child to measure ingredients or pour them in than to just do it yourself.

But typical kids get the benefit of being part of the team through such laborious coaching, and so should kids with ASDs.

Also, typical kids are often assigned small, even tiny, subsets of chores that they can do without help; a child too young to set the table might be assigned to get a package of napkins out of the cupboard, or to carry one specific item to the table (with careful supervision).

When my little sister was very new, my mother had me fetch a damp washcloth so that I could "help" with changing the baby. She didn't need me to do that, and she probably could have changed a diaper faster without waiting for me to come help, but she did it to make me feel that I was part of the whole baby-care process, rather than being shut out of the new family circle.

Think of the pride children get when they do these small tasks that feel important to them. Those small tasks *are*, in fact, important, since they create both the habit of doing chores and the sense of taking part in a bigger project.

FIND YOUR CHILD'S LEVEL

Kids with ASDs miss out when they are not given tasks at their level. Academic slowness or slow emotional development should not mean shutting a child out of the whole chore process. A child who is nonverbal and several years behind in reading may well be able to set the table, *if* that child is given examples and/or pictures to work from and learns to do a little more each day over time.

And what if that child cannot set the table? Then she brings the napkins or the plates to the table. That's what unbreakable plates are for, darnit.

For the record, my Corelle® plates do occasionally jump out of my hands and hurl themselves onto the floor so hard that they shatter. If you want someone to help around the house, you have to tolerate such incidents. I swear, the plates do themselves in without me doing a thing!

Again, figure out which little parts of chores may be doable when an entire chore is not. A child who cannot even begin to pack his own lunch may be able to get his lunchbox and put it on the counter to be filled.

SOME CHORES ARE DIFFERENT WITH ASDS

Mealtime preparations can be different when you have an ASD. Some of us on the spectrum have delicate digestions; some cannot tolerate more than a few foods. Find ways to work coping skills for those realities into your child's consciousness.

A child who can tolerate only a few foods can learn to signal the need for alternate foods. When possible, make it the child's job to check what is for dinner and to put one or more of the ingredients for an alternative on the counter if he can't eat the meal as served.

A child who has learned to ask (in words or with PECS) what is for dinner and, if the meal is too scary to try, to put the jars of peanut butter and jelly on the counter to signal the need for a PB&J is making a step towards providing for his own needs. Eventually, he or she can be assigned to prepare the needed sandwich.

With the added step of learning to deal with the common meal being inedible, a child learns that he or she has some responsibility for dealing with the problem of food restrictions. As an adult who has to deal with this all of the time, I can tell you that it is important to be alert to what food is available and be able to make alternate plans.

After years of coping with a limited ability to tolerate food tastes and smells, I've learned to scope out restaurants and food courts ahead of time. I've also learned to carry trail mix and Pop-Tarts® with me as necessary, and to politely participate in a group luncheon when I can't eat what everyone else is eating.

Step One of coping with food difficulties is learning to politely and kindly handle them at home. This means learning to provide one's own alternate dinner (when appropriate), remembering not to make negative comments about others' food choices, and handling the situation calmly when one cannot eat what is served. These are all vital skills for functioning, not just as part of a family team, but in the working world as well.

ENCOURAGEMENT IN TEAM SKILLS

There are many team tasks around the house that can be accomplished as a group. In addition to meal preparation and house-cleaning, you can add raking leaves, pulling weeds, and shoveling snow to the list of activities in that allow a child to be part of the group that accomplishes the job.

Don't fail to encourage a child who puts in a good effort, but don't be unrealistic either. Letting someone who is functionally three years old throw snow around with a small shovel is okay, and it's fine to praise that child for the sheer amount of effort that he or she has put into moving perhaps a cubic foot of snow. It is certainly okay to focus on the positive effort and ignore the little detail of actually getting the job done when a child is first learning to help.

Rewards and praise should *always* be given for strong efforts and real contributions in team tasks. If a child is doing his or her best but makes mistakes, praise is in order, and the correction of mistakes should be treated as a normal, expected part of the process.

Let's face it, making mistakes and correcting them is part of every real learning process, so no child should be rebuked or shamed over them. After all, the only way the child can avoid all mistakes is to not do anything new, challenging, or different. It's important to encourage the child who is stepping up and trying.

So it is important to give that positive feedback and praise for real effort, and to make fixing mistakes something that is expected and normal. If you freak out over errors, your child will learn that errors are disasters.

Of course, there is a big difference between a child who is learning or is extending himself to do something new or difficult and the child who just decides to phone it in because "I'm disabled, so I shouldn't have to do this."

Encouraging a child who is just starting a new kind of task—regardless of that child's lack of skill—is something I encourage, as per above. Encouraging someone who is functionally twelve years old in the same way you would encourage someone who is functionally three years old is just plain indulgent and leads to coddling someone who is far beyond the coddling stage.

If a child is old enough and capable enough to do something properly, don't give them huge amounts of praise for just showing up and making a tiny effort. Regularly doing that can lead to disaster, both on the job and in life.

Trust me, I see this often. There are adults with Asperger's who got so much encouragement and positive praise for the slightest little effort that they expect a gosh-darn medal just for showing up.

Nothing hurts a person's chance of keeping a job as much as when that person requires constant praise for everyday tasks. Okay, that's hyperbole—there are actually things that can hurt a person's employability more, such as showing up for work wearing nothing more than a few strategically placed cheerleader's pom-poms and a surly grimace.

It does, however, hurt if someone does not understand that real effort is important. There are men with Asperger's whose wives get totally burned out when said men give them only the slightest bit of help and then expect ample praise for it.

So, let's review. Teamwork = good. Finding tasks at the child's level = good. Positive praise for real effort = good. Over-praising a child for minor efforts = not on your life!

Chores Part Deux:
How to Tell your Child What to Do

MORE ON CHORES

While I do believe that doing small things can help children learn to be part of a team working towards a larger goal, I also believe strongly in giving children bigger tasks to learn and conquer.

The reality is that children do not have to be at grade level to learn household tasks. Children who are not ever expected to get beyond grade-school academics can learn a lot about what to do around the house. And children who are in the 150+ IQ range can also benefit greatly from learning to do good old physical work around the house.

There is good evidence that doing physical work that has a visible, tangible result—such as cooking a meal, mowing a lawn, or even taking out the trash—can help us feel better about ourselves and about our lives.

GETTING KIDS ON THE SPECTRUM TO DO CHORES

Two important facts: (1)It can be hard to get kids in general to do their chores. (2) When a child has an ASD, regardless of their "level," they often need extra help to be capable of getting chores done at all.

For one thing, kids with ASDs need a clear schedule and plenty of warning as to when they need to do chores and what they need to do. For another, they need to know what set of actions are actually involved in doing the chore, and in what order to do those actions. With those two supports, your child has a good chance of successfully coping with and doing his chores.

Informing the child of what chores need to be done and when to do them has to be handled in a matter-of-fact, literal way. That doesn't mean you can't use fun stickers and colorful charts, but the information has to be clear, factual, and literal.

When I was a kid, I didn't clean my room when my mom said, "Your room looks like it needs cleaning," or "Your room is getting pretty messy," or "You'll have to clean your room this week sometime."

I cleaned my room when my mom said, "You have to clean your room today, right after lunch [or breakfast]."

Yes, I did grump and grumble when she said that I had to clean my room at a specific time. But I did it because I now knew that it actually needed to be done and at what time that had to occur.

"Your room needs cleaning" and "your room is messy" are general statements that do not include any real information about what *I* should do and when I should do it.

This is actually important. You can tell a child that his room needs cleaning or the trash "isn't going to take itself out" a dozen times, and it isn't as effective as saying, "You have to clean your room starting at 1:00 P.M. today," or, "You have to take the trash out and then wash your hands, and then you can have a snack."

Now, I often will imitate and emulate NT behaviors when those behaviors enhance my ability to communicate with NTs. Occasionally, though, I get jumbled and use the NT kind of communication with an Aspie. I have even used the communication methods typical of NT females when those methods are completely inappropriate.

When my husband and I got married, one of the chores he took responsibility for was taking out the trash. Sometimes I'd say to him, "The trash in the kitchen is full," or "There sure is a lot of trash," or "It won't be long before the trash will need to be taken out."

He would generally nod agreement, and then, being as I'm a bit thick, I'd be surprised to note that the trash did not subsequently get taken out.

Fortunately, my Aspie brain kicked in at some point and told me, "Hey, Jenn, stop talking like a TV wife and tell him what you want."

So, when the trash got full, I started saying things like, "Gary, please take the trash out."

Being as Gary is very responsible and does the chores that he has previously agreed to do, that worked.

As for my brain-lapse of using non-literal language, well, I'm not at all surprised that all of those very silly, very non-literal statements like "the trash can is full" got me nowhere. I must have learned them from bad examples, like TV sitcoms and women's magazines. These days the main sitcom on my "must watch" list is *The Big Bang Theory* and I don't read women's magazines at all, so I'm all better now.

The point is, if you tell me (or my husband, or anyone on the spectrum) that the trashcan is full, that is merely a statement of fact. If you tell me that it is time for me to take out the trash, I may grouse about it a bit, but I will probably do it, unless there's a problem like killer robots attacking the garbage bins or something.

Don't assume that people on the autism spectrum can infer that they are required to do something from a simply statement such as "the trash is full." Give them directions, such as "take the trash out now."

Mind you, if you say, "Stop playing that video game and take the trash out now," there may well be whining involved. But they will know what they are supposed to do, and that is an important step in the chore-learning process.

Be literal, be clear, and make sure that your child(ren) know(s) exactly what chores must be done and when they are required to be done.

BEYOND LITERAL

Don't just be literal when teaching a child with an ASD to do chores on time: be thorough, be visual, and be ultra clear. Assume that the child may need visual *and* verbal cues.

That means posting a list of what-must-be-done-when in a prominent space. Yes, back to that section on visual aids. Without a clear schedule and clear visual aids, your chances of getting your child to cooperate are small.

In general, kids don't want to interrupt their days to do chores. And yes, kids should have adequate time for play, rest, reading, and whatever else it is kids do. All I did many days was read, ride my bike, read, spin, read, and play records, but I'm sure other kids do more stuff than that.

But a reasonable set of chores has to be clearly set out in visual form and with plenty of clear verbal warnings, as in, "You can play video games for ten more minutes, and then it's time to clean your room." And there should be a timer set for ten minutes so that there is no debate about when ten minutes have gone by.

WHAT TO DO?

Of course, all of the visual schedules and clear, to-the-point instructions in the world won't help if the child does not know what to do: specifically, how to get started and what the steps are to complete the task.

There are many, many chores that "typical" children learn to do without a lot of specific instruction. Once they've learned to pick up their toys after playing, they seem to understand that any time they are asked to clean up their rooms, they must pick up all the toys as part of that process.

They are also fairly likely to figure out that if they need to vacuum their rooms, they will need to pick up the toys and get all the trash off of the floor first.

Please do not expect that level of independent organization of seemingly unrelated facts from any child on the spectrum.

For years, if my mother wanted me to actually clean my room, she would have to do it with me. She was pretty frustrated about this at times, because she didn't fully realize that I had no idea of what the steps are that go into cleaning a room, nor of how to keep track of those steps and pick up the pattern from her.

That's right—while I picked up algebra and symbolic logic in a snap, I did not know how to clean my room even after my mom led me through the process dozens of times.

When Mom cleaned my room with me, she'd get a couple of trash bags, some dust rags, and then she'd round me up and take all of the above up to my room.

She'd lead me through the process of picking up toys and putting them in toy boxes, of pulling bits of crumpled paper and hand-shredded sketches out of the toy boxes, and of figuring out whether various pieces of clothing, magazines, newspapers, and Halloween costumes variously strewn around the room were to be cleaned, to be put away, or to be buried in an unmarked grave at the crossroads.

Note that even when I seemed to be utterly unable to clean my own room, Mom still cleaned it *with* me, not *for* me.

Importantly, while she led me through this staggering process time after time, at no point did I see it as a pattern of behaviors, nor as a set of activities. To me, I was just following my mom, who magically knew what set of strange actions could be performed over a series of minutes or hours to cause the room to somehow become clean.

It took a *lot* of years of her help for me to start seeing anything resembling a pattern. But I didn't actually start really cleaning my own room until a friend loaned me a book about "growing up" for teenage girls.

It was rather an old and outdated book that only briefly and obliquely referred to issues of puberty and other difficult stuff. But it had some magical, brilliant things in it that changed my life.

It had instructions on how to clean one's own room! It explained what order to do the steps in—that it was important to first remove all *tchotchkes* and bric-a-brac in order to dust the flat surfaces, then pick up all debris on the floor. It explained the categories of debris, and instructed me to put laundry in the hamper, trash in the trashcan, and books in the bookcases.

It even explained that one should dust at least ten minutes before vacuuming, so that any dust that gets kicked up into the air (instead of getting on the duster) will have a chance to settle to the floor and be vacuumed up.

It also gave a brilliant piece of advice that solved my closet issues: to clean a closet, take every single thing out of that closet, then put it all back in where it belongs. It actually works.

Most of this was stuff my mom was telling me and demonstrating to me time after time as she slogged through the process of helping me clean my room. But none of it really sank in until I had it in a clear written form that I could go over dozens of times in a short space of time.

Of course, it would have been harder to follow the written instructions if I had not had all of the steps demonstrated to me by my mom. And it would have been impossible to actually clean my room if she hadn't already taught me to do each component part of room cleaning.

But putting it all together required something other than hours of my loving mother's time and energy and glowing. (Horses sweat, men perspire, ladies glow. Ladies who are cleaning my room glow like the Disney Electrical Parade.)

I needed a clear plan that I could refer back to again and again. I had borrowed that how-to book, and it was months until my friend saw it again, because I went over the darn thing about a gazillion times.

So if there is any chore, no matter how large or small, that your child is stubborn about starting, and seemingly can't do without someone walking him through every step, make sure that you give him instructions. Written instructions, pictorial instructions, a combination of both—whatever works best for you and your child.

Make sure all instructions come with a very clear Step One, so your child will know where to start. You may have to choose Step One somewhat arbitrarily, but it must be there! We on the spectrum are notorious for having difficulty getting started!

I will put here a solid plug for Carol Gray's Social Stories™. She has done a great job of coming up with good, solid parameters for creating a "story" about what to do for almost any child with autism. Her Web site is TheGrayCenter.org and she is a goddess, even if she is one of the most NT people I've ever met.

Chores Part Tres:
More on Teaching Chores

Since it is often trickier to teach chores to children with ASDs than to teach chores to "typical" kids, it is important to be prepared to provide more than one kind of training in a given chore.

Mind you, I do *not* mean that you need to be ready to provide all of the below kinds of training for every little chore, nor that it is hard to teach all chores to all children with ASDs.

In reality, the level of difficulty varies in ways that are hard to predict. For example, a very visually-oriented child with a low testable IQ may easily learn to put groceries away in the cupboard after a few demonstrations, while a very verbally-oriented Aspergian like myself may have great difficulty putting things away.

In my case, my poor mother often had to help me put things back in the freezer after I took one thing out, because I just couldn't figure out how the things fitted. Poor spatial reasoning.

Meanwhile, there are kids who could never hope to beat me on a test of symbolic logic who could easily clean my clock when it comes to good old-fashioned freezer Tetris®.

Your child may be considered mostly "low functioning" and still be able to learn to do quite a few chores pretty darn well; your child may be considered very high functioning and have difficulty learning to do chores. Neither is a good enough reason to skimp on teaching how to take care of oneself and one's surroundings.

Remember, a person who can tidy up after him- or herself, who can load and run the dishwasher, who can do laundry without destroying either clothing or the washer, and who knows to keep track of the days the trash is taken out so as to always take the trash out on time will be more welcome and able to function in your home, a group home, or a dormitory, either with roommates or on his or her own.

Heck, if you live in a dorm and can remember to empty all of your trash into the hall trashcans early Friday to avoid having to keep your trash in your room (due to the heaping piles of pizza boxes and flotsam that will build up in those trashcans by Sunday night), you have one less little problem in life. Also, your room will stink less.

All dorms should have trash pick up on Sunday morning. I'm just saying.

Back to teaching kids. I know darn well that there are going to be times when you have to pick your battles and decide that a child who is going through the process of learning to use PECS cannot simultaneously handle learning to sort laundry. That's okay. You do what you can, and you learn as you go.

After all, while your child probably needs to be able to do a lot of household chores, he does not need to learn them all by next week. Work these skills out over time as opportunity presents itself. And maybe give opportunity a little push once in a while.

LEARNING BRAIN SKILLS IN THE WORLD O' CHORES

Don't forget that many of the skills that are taught in school can be better taught at home in the world of doing chores.

When a child with autism learns to sort the official set of approved educational toy objects by color, size, or shape, that child has learned to sort those objects, period. The skill does not necessarily generalize, because we on the spectrum do not generalize things easily.

When a child helps sort the laundry (clean or dirty), he or she learns how to sort objects that vary greatly from week to week and can be sorted several different ways. This can help broaden their thinking quite a bit.

Obviously, you can't just tell your child, "Hey, could you sort the laundry now?" And you may not always have time to help your child help you.

But by starting with simple tasks and moving on up to more complex ones, you can help your child master this real-life sorting and grouping problem.

For example, you can start with asking your child to do one sub-task of sorting laundry. You might start by asking him or her to find all the socks and put them in a pile. Or to find all the black clothes.

Eventually, you can work your child's way up to sorting "light" clothes from "dark" clothes. Or button-front shirts from knit tops.

This is one of those good opportunities to challenge yourself to help your child to find different ways to sort things. After all, you can do all of the button-front woven shirts in a load together, or you can put the white ones in with other white clothes and the light-colored ones in with other light-colored clothes.

It's an opportunity for an extension of Temple Grandin's suggested game of providing objects that can be sorted several different ways into several different categories.

For anyone who thinks that their child is too "high functioning" to need this kind of training, think again. I live in an apartment complex near a university. I share a laundry room with college kids. You would be amazed how much money these kids unknowingly lose by ruining clothes by washing them in the wrong cycle, or by putting stuff into a hot dryer that should air dry.

When I was a college student, I got to save money and the time I would have spent shopping by simply never "cooking" my bras in a dryer and always either hand-washing them or using a lingerie bag. Thank you, Mom!

Here's a question whose solution is left for the reader to generate: how many household tasks are there that involve sorting, adding, subtracting, and other brain skills that we all need in everyday life? How can you get your child to sort toys, dishes, books, and other household items so as to teach him how we as humans organize objects?

INSTRUCTIONS PLUS DEMONSTRATIONS

I mentioned above that once I had good written instructions, I could clean my room pretty well—but that I wouldn't have been able to if my mom had not done those things with me repeatedly.

Written (or pictorial) instructions plus repeated demonstrations equal GOOD. That's what you could call education through multiple methodologies and sensory pipelines.

Okay, you don't have to call it that. But it is important to realize that information is more likely to become useful to children on the spectrum if that information is presented in several ways.

This principle was dramatically demonstrated by an experiment I was privileged to see on videotape. It was presented at a conference by Howard C. Shane, PhD, who had been looking at the ability of children with poor language input/output to follow instructions.

The video showed Dr. Shane and a child with autism playing with some toys. Dr. Shane then told the child, "Put the baby in the stroller and have Kermit [the Frog] push him."

The child went on playing. Repeating the instruction had little effect except to make the child twist and turn in his chair, turning away from the researcher—the kind of behavior seen as a hallmark of non-compliance.

Then Dr. Shane turned on a TV and played a video for the child. The video showed someone putting the baby in the stroller and having Kermit push the baby. And the voiceover repeated the same instruction.

Instantly, the child complied. As soon as he saw the interaction in the video, he did the same. No non-compliance, no muss, no fuss, no problem.

Two things struck me immediately about this experiment. One was that Dr. Shane, by providing videotaped instructions, had changed who the child was. One minute you saw a child who would have been considered difficult and non-compliant, and the next minute you saw a child who was happy to follow suggestions for playtime.

The second thing that struck me is that this is not just a problem for kids with poor receptive language. Many children who are nonverbal have great receptive language, but they might not be able to follow purely verbal instructions for a "novel" task—that is, for a task they aren't familiar with.

Many children (and adults) who have great receptive language and can speak quite well can have that same problem. New tasks, or tasks that they have never noticed or thought about much, can require more input.

In the example about cleaning my room (see previous chapter), it didn't matter that the task was familiar and that I had participated in it many times. I could not see the pattern in the behavior. It didn't fit my brain's definition of a pattern.

For example, my mother did not start at the same place in the room each time we cleaned it. We did not do exactly the same activities in the same order. Some activities, like picking up toys, might be started, then stopped while we did something else (like sorting my papers from school), and then resumed. The pattern of stopping and resuming various tasks was very inconsistent.

When I started to build up an idea of a pattern by deciding that a particular task—say, dusting—could not be interrupted and must be done from beginning to end, then the next time we cleaned I might find that task did get interrupted. If that happened, I'd pretty much throw up my hands and decide that it was just impossible to figure out the pattern.

So in addition to my mom showing me what to do and doing it with me, I needed written instructions. My mom could have saved herself a lot of time and trouble if she had just invented a time machine and traveled to the future to take a Carol Gray seminar on creating Social Stories™.

(Incidentally, the proper title for such Social Story would be something like "What People Do When They Clean" or "How Jenn Can Clean Her Room," *not* "Clean Your Room, Dammit!" The instruction process should be as positive as possible.)

Thus, while receptive language skills can loom very large indeed in teaching chores to kids on the spectrum, children with all levels of communication input/output often need more than one kind of teaching.

You don't actually need to attend a Social Stories™ seminar or own a video camera to begin teaching. You can start by simply doing one part of a task with your child—you demonstrate, then you help them do it, then they do it on their own. Repeat any and all steps as necessary.

Oh, and don't underestimate the power of the written word. If you write down a set of steps (in a simple, friendly way) and read it to your child, making sure they can see the paper and see your finger underlining the words as you read, you can get good results even if the child is not yet literate.

Why? Well, for one thing, writing them down forces you to give the instructions in exactly the same way, over and over. It means the child does not have to try to parse a new set of instructions that may or may not be the ones he is familiar with. Change the words, you force the child to re-parse every phrase, and he may not be able to tell that they are the same instructions.

For another thing, we on the spectrum are good at rote memorization. If we know what the piece of paper says, we will refer to it even if we can't read it. Non-readers can still understand that the paper "contains" the instructions given. Heck, I only know a tiny bit of French, but I actually "read" *Les Liaisons Dangereuses* in the original French. I know what it says, even though I can't read it, and going over the familiar is pleasant.

Getting actual pictures of people doing specific chores, or taking pictures of your child(ren) doing chores and using those to make instruction sheets are great ideas too, as is the liberal use of clip art and pics grabbed from magazines, newspapers, and the Internet. All of those can enhance your written and verbal instructions like crazy!

This is another one of those times when you might want to try strong-arming any devoted crafters and/or scrap-bookers in your family to help you create something that has lots and lots of visual POW!

When the world comes to its senses and puts me in charge, I will create a program in which all of the nursing homes will have regular crafting sessions where the residents will be offered the chance to put together visual instructions and communication aids for kids with autism. That way the residents will have something to do that is way cooler than daytime TV, and can continue to have a real impact on children's lives and thus the future.

And if you find someone who wants to take that idea and go with it, you and they are welcome to it. I don't even want credit—I just want a world where everybody gets to be useful and kids with autism get all the visual aids they can possibly handle. That, and all the chocolate I can eat.

YOU HAVE NOTHING TO LOSE BUT YOUR PERFECTIONISM

As a parent of a child with an ASD, you may be used to letting go of expectations you have had for your child. Here's something else you may have to let go of—*perfectionism.*

One of the most difficult things about teaching children to do chores and letting them do things for themselves is that, in general, children are not all that adept.

In general, children are born without much in the way of everyday skills. Ask *any* baby how to locate a stud when putting a painting up on a wall—they don't know. Oh, sure, they may find a stud by bonking the wall repeatedly with a random blunt object they have found, but they will have no idea of the significance of the discovery.

What does this mean? First, it means that you should never allow a toddler to help you redecorate. Second, it means that you have to cut children a large amount of personal slack.

If, after you have a visual morning schedule, a chore chart, and a plainly labeled and prominent list of what privileges can be gained or lost by doing or not doing chores, your child actually makes his bed all by himself, there is every chance that it will be pretty much a mess.

And that's where letting go comes in. There are a *lot* of parents who will, once the child is occupied with something else, remake the bed. After all, it's a mess, and it'll look way better if you do it yourself.

Don't. If your child has the pillows at the head of the bed, the top sheet under the blanket, and the blanket under the spread, you are doing just fine and can leave it.

A child whose work is constantly redone and fixed by well-meaning parents gets two clear messages: (1) they are not doing a good enough job—in fact, they aren't doing it well enough to even count it as being done—and (2) if it isn't perfect, Mom and Dad will always fix it.

Ugh! I hate those messages! In fact, I just got a creepy chill up my spine just typing that last paragraph. No, I'm not kidding. It really gives me the creeps.

We on the spectrum tend to be perfectionists—something is either right or wrong, good or bad, and there is no in-between. What's more, we tend to see our own efforts as either right or wrong, good or bad, worthwhile or worthless.

It is a powerful and important lesson if you can in some small way communicate to your child that doing things badly is the path to doing them well. If every day there are a few little things that they don't do so well and you say, "Hey, that's a great effort! You're learning to make your bed a little better every day!" then you are providing one of the multitudinous small doses of that message that we on the spectrum need in order to be mentally healthy.

Plus, the reality is that parents of aut-spec kids sometimes get overwhelmed. Heck, some years "sometimes" is every darn day, ten times a day.

So let your child learn that doing badly is the path to doing well, and at the same time save yourself a little effort. Maybe you'll even manage to teach your child that he or she has the ability to make life better for other family members by pitching in—and what a big chunk of power that is for a child to acquire! Let us hope they learn to use their new-found powers for goodness and niceness instead of evil.

An extra note or two here: while we on the spectrum can take years or decades to learn to read faces, pick up on the meanings that others communicate using changing vocal tones, and otherwise interpret emotional communication, we are super-good at picking up on stuff like "Mom re-does it because I don't do it well enough. And no matter how hard I work, she's going to redo it, so I might as well phone it in."

And if Mom, Dad, Grandma, Aunt Kate, or whoever just can't let go of the need to redo anything that isn't perfect, well, then it's time for some serious cognitive behavioral therapy. And maybe a screening for Asperger's. I'm just saying.

BONUS TIP

Hey, as long as I'm giving out tips on how to get your child involved in household chores, here's one more you can try.

One mother of an Aspie teen of my acquaintance (who is an Aspie herself) has an unusual but pretty darn clever way of giving her son new household responsibilities, as he gets older. For each birthday, in addition to the usual presents, he is given one new privilege and one new responsibility.

I just love this one. It clearly connects privilege and responsibility, and additionally makes the connection between getting older and becoming more responsible for yourself.

Having the words "With Great Power Comes Great Responsibility" written on the birthday cake is optional.

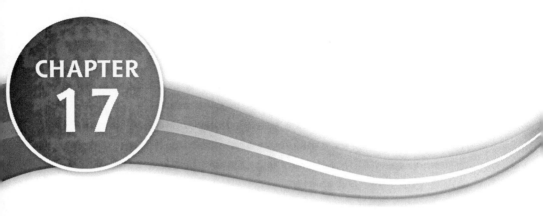

Punctuality

PUNCTUALITY IS A BIG LIFE SKILL

Being able to be on time is a huge life skill. It can take years of patient reinforcement and age- and ability-appropriate coaching to teach a child to be on time outside of a fully controlled classroom situation, but it is worth it.

This, like being able to cope with mistakes and being reasonably polite, is one of those life skills that really can't be skipped. These are vital work skills—the skills that allow a human being to have a decent shot at getting and keeping a job. Habitual lateness will have a negative impact socially as well. Even though being late is usually simply a bad habit on the part of someone who doesn't properly know how to monitor time, it looks bad—really bad—and upsets people.

Unless a child has the most severe impairments and will always need near-constant supervision, he or she will need to learn to be punctual. Even a person who is incapable of living independently will benefit from being able to get ready when told to.

TELL THE TIME

One important step to teaching a child to be on time is to *tell* the child when he needs to do things. We adults as a group have a bad habit telling children to be ready in "five minutes" without setting a timer or giving any clear idea of what "being ready" mean.

Saying "I need you to start getting ready for school" is not a clear directive, especially for someone on the spectrum. It is really important to provide specific prompts in a way that will be understood, depending on the child's age and ability.

Even really high-functioning kids can have tremendous difficulty getting ready for school if they have a hard time keeping track of how much time specific activities take and how many of those activities are necessary to be ready for leaving the house.

In English—those of us on the spectrum have a great sense of what *should* be done, what is usually scheduled, and how a process should go. What we *don't* have is any idea of how long it really takes to brush our teeth, what things we really need to do before school, and of how easy it is to burn time on unnecessary activities.

Even more directly—it's really normal for kids to think they have time to play a video game for "a few minutes" before school and then wind up spending all the time they have on it. Those of us on the spectrum are *even more prone* than typical kids to do this, and to get in trouble for being late all of the time.

Teaching kids on the spectrum to be on time can be broken down into several steps (the order and intensity of the steps can be altered according to need):

- Set a good example.
- Give clear directions about what needs to be done by the specific goal time.
- Give clear and frequent information about how much time there is.
- Engage the child by using timers and alarms (mechanical devices help).
- Use appropriate consequences, not yelling and freaking out.
  Natural cause and effect means more than any amount of scolding.

- Really, don't freak out. You have every right to feel like freaking out, but don't.
- Be persistent.
- Let real life dictate consequences when appropriate (especially for older and higher functioning kids).

SOME STICKY WICKETS

If you're going to work on the problem of being on time, you should know some of the basic problems we on the spectrum have. As usual, our problems are a lot like other people's, but in more intense and trickier versions.

One of the major problems we have with being on time is that we on the spectrum are often super-literal about the time we are supposed to be somewhere. If we are supposed to be at the dentist at 2:00 P.M., then 2:00 P.M. is the time that is fixed in our minds, and we try to be there not at 1:55, not at 1:45, but at exactly 2:00 P.M.

Many of us have difficulty making the connection between the time we have to be ready and the things that have to happen before then. We will look at the clock, see that it is not yet 2:00 P.M., and not get ready.

If you want your child to be ready at 1:45, then you have to tell that child so. If the child can't tell time (and usually even if he can), you can use timers to let him know that he has to be ready "in fifteen minutes" or five minutes, or whatever. A countdown is a big help.

One thing that I have noticed as being common in "spectrum folks" is that we are often terrified, in one way or another, of "wasting time." Kids who hate waiting for whatever reason do not want to sit in the anteroom at the doctor's, nor to have to wait for a haircut.

The logic is clear: if I stop watching my video, playing my game, or otherwise occupying myself pleasantly, and then get ready and wind up being *early*, then I have lost precious viewing or play time, which is just so terribly, terribly tragic.

Convincing a child that being late is a bad thing, and that being on time is good, is often a matter of reiterating and enforcing rules related to that fact, over and over and over and over.

There is one other reason for dreading being early that I should bring up—there are children for whom waiting on the playground to go into school is sheer torture. It's a loosely organized period with little or no supervision, and bullies are full of energy, pep, and Phrootie Phlavored Kokoe Bombs. Sitting in homeroom before school starts is a similarly loaded *Lord of the Flies* type situation.

It wasn't until I got to high school that I was able to beat the before-school miseries by joining the choir, which rehearsed before school. I got there early when there was no one there; had an organized, supervised activity almost up until the ring of the bell; and avoided all sorts of hallway chaos and social inconvenience. Plus, the girls' rooms are much less smoky then.

TIME LINE

How long does it take you to brush your teeth? How about dressing? What about scarfing down a bowl of cereal, washing your face, or driving to work or school?

You probably have a good idea of at least some of these, but only really time-obsessed Aspies keep track of them. Chances are that your autie or Aspie thinks of those things as taking no time at all.

I've made bacon and eggs for breakfast every Saturday for ages, and just last weekend I decided to find out how long it actually takes. Usually it is a race with the devil for me to get both the bacon and eggs to be ready at the same time, so I figured timing it would help.

I'd thought that there was about a fifteen-minute discrepancy between bacon cooking and eggs cooking, and that the whole thing took a bit more than half an hour. To my surprise, there is less than a five-minute discrepancy, and the whole thing takes less than twenty-five minutes.

(Again, your mileage may vary.)

Similarly, I have had to work hard and make frequent notes to determine how long it takes me to walk two miles, do the laundry, brush my teeth, and write three pages. I just don't have any natural sense of time.

In fact, I only recently learned to add the time it takes to find my backpack, throw appropriate stuff into it, get my hat and shoes, and walk down to the carport into the time slotted to get somewhere. Previously, I was just using a Google or Yahoo map to estimate the time needed for travel and setting an alarm to get me to leave at the time indicated. I've been late to a lot of stuff.

ANNOUNCE TIME IN REAL SITUATIONS

If your child doesn't know how much time things take, you must either provide information about what he must do when, or teach him how long things take.

If your little one needs to brush his teeth, wash his face, and get dressed by 7:20 A.M., then you have to figure out when to tell him to do each thing.

As in, "We have twenty minutes until you need to be ready. Go brush your teeth now." And then you shove his little butt into the bathroom, put some toothpaste on his brush, and have him do it.

Note that I said, "Your little one." You should work on this with young children, so that your child is able to eventually function without it. You do not do this with your child who is at a tenth grade level in all classes. You do not do this with your kid who works a full-time job. You do not do this with your college student.

As the age and ability of your child dictates, you start by figuring out what steps to tell them to take, how many of those steps they can handle hearing at a time, and how much time you need to tell them they have.

You can write up a nice little A.M. schedule for "getting ready for school by 8:00 A.M." and you can get a clearly readable timer. Analog timers (the kind that tick and have a dial that moves towards zero) are sometimes really helpful because there is a clear link between the visual of the timer moving and the passage of time. Time Timers® are a brand that makes this super-duper clear for any child, with a big red swath that disappears bit by bit as the zero moment is approached. They cost an arm and a leg, but if you are having an impossible time getting your child to recognize the passage of time, it may well be worth it.

The point is that the average child with an ASD needs support to get ready on time, and if you give your child that support, you will help him build up the ability to get ready on time by himself.

If you have a child who really, really, really can't get ready on time, it might help to have him go through each task separately (at a neutral time) and time him (or have him note the time taken) so that he can experience in a clear way how much time each thing takes and how much transition time is needed in between.

LITERAL TIME

Do be aware that we on the spectrum are often so anxious about time that it makes us late. We are so very, very literal.

As mentioned above, we will try to get someplace at exactly 2:00 P.M. or exactly 4:47 A.M. or whatever it is. We will read a schedule that says "11:30 A.M.—Lunch" as meaning we absolutely must do the previous activity until 11:30 A.M. and then absolutely must be at lunch at 11:30 A.M. Not 11:31, not 11:29, but absolutely, specifically, at 11:30 A.M.

Because of this, schedules and information may need to explicitly state what is obvious to most typicals—if Math is scheduled for 10:30 A.M. and lunch is scheduled for 11:30 A.M., you don't stop Math at precisely 11:30 A.M.

Words like "approximately" or "about" can be used in schedules. Transition time can be specified, so that Math is scheduled from 10:30 A.M. to 11:20 A.M. and getting ready for lunch is scheduled from 11:22 A.M. to 11:29 A.M.

And children can learn that while being late is usually not a good thing, it is usually perfectly okay to be a little early or a little late for non-crucial activities.

WORK SKILLS ABOUT TIME

It is pretty important to specify the work skills needed in relation to being on time. For example, being late to work and leaving early are usually serious problems.

I knew one guy, call him "Homer," who had a real jackass of an HR guy at the small company that employed said Homer.

Homer was habitually coming in just a few minutes late and leaving just a few minutes early. A smart HR guy, boss, or coworker would have told him that this was a problem and to knock it off already.

Not this HR guy. One day, Homer got to work and his HR guy was waiting for him. HR guy had a little announcement.

He informed Homer that his being just a little late and taking just a little extra time at lunch had, as of the day before, added up to eight hours, and so Homer would have to come in Saturday and work an eight-hour day—that is, if he wanted to keep his job.

Okay, so it was a jackass move and not really appropriate. You don't pull something like that unless more direct methods have failed miserably. But Homer was on time thereafter.

People get fired for being late. People get fired for taking more time on their break than scheduled or for leaving just a little early each day.

Sure, there are companies that are somewhat flexible on hours, and even companies that are insanely flexible on hours. But being on time is soooo useful and likely to be necessary that it is worth pounding it into your little snowflake's head that being on time to work is not optional.

("Little snowflakes" are our oh-so-preciously unique children whose self-esteem and delicate feelings must be protected at all costs. But protecting self-esteem and delicate feelings too much can produce a child who can't function in a world that expects basic courtesy, punctuality, and hard work as the price of actually having a job.)

OTHER WORK-RELATED TIME TIPS

I was probably five the first time my dad explained to me that you always need to get to the airport at least an hour before your flight takes off. Dad wanted me to be successful, and he knew that there are people whose sales calls, meetings, or even careers had been wrecked by missing a plane.

Of course, nowadays you have to be at the airport—physically be in line for security—about two hours ahead of when your flight boards. If my dad hadn't taught me specifically and explicitly that waiting around in the airport is infinitely better than missing a flight, I would have suffered some very severe consequences. Yay Dad!

Knowing when to get the bus, when to get in the car, and when to simply get moving is vital, and you can start working on that any old time. Dad may have been a leetle early, but I don't wind up freaking out at the check-in desk or having a meltdown in a big airport at the podium by my gate.

And oh, yes, adults without ASDs—businessmen in fine suits—do indeed have tantrums and meltdowns at airports. But I don't. I was taught the rules early. I just watch and then marvel at the teachers and parents who tell me that "eight years old is too old to start screaming when something goes wrong." Actually, fifty-eight years is not too old to burst into obscenities if no one actually taught you the unwritten rules of airports.

A BRIEF ADVISORY

I'm going to continue here with some more examples of how to get older children to do something on time. I want to make it clear, though, that these are things that have to be age- and ability-appropriate if used. There is no use punishing a two-year-old for failing to watch the clock, nor for letting an eight-year-old get in serious trouble for truancy because he hasn't mastered getting ready in the morning. Pick your battles and choose your weapons with care.

OH, YOU WILL GET UP

When I was a kid, and even now, I was/am terribly bad at getting up in the morning. I just don't do transitions well.

Every morning, my mom would wake me up for school, and I would burst into a huge tirade. I don't remember the details, but I think it was something about conquering her land and relishing the lamentations of the women as they were driven before me. Also something about life sucking.

Various punishments, scoldings, and other inducements to be nice when I woke up were applied to no effect. Eventually my folks realized that I just could not be pleasant when I woke up in the morning. My speech and yelling function turned on before my brain was working well enough to understand the situation.

So, when I was in second grade, my parents got me an alarm clock. An electric one, I might add, not one of those bleeping ticking ones. Ticking is bad, very bad.

Mom made sure I knew how to set it, checked that I had it set, and explained that I was going to get myself up. I'm not sure what consequences there were for failing to get up, but I'm pretty sure I wouldn't have gotten to watch *Match Game* for about a decade.

(Oh, *Match Game,* how I miss your many single entendres and Charles Nelson Reilly.)

I never did get good at waking up, but I did it. I learned to get up before my mom had to come into my room. After all, I didn't want to *see* a human being first thing in the morning, so I really liked having a grown-up alarm clock that allowed me to get myself up without the interference of any mammals whatsoever.

And yes, it did take some effort to really make it work. Getting me out the door was no picnic, even with the alarm clock in place, and one day in fourth grade I did, in fact, miss the bus.

And my mom did, in fact, inform me that I could walk to school and she was not going to give me a note to take with me.

Knowing that Mom meant business (she always did), I started trudging. My brain was consumed with the issue of when I would get there, what I would do, and whether I would get in trouble, but gosh darn it, I walked. Well, part of the way.

When I was only about a quarter mile from home, my dad drove by on the way to work and pulled over. He informed me that Mom felt that now that I had been punished, he could give me a ride this one time only, in order to prevent me from getting into more trouble.

Oh, I got a lecture in that car. And because my parents were super-consistent about discipline, I knew that when he said this was a one-time thing, he meant it. I certainly didn't want to find out the hard way.

I got to the bus stop on time from then on. By high school, when I got the early bus for choir, this often meant going out with my hair soaking wet in freezing cold weather, but I got there.

Of course, at that age, I thought it was fascinating that after just a few minutes outside my hair could be broken by simply bending it, and I'd snap individual hairs one after the other just for the fun of it. So I still wasn't normal, nor was I doing personal grooming at the typical teenage girl level.

In fact, I didn't start actually drying my hair on time in the winter until I understood the link between my soggy hair and frequent swimmer's ear. But that's another story.

MY SISTER GETS REAL

Older kids, especially high school kids functioning at grade level, sometimes need harsher, reality-based consequences to push them to where they need to be.

This is serious business. There are college students—and twenty-somethings with jobs— whose parents call them each morning to wake them up so they'll be on time. Apparently these parents don't know that

(1) they are not supposed to be doing that and (2) their kids will outlive them. It'll be a shame when precious snowflake Dillon or Agape loses that big promotion because Mommy had to have a hip replaced and no one got him (or her) up on time to meet that major client.

And it'll be a shame if you spend the rest of your life getting your stay-at-home child up for the job you worked so hard to get them through intensive state services. The more independence a child has, even in an at-home or other sheltered situation, the more they should stop being a child and start being an adult while they still have parents to teach them.

My sister Catherine (the "normal" one) has a son named Pete. Pete is really smart, has no autism, no learning disabilities, and is social, charming, and he even got a nice scholarship for college. So yay for him.

However...Pete has been, through several years of the extremely recent past, a teenage boy. A disorganized, not tremendously tidy, occasionally extremely flaky, teenage boy.

Getting Pete ready for school was quite a production number, being as he had to actually find assorted necessary items in the labyrinth of chaos he calls a bedroom, and avoid the various distractions of video games, TV, and staring at random objects for no discernable reason.

When he was little, I distinctly heard my sister tell him, "When I said put your socks on, I meant BOTH FEET!" A genius IQ and "neurotypical" brain do not guarantee good organizational skills.

Note that I said "neurotypical," not "normal."

When Pete hit high school, my sister realized she had a choice. She had to get him to the point of getting himself where he needed to be when he needed to be there, and she had to do it before the lack of that skill would have catastrophic consequences.

So she did what she had to do. She told Pete that it was now his job to get himself to school on time with all of the necessary items on his person. She would not intervene, and he would suffer whatever the consequences were by his own self.

She could have taken the easy way out. Trust me, the infinitely easier way would have been to wake Pete up herself, nag him into being ready, and then drive him to school if he didn't have time to bike there.

It's easy, oh so easy, to protect that precious snowflake. All it takes is a raised voice, the ability to nag, and gas in the car.

But Cath was not going to take the easy way out. She made getting to school Pete's responsibility. And she tore her hair out and white-knuckled it for months while he made a mess of it, but she stuck to her guns.

Pete was not immediately inclined to get himself to school on time. He got called to the assistant principal's office. He got detention. He reached a point at which he was told that if he continued to be late so often, he would have to attend a proportionate series of "make up days" over the following summer.

One of Pete's teachers even called Cath up and told her that Pete had not brought his homework that day. Catherine calmly explained to her that it was Pete's job to bring his homework to school, and if he did not, he should suffer the appropriate consequences. She pointed out that it was the teacher's job to mete out detention, extra work, or zero grades for homework if this happened.

The teacher was pretty indignant. After all, she was sure that it was Cath's gosh-darn *job* to get her kid to school on time, and with his homework.

But Catherine knew something that maybe that particular teacher didn't—that high school might well be the last chance Pete had to learn to get himself to where he had to be and to get his own work done. In college, going through the same learning process might mean losing a scholarship. In the working world, going through the process might mean losing a job and having a hard time getting a new one.

And Pete did learn. He did pay some consequences, and I'm pretty sure Cath lost about ten years off her life and about half her eyelashes from sheer stress, but he learned it. When he himself had to be responsible or take the logical, innate consequences of being late or not having his homework, he learned.

Now the disclaimer—this is not something you just drop on a kid with an ASD, no matter how high functioning. If you haven't been teaching punctuality skills or basic organizational skills, you don't just throw the kid into a hardcore, consequence-filled situation.

It is really important to take the time to teach and demonstrate things like working out a schedule, using an alarm clock, keeping track of homework, and keeping lists of what needs to go to school (or work).

Work with your child on these things. Your child needs examples and coaching on things like to-do lists, time management, and putting the things he needs where he needs them to be.

Don't ever expect a child on the spectrum to intuitively grasp that completed homework must be promptly put into the appropriate folder that must then be immediately put into the backpack, which is then hung on its designated hook so that it will go to school with the contents intact.

But once you teach the skills and do the appropriate amount of support, you need to let the child actually do things for him- or herself. If you catch your child every time he falls, he won't learn to catch himself.

I learned to get myself to school on time, even with Asperger's. My sister learned to get herself to school on time. My nephew (eventually) learned to get himself to school on time and gets himself to his job and to his college classes (mostly) on time.

And my brother Jimmy, who has autism and had not yet graduated high school at twenty-one, can gosh-darn well get himself up and prepare himself for his day. Heck, the only reason he wakes my mom up is that he is really friendly and social first thing in the morning. I have no idea where he gets *that*, but the point is that it is possible, really possible, to teach kids with (and without) ASDs to be on time.

Anyone who learns to be on time has a skill that will serve him or her well every day, forever. I don't want to miss school, I don't want to miss meetings, I don't want to miss work, and when I'm old(er) and gray(er), I don't want to be late for bingo.

So thanks, Mom, for teaching me to be on time. You truly are the Alpha Mom.

Appropriate Attire

It is incredibly important for all children to begin to learn what clothing is appropriate for what situation. This is not a one-time thing; it takes many years to acquire the basic concepts of what is casual and what is formal.

Heck, here in Southern California, there are approximately twenty-seven different levels of "casual dress" for different situations. Getting the basic idea of dressing for the activity or occasion is a vital skill for work and play, so start when you get the chance and keep at it.

Unfortunately, there are some issues with clothing that are pretty common to people on the autism spectrum. It's not really possible to teach a child with an ASD about appropriate dress without taking into account the sensory and emotional issues that can come with clothing.

PROBLEMS WITH WEARING APPROPRIATE ATTIRE

Wearing functional and appropriate clothing is an important life skill for all children to learn; however, when it comes to children on the autism spectrum, allowances have to be made for sensory issues as well as for social and emotional needs.

Sensory issues are weird, difficult to understand, and very important. You can't argue with sensory issues, you can't punish or scold away sensory issues. Sometimes, they can be mitigated by an occupational therapist or what's called a "sensory diet" (see suggested reading for more information). But to some extent, sensory issues just *are*. You can't overcome sensory issues by forcing discomfort or pain on a child.

Knowing that sensory issues are an ongoing problem for most of us with ASDs, we have to work from there. We literally don't *feel* the way others do. Some of us are incredibly sensitive to light touch, and to the textures of clothing; others have a very low sensitivity to feedback from their own bodies and like to use tight elastic at the wrists and other key body points to help keep track of where their bodies are.

Another issue in sensory sensitivity that affects some auties and Aspies is being upset by the feel of air moving across the skin; I know people who have difficulty shifting from long-sleeved tops in the winter to short-sleeved ones in the summer because the feeling of air moving through the hairs on their arms is so very disturbing when they've not felt it for several months.

Some children have extreme visual sensitivities and are upset by certain colors or color combinations. Other children are super-sensitive to smell and will be genuinely upset and disturbed by the smells of some fabrics and dyes.

Of course, as you likely already know, sensory issues can go both ways. Some people on the spectrum are so insensitive to smells that they will attempt to wear a favorite piece of clothing over and over without washing it because they don't know that it makes them smell really, really bad.

When my parents were at Drexel Tech, they knew one of my father's fellow engineering students who always dressed smartly, looked tidy, and smelled very odd. (There is a disproportionately high percentage of Aspies in engineering.)

This little mystery was eventually cleared up by a conversation with said engineer's roommate. It turned out that every evening, this smelly but tidy engineer would take off his button-down shirt and carefully place it on a chair so that it would stay tidy-looking for the next day. Every single night. He just never washed it (unless perhaps he took it home at the end of the semester for his mother to wash).

There are other issues with clothing that are unique to people with ASDs. A child on the spectrum may get a really strong emotional boost from wearing clothing related to a special interest, or refuse to wear clothing that is associated with some part of a special interest. If a well-meaning relative buys a shirt representing a hated character or problem area of a special interest, the child may well refuse to wear it even when that thoughtful relative visits.

In other words, if Gamma buys little Timmy a t-shirt related to Episode I: The Phantom Menace, and little Timmy is among the right-thinking people who refuse to acknowledge that Episodes I through III even exist, then trying to get Timmy to wear the shirt to show Gamma how much he appreciates the gift may result in a knock-down drag-out fight. And if you "win" the battle and Timmy wears the shirt, he may resent Gamma (and you) for weeks thereafter.

Forewarned is forearmed.

(To my fellow Aspies: Yes, little Timmy's attitude towards Episode I is, in fact, mine. I don't care if Kevin Smith says I'm a hater. Eps I through III simply never happened—even though George Lucas is a deity and deserves any and all People's Choice Awards® he may have gotten for non-existent films that I do not remember seeing over and over.)

(Pod racing sucks.)

Sorry, non-Aspies. I needed to talk to my peeps for a moment.

APPROPRIATE DRESS IS STILL IMPORTANT

Despite all of the above caveats, teaching children with ASDs to wear appropriate clothing is still important. It is important to make allowances, but we on the spectrum need lots of coaching from our parents (and occasionally other family members) to have a chance in this area.

So how do you do that? How do you balance teaching children that what they wear to school, to religious activities, to club meetings, and on holidays actually matters when there are so many things that get in the way?

As with so many things, there is no magic formula. The main thing is to figure out what is important, and then take what is important and narrow it down to what is really, really, really important, then work from there.

This is an area where visual aids can help. Cutting up catalog pages with children's clothing in order to match the clothing to various activities can be a good visual way to help children figure out the mystery of clothing. It is good to acknowledge that some clothing can be worn in many situations, and some clothing is almost never appropriate.

Clothing is a mystery, and a complex social and emotional issue. Please don't forget this. Those of us on the spectrum need to see a very large number of examples of appropriate clothing for different situations.

Why are some trousers casual and others formal? Why are comfortable, practical "mom jeans" viewed with such derision while hideous and expensive pencil jeans are lauded? Why on earth are men's ties so important? And why, oh why, does women's underwear so often come in itchy, extra itchy, and itchier-than-heck?

These are difficult questions, and even more difficult ones face children with autism or Asperger's every day at school. The clothing that is extra-cool when an "alpha" child wears it is mocked cruelly when the low kid on the totem pole tries to copy it. People who give lip service to "it's what's inside that counts" treat expensively dressed people better than cheaply dressed people. It's crazy.

And it's enough to drive a child up the wall. Let me give some examples of teaching the ins and outs of what to wear to help you sort through the chaos.

THE MYSTERY OF CLOTHING
EXPLAINED BY EXAMPLES

For those children who have Asperger's like me, detailed verbal explanations of visual examples can be a big, big help. (This technique can be adjusted to be less verbal and more visual for children who can't process a lot of words.)

For all of us on the spectrum, the more concrete, memorable examples we get, the more likely it is that we will be able to generalize clothing concepts.

My dad didn't know about all of this, but he did want me to be successful in my profession as an adult, so he started teaching me this way very early.

Whenever we would be on an outing of any sort, he would point out various women to me (not in their hearing) and discourse on the effect of what they were wearing.

"See that woman? No matter how smart she is, she would never be taken seriously in a business meeting. Her clothing is too revealing and too tight, so people, both men and women, will see her as a lightweight, or even a bimbo.

"That woman over there is wearing the right clothing for a business meeting, but it's all too tight. Some people think wearing the smallest clothes they can fit into makes them seem thinner, but actually it makes them look fatter and also unprofessional.

"There's a woman who looks really smart. Her outfit sends a clear signal of professionalism and intelligence. If she's not smart, it won't fool people for long, but since she looks smart she'll have a better chance of being listened to and heard. Getting that chance to prove yourself is very important."

And when I was watching the Miss America pageant on TV (a fascinating social phenomenon I never did figure out) he would say things like this:

"See that girl right there? If you look closely at her features, she doesn't have a very pretty face, but you wouldn't know that because of how she presents and packages herself. Her smile helps too—smiling can make people seem more attractive. But the way she packages herself is very important. People are influenced a lot by how you package yourself."

So over and over, my dad talked to me in a very direct, factual way about the way in which people dress affects how they are seen by others. This meant that I knew darn well that other people have a social and emotional reaction to clothing. It doesn't mean I understood how to dress every day, but it meant I knew what I was aiming for and I had a really good idea of how to dress for an interview.

It is hard, really hard, for most of us on the spectrum to work out those social and emotional issues of clothing. In fact, without specific instruction, we are unlikely to really understand that there are serious social and emotional communication issues involved in how we dress.

By making me aware that those issues exist, my dad did me a huge favor.

Of course, I also went through the usual thing of having my mother and sister question my fashion choices, but if I didn't understand that those choices had meaning, I wouldn't have listened much.

And when I say "questioned my fashion choices" I mean that there were many, many, many days when I came down to breakfast and one or both of them said, with an expression of horror, "Are you going to wear *that?*"

Tactful, huh? But I wouldn't have gotten a subtle hint. And many Aspies and auties need even firmer hints. Okay, not hints. Direct, clear statements.

But sometimes we do need to be cut more than a little slack. Sometimes the game is not worth the candle.

THE PRE-SCHOOL RED TURTLENECK BLUES

When my brother was about four, he developed a love of red, long-sleeved turtlenecks. In fact, regardless of weather, season, or anything else, he would choose a red, long-sleeved turtleneck to wear every day.

His pre-school teachers objected. They complained to my mother, "Can't you make him wear *something* else? It isn't normal. He's going to have to learn to dress normally sometime."

But my mom decided that if Jimmy wanted to wear a red long-sleeved turtleneck every darn day of the week, then she would just have to buy some more red, long-sleeved turtlenecks and make sure he always had a clean one.

But why? My mom is a firm believer that a parent's job is to prepare his or her children to be the highest-functioning adults that that parent-child combo is capable of developing. And she certainly wanted Jimmy to be able to hold a job, fit in socially, and make good choices.

She let Jimmy wear what he wanted because that was not the right battle to fight at that time. He was learning social skills and improving his ability to speak by leaps and bounds. He was growing mentally and socially. She knew that all of that learning and growing was pretty intense and that Jimmy was loaded with all he could handle.

She also knew that Jimmy's sensory issues were pretty severe at that time. Having a soft cotton top that covered his neck and arms was comforting to him. It meant he was less likely to get upset by sudden breezes, and it protected him from the fear of feeling a sudden light touch on his arm from a teacher or classmate. This helped him be calmer.

And he loved red shirts at the time. He was not into *Star Trek,* so wearing a red shirt held only positive associations for him, such as reminding him of the Red Power Ranger. Red made him feel happier than any other color at the time.

So Mom let Jimmy wear his red, long-sleeved turtlenecks. She figured that as long as it was really an appropriate shirt for the situation anyway, and as long has he had so many new things on his plate, she could and would be flexible enough to let Jimmy be a little inflexible in that one area.

Eventually, Jimmy outgrew his red turtleneck phase. Partly it was because Mom weaned him off of them gradually with other colors of turtlenecks. Maybe it helped that his OT was working on his sensory diet and taught Mom to "brush" him to help makes his skin less sensitive. Maybe the other colored Power Rangers became more appealing to him. Maybe he just matured a little and wanted more variation in his dress.

So Jimmy outgrew his phase of wearing a turtleneck of the same color almost every day. However, I don't want to give you false hope. As of this writing, Steve Jobs is fifty-four years old, and he still hasn't outgrown this particular problem yet.

REASONS FOR CLOTHING

The reasons for wearing certain kinds of clothing are very odd and hard to understand. Just as "one pill makes you larger and one pill makes you small," one outfit makes you chic and one makes you look a fool. It's a really difficult thing for anyone with an ASD to wrap his/her head around.

This is sometimes easier for lower-functioning kids. Simple repetition with visual aids, such as "fashion shows" made up of photos of typical children on the playground, at church or temple, and so forth, may well be enough. Once a child has learned the clothing rules for 2nd grade, it may be hard to get him or her to understand that the rules on the playground change for 3rd grade, but other children may be coached to give the obviously disabled child some slack in this area.

If a handful of well-liked children or a classroom full of typical kids is coached to be thoughtful and supportive towards disabled children, whether mainstreamed or not, it is possible for a disabled child to get kind feedback and encouragement for all sorts of things, not just clothing. Something to think about.

(Don't assume that children will naturally be kind and flexible with disabled children. This varies tremendously, and one or two mean-spirited children can influence a whole school to be less than kind.)

If another child says, "Those are great jeans but your top doesn't fit," and the child says it kindly and helpfully, that can go a long way towards getting any kid, not just one with autism, to accept the weird and arbitrary standards for clothing in our society.

But sometimes children just have to learn to accept that human fashion choices and their social impact are just rules that *are*, not logical constructs. My mom communicated this to me quite clearly.

My parents always took us to church, every Sunday. We attended some kind of Sunday School for as long as I can remember. This attendance at religious rituals is not a necessary part of bringing up children on the spectrum, but it was part of my upbringing.

Having paid a great deal of attention in Sunday School and being inclined to think about these kinds of things a lot, I went to my mother with a conundrum. It was, I told her, illogical that we had to dress up for church instead of wearing our ordinary clothes.

"Why would God care what I wear?" I asked her, quite pointedly.

"God doesn't care what you wear, but *I do*," she responded with thorough finality.

By then, I had learned that even if I won an argument with my mother on points, she won because she controlled the TV, cookies, and general access to fun stuff. So I stopped asking questions and dressed up for church.

Later on, she explained to me that the main reason she had us dress up for church is so that we would get practice in being dressed up every week. By having us wear dressy clothes regularly, she was ensuring that when we dressed up for special occasions and, eventually, for job interviews, we would seem comfortable, natural, and competent in our clothing.

Having seen what happens when a woman who has never worn dressy shoes or a skirt tries to wear those things for the first time at an important occasion, I think my mother was very wise. If you can't walk in relatively low heels and don't know how to cross your legs in a skirt, you will look foolish dressed up. And who needs to look foolish because of their clothing? I look foolish on my own often enough!

HOW TO MAKE CLOTHES WEARABLE

The dressing up for church thing is a good example of how to teach something to a child with an autism spectrum disorder. I had to dress up once a week no matter what, so I got lots of practice over a long period of time, but with enough time in between to recover from any given bout with a bad fashion choice.

Constant practice in finding clothing appropriate for various occasions can teach children a lot about selecting clothes. More important, it will teach the parents what the child can tolerate. It's much easier to teach a child to select appropriate clothing once you have a good idea of what his or her limits in the area of clothing are.

Fortunately for me, my mother was alert to and understanding of some of the problems that came with sensory issues because of her own sensory issues. She looked for clothing for us that fit a safe sensory profile.

The "safe" clothes were ones that were not itchy. Lace and other details on the outside, where they never touched the skin, were okay. Itchy and close to the skin meant the outfit was a no-go.

Also, the safest clothes, from a sensory standpoint, are machine washable. This is important for several reasons.

When you go clothes shopping, you may notice that brand-new clothes have a distinctive smell from the dyes and from the chemicals that are applied to make the dyes stay put. One popular chemical that is often applied to new clothing is formaldehyde. No, I'm not kidding. It "sets" the dye and prevents the dyes from different pieces of clothing from getting on other clothes during shipping. Thus, most new clothes are very smelly to anyone with a sensitive nose, and very irritating to anyone with sensitive skin or skin allergies.

So new clothes, *all* new clothes, should be washed before wearing. If it's machine washable, that's easy.

Additionally, machine washing and drying softens clothing slightly each time. This can be a big help, as people with sensory issues often need to pick their softest, most comfortable clothing on stressful days.

Knowing that an old, frequently washed shirt is softer than a new one, you can pick what is most likely to work for a difficult situation.

Of course, the most important thing is that children with ASDs will eventually need to learn to help care for their own clothing, and machine washing is easier and faster than hand-washing and dry cleaning. If you hope that your child will be able to help with this kind of self-care someday, then get him or her in the habit of choosing machine washable clothing.

Okay, maybe that wasn't the most important thing. Depends on your point of view. My mom restricted our ability to choose non-washable clothes because, for most of her adult life, she has been trying to raise one or another really difficult child. (My sister wasn't so difficult, she's just really smart and cute, but she overlapped me, so Mom never had an escape from the diffi-kids.)

When you are raising a difficult child, you need to save time and energy where you can. Doing wash by hand or running to the dry cleaners is time-consuming. Save yourself the hassle.

WHERE ARE THE LIMITS?

For many, many parents of children with ASDs, at some point what the child wears becomes a subject of fights and struggles. This can be common among teens with Asperger's and high-functioning autism.

The question is, when do you switch from saying, "Is that what you are planning to wear today?" to saying, "You are *not* going to wear that today."

Be thoughtful, be judicious, and be sympathetic. If a child has only one or two outfits that fit his or her current sensory needs, then don't expect a lot of variety (see red turtleneck story above). You really cannot fairly expect someone to wear clothing that is seriously uncomfortable, scratchy, or even painful to them. If you do decide to expect that kind of clothing to be worn, don't expect much in the way of good behavior, social awareness, or learning to occur.

If a child is going through a very stressful time and is greatly comforted by items related to a special interest, don't try to ban those tattered "Transformers" t-shirts or whatever it is. Work with the child on finding other comforting items that can be carried more subtly, such as printing out wallet-sized pictures of beloved characters and then laminating them for safe carrying. Get the new comfort in place before trying to phase out the old one.

When serious questions arise about a child's clothing, you will seldom go wrong if you address the whole child rather than just trying to cram him or her into the right outfit.

If necessary, go back to the idea that you are trying to teach the child a life-long skill, not get him or her to fall into line instantly. Get some more catalogs and sale ads and start cutting out pictures of different clothes (with the child's help, if he can manage it). Go through the pictures with him and work on matching the clothes to categories like "at home," "at school," and "at formal occasions."

Then try helping him sort the clothes in his closet into the same categories. Work on helping him learn to see where the actual clothes he has can be worn. Give him a chance to learn the big picture.

If that's too much for your child, maybe you could simply try taking a few of his clothes and two signs labeled with a picture of a school and your home. Help him figure out which clothes go where, but only work on one or two outfits at a time.

If you just can't do that, try getting a camera, any camera, and taking pictures of your ASD child—and any siblings who might be game—in different outfits. Post some pictured outfits on his closet under those "school" and "home" signs so he has an easy visual way to find clothes. Add more pictures as you get a chance. Do this with other young children in the family, because it sure won't hurt them and then they won't be left out of the picture-posting stuff.

In short, use every visual means you can think of to help your child select appropriate clothing. Instead of scolding him for doing the wrong thing, set him up to succeed so you can tell him how great he looks.

BUT WHAT ABOUT GOTH AND EMO AND OTHER SCARY STUFF?

I know, somewhere one of you is harumphing over all this. Never mind the young kids, you think, what about my scary, scary teen who is eager to pierce everything and dress like something out of a Tim Burton movie?

First of all, if your child has the design and sewing skills to actually dress like something out of a Tim Burton movie, congratulations! Get that kid into classes in drawing and computer-aided design! This December, buy him/her a sewing machine and stand back!

With the "high-functioning" kids, the whole issue of teaching a child to pick or at least accept appropriate clothing can get very messy around the tween and teen years. A child who was always content to wear a variety of fairly typical styles and colors may suddenly decide that a black-mesh faux straight jacket is the height of self-expression.

I tried to express myself in that way a lot. While I would have killed to dress like Winona Ryder in *Beetlejuice,* I wound up simply trawling through the local thrift shops in search of weird, weirder, and weirdest.

In the early-to-mid '80s, I decided that bell-bottoms were for me— at exactly the time when pants were tightly pegged and the paper-bag waist was on the fashion horizon.

There was a pair of paisley velvet bell-bottoms that my mom said made me look like a middle-aged woman in Vegas in the early '70s. There were a variety of odd and tattered shirts, including my beloved Marx Brothers T, which had seen better days perhaps several years before I found it selling for fifty cents.

And then my sister and I discovered MTV. The resultant explosions of eye makeup, big '80s hair, and mesh over-vests can scarce be described in mere words.

(Aside to Cath: I'm really sorry that I never let you borrow my pink mesh over-vest. You would have looked way cuter in it than I did.)

So what did my mother, who was determined to make sure I knew how to dress for any occasion, who made me dress up for church, who could lay down the law like an old-timey sheriff, do?

Not all that much, actually. As long as the clothing was clean, neat, and appropriate to the occasion, she simply let me wear what I liked, no matter how *outre.*

This meant that I got to wear some truly awful clothes to school. As long as they provided adequate skin coverage and were, basically, within the realm of school clothing, I could wear them. Even the dreaded paisley bellbottoms.

If something I dug up at a thrift shop was dressy enough, clean enough, and generally appropriate for church, I could wear it there. If it wasn't really dressy/tidy/etc., I could wear it around the house.

My mom chose her battles carefully. If I knew I could wear the mesh vest and the Marx Bros T at home and to school, then I was more flexible on what I wore to church.

She was still strict on some things. Showing an inappropriate amount of cleavage was still a no-no. She also very clearly and repeatedly explained that the fad for showing bra straps only worked if you bought bras with straps that were designed for show, and she was not going to pay for extra bras. Broad, comfy bra straps, she explained, always look tacky and cheap when they show, regardless of fashion. And there was no such thing as wearing a bra as a top in her world, thank you very much.

Additionally, things had to fit properly. No squeezing into an outfit I liked the style of just because it was the only one I could find—if it was too tight, it wasn't to be worn.

I really strongly feel that my mom's choice to be flexible where she could be had a positive impact on my style choices and my growing-up process. Now that I am all grown-up, I understand that it takes money and/or time and/or skill to be good at being *outre,* so I tend to be extremely dull in my clothing choices. But I wouldn't have been able to get to the point where I see the advantage to having my clothes say as little as possible if I hadn't had the chance to have clothes that said, "I'm a TEENAGER and I'm EXPRESSING MYSELF."

And I do enjoy the annual unofficial "Goth Day" at Disneyland. Many of the people who show up in serious Goth regalia would have easily met my mother's standards. I find myself rating their outfits by those standards now.

What would I ban for the teen who has decided to express that they belong inside a group of outsiders? The same things Mom would have.

"Goth Day" gives me plenty of examples. The girl who doesn't want to have to buy the fancy corset twice, so she buys it in the size she thinks she'll be once she gets a chance to work out more often. No, no, no. If you're going to wear a corset, get one that fits you now, and if you lose or gain weight, sell it on Craig's List, but don't wear it.

And, of course, if you wear a corset as outerwear, it better darn well have a nice black layering tee under it. Or maybe lavender. Or blood red. But the world does not need to see underage boobies being flaunted/strangled via a too-small corset.

So if your teen is going to wear all black to Disneyland, it should all fit, it should not be revealing, and it should be appropriate to the weather. Wearing your super-cool long black leather coat on a 90-degree F day results in unattractive smells, so unless you intend to shower at midday and then pay for the dry-cleaning yourself, leave it at home.

In other words, I do believe that teens have the right to choose to dress according to whatever odd group they feel comfortable in. They just don't have the right to wear inappropriately warm, revealing, tight, baggy, or dry-clean-only outfits.

And that black dress with the full crinoline is only okay for church if there is plenty of pew space to go around. Crinolines mean taking up three places instead of one, and it is not polite to crowd people out for the sake of fashion.

Oh, and while I'm imagining I'm parenting a teen, he/she is *not* allowed to wear heels over two inches, or to wear platform shoes. Not while I'm paying the podiatrist, darnit.

Manners, Manners, Manners

POLITENESS IS A LIFE SKILL

I often see teens with autism or Asperger's with their parents at various conferences and conventions. Some are dragged to an autism conference in the hope that they will somehow pick up on some of what is covered; some are there because the parents could get no respite care. One adorable young girl was in Pasadena to meet her hero, Temple Grandin.

Some of these teens, when introduced, will look more or less at (or towards) me. Many will shake my hand, and say something fairly appropriate, such as, "Pleased to meet you." Some can only get out a "hi" or perhaps a wave. Some wave with their left hand while shaking with their right.

And some of these teens will just not look up, not look at all in my direction, and keep playing whatever portable video game they have in hand. The most I get from them is a grunt. They have Asperger's (this doesn't happen much with autism), they don't like dealing with people, they can't cope in a crowded place, they didn't ask to be introduced to me, and they don't want to interrupt their games.

What I'd like to say to all of the latter group is HEY, THERE'S A REASON THE GAME HAS A PAUSE BUTTON!

Here's the deal: if a nonverbal kid who, despite being able to read, write, and use PECS, still has a testable IQ well under eighty, can, in fact, manage to look towards me (or towards my feet) and form a barely-comprehensible "hello" while pulling back and waving to avoid the feared contact of a handshake, IF all that is true, THEN, my fellow Aspies, those of us without those problems need to rise to the occasion.

Yes, it's true. I expect a teen with Asperger's to be able to look in my general direction and say, "Hi." Or, "Pleased to meet you." Or, "Hail, fellow well met." I don't care about the details; I care about the basic acts of courtesy being there.

A disturbing trend seems to be taking place these days. More and more parents are letting kids of all levels of developmental functioning simply not be reasonably polite.

If you are raising a child who cannot look at faces or manage more than a wave, that's okay. We can all accept that people with ASDs have some limitations.

But more and more, parents seem to be excusing children from working at the level they are capable of. "He's disabled, so it's too hard." "He has Asperger's, he's not very social." "I don't feel like pushing him right now."

Look, the reality is that it is totally unimportant to me as an individual that some people who are introduced to me do not acknowledge the introduction. As a person who cares about the lives and well-being of people on the spectrum and the society we live in, it does matter to me. In fact, it matters a lot.

WE'RE ALL IN THIS TOGETHER

The reality is that waving, shaking hands, saying "hi" and making small talk are very, very unnatural things for people with ASDs to do. The bigger reality is that all of those are unnatural things for *everyone* to do.

Yes, NTs do have an easier time learning all of those little social greetings and mannerisms. They can learn more of them, they can learn them faster, and they can generalize them well enough to usually get the right gesture or phrase in the right situation.

That doesn't mean any of it is "natural" to anybody.

Natural behavior would be very different. Many people have pointed out that the world would be very different if people were just completely honest, didn't use artificial social phrases, didn't "put on airs," and generally acted in a way that expressed how they truly felt.

It would be different. It would also be a lot smellier, messier, and generally non-functional. You, yes you, would know exactly who thinks your nose is too big or too small. You would know exactly which of your relatives thought your sister, brother, or cousin turned out better than you did. You would know why and how people rejected you for stupid, stupid reasons.

A few of those reading this already know those things, because they are surrounded by people who do not understand that manners make society run. My sympathies go out to them.

We need manners to make the day functional. For example, we need a set of phrases for interactive greetings, so that when we see the people at work or school we can acknowledge their existence and that we have a generally positive desire to work smoothly with them. Or at least that we want to get through one more day without strangling them.

So, for all of the parents and others with Asperger's and the like that may be reading this: when someone says, "Have a nice day," that does not mean they are telling you what kind of day you should have. Do not get angry because you don't want to have a day that fits what you think that person means by "nice." It is only a very mild positive wish that your day would be such that it would suit you. And it is not considered to be an order or a restricting instruction.

OKAY, I'LL GET TO THE POINT NOW

All of that hubbub above is meant to convey two important ideas to people who have to raise or teach people on the spectrum: first, that politeness and ordinary kindness are important skills that we all need and, second, that there are a lot of people on the spectrum to whom this is completely non-obvious.

This means that it is pretty important to teach children with ASDs basic manners (at the level they can manage) from a very early age. Whatever the current age of the child or teen you are raising/teaching is, that's where you start.

While being polite and kind are things that we as a society often feel should come from the heart and not be artificial or strained, sometimes they have to be. You see, being polite and kind is a habit that can be developed. And, as I've pointed out before, those of us who happen to be on the spectrum learn well by rote and repetition.

During my childhood, and again during my brother's, this meant being polite and kind was reinforced a lot. I know that there are a lot of highly qualified and smart teachers, OTs, and speech-paths out there who are working with children on having good manners and good social skills.

For the most part, those teachers, OTs and speech-paths are working on those skills one-on-one or in small groups. They will role-play with children and then send them out onto the playground, confident that the child is well-rehearsed. And when the child gets or gives a black eye, they will say, "He just won't do what we went over. I don't know why, but he just won't do it."

Having read the previous chapters, you say, "Well, of course he can't do it on the playground. He can't very well transfer a skill learned in one kind of place to a completely different kind of place."

You are right, astute reader. I am about to repeat information I've given before. The ASD child who is trained to do a certain skill in a classroom with an adult will have a heck of a hard time transferring it to the playground. In fact, expecting such transference is like expecting the average child to explain Richard Feynmann's QED after a few hours of coaching.

(If you don't know what Feynmann's QED is, that's kind of the point. Heck, I'm pretty bright for my age—I'm forty-four, but read at a forty-five-year-old level—and the whole thing is Greek to me.)

Manners are like that. A child will only be able to use the manners that he has practiced a lot and has seen his parents use clearly enough to have a good idea of who says what when. The degree of practice needed varies, as does the degree of exaggeration and pointedness the parents (or other family members, or teachers, or the local community theater group) need to use when acting out examples.

If the folks who were introduced to me at conferences had basic greeting behavior pounded into them the way I had it pounded into me, it would have been automatic for them to pause the game and go into "official greeting mode" for about fifteen seconds. No muss, no fuss, no big deal, and it's a habit that pays off big over time.

And if I, as a teen, had failed to go into official greeting mode and had continued to play a hand-held game (which didn't exist at the time, but bear with me anyway), my mom would have had that game to herself for a few days. Capisce?

LEARN TO SHAKE HANDS THE ROY MCILWEE WAY

Okay, you say, but how about a practical example?

I thought you'd never ask. The following is about how my dad taught me to shake hands. Shaking hands may or may *not* be what you want your child to do; ASD kids who are taught to shake hands with other children in a social skills classroom tend to wind up being made fun of a lot for then trying to greet other children in the regular classroom.

However, this isn't just about shaking hands. It's about teaching the entire skill, so that the child can actually be polite by using the skill when it is appropriate.

For several years, from when I was about four to about eight, my dad frequently worked with me on my handshake. It was important to him that I be able to make a living as an adult, so he wanted me to have this handy and extremely useful behavior down for business purposes. After all, most job interviews and sales calls do begin with a handshake.

At first, he just worked with me on my grip, starting with, "Okay, honey, I want you to shake hands with me now." (I knew what shaking hands was—I watched *Bewitched* and *The Addams Family* all the time.)

And as soon as I did shake hands with him, the lesson began.

"No, you don't want to just put your limp hand in mine. If your hand is limp or your grip is weak, the other person will think you are weak or unsure of yourself.

"No, don't squeeze really hard. When you use a lot of brute strength in a handshake, the other person will think you are pushy and too aggressive.

"That's more like it. Use a firm grip but not too hard. Don't squeeze my hand, but don't let your hand go limp. A firm handshake will convey confidence and friendliness, but don't shake for more than a few seconds."

And on and on and on. He went over it with me, seemingly spontaneously, on many different occasions.

I might mention that Dad was really careful to be clear in his explanations of how my handshake would affect how I was perceived by the other person. Dad just wanted me to make a good impression, but without knowing it, he was giving me a GIANT clue to the magical and much-misunderstood realm of "theory of mind."

Yes, if you want your child to know that other people have different perceptions of them and each other, you might try using spoken language, written language, or pictures to communicate exactly that. My dad didn't know that I desperately needed an intellectual understanding of how different people might think, but he handed it to me on a silver platter.

After he was satisfied that I had a good grip, and that I understood how long a handshake could last, it was time to up the ante.

Dad explained it to me in detail. "I'm going to introduce you to some of my friends at church. Church is a social occasion, so if I introduce you to a man, you should extend your hand first.

"In social situations, the woman always extends her hand first. If you shake hands with a woman who is significantly older than you, you should allow her to extend her hand first. If you shake hands with a female who is about your age, either of you can extend a hand.

"Don't forget, the rules for social handshakes are different than business handshakes. In business, the person who has the highest rank in the company extends his or her hand first. If you are dealing with a customer, you wait until he extends his (or her) hand first. If you go on a job interview, wait until the interviewer extends his or her hand first."

WAIT A MINUTE

But, some of you are saying, what about my average autistic kid who does not understand huge amounts of speech and wouldn't know or care about the difference between a social and business situation? What about the kids who aren't weird little hyper-verbal mutants like you were? Huh, Jenn?

There are a lot of kids who are completely different in their ability to parse verbal directions, and that is totally cool. The difference is not in the overall kind of teaching, but in the specifics of transmitting the information.

If you were trying to teach a child/teen/adult with low receptive verbal skills to shake hands, you would have to use few words and highly exaggerated responses.

First, you might want to make sure you started with a simple demonstration with just that one word: "handshake." As in you enlist a spouse, friend, or cable-installation guy to shake hands with you for the child to see, repeatedly doing so while saying that one word once for each shake—"handshake."

Then you would warn the child that you are about to shake his hand, and do so. If his handshake is limp, you tell him "harder" and give a little bit of a firm grip so he can feel what "harder" means. If his handshake is too firm, you would need to say, "Ow, too hard!" and possibly overact badly, writhing in pain until he released his grip.

If you use "The Incredible Four-Point Scale," you can use the numbers 1-4 to teach your child that a very limp grip is a 1, an overly firm grip is a 4, and a 2 or 3 is just right.

It's not too hard to use pictures, simple phrases, and repetition to teach a child that handshaking is something you do upon meeting an adult at work or church, temple, or the skeptics' club meeting, but not at school. You really can cover the whole nine yards if that's what you'd like to do.

The point? If you choose to teach handshaking to a child on the spectrum, it doesn't matter whether the child needs words, pictures, or demonstrations to get it. What matters is that you decide that, for the politeness skills you teach, you are going to teach all of the needed information. The needed information includes with whom to use the skill, where the skill is used, and any other little details that might be involved.

Yes, you do have to pick and choose your details. Some of the below stuff (in the continuance of the Roy McIlwee Method) could be overwhelming and confusing. But you do need to work on those whens, wheres, whys, and whos. You do need to give the details that matter for that child and for that skill.

This, by the way, is why I think it's just super when a teen who has an official "cognitive age" of two greets me with a "hi there" and a wave. That means he's been taught politeness skills that can be used in a whole bunch of situations so that he doesn't wind up greeting a stranger in a men's room with a hearty hug or squeezing the hand of an astonished checkout clerk. His skills respect his own verbal level and his need not to be touched, and they also show respect for the other people around him. Awesome!

Plus, it's just nice when people who have a heck of a hard road to follow in life are able to be polite and friendly. It makes the world seem a little brighter, and it reminds you that everyone around you has that same core human value, regardless of verbal skills, testable IQ, or ability to remember detailed instructions in social situations. It's a happy thing, you know?

BACK TO THE ROY MCILWEE SCHOOL OF BUSINESS

My dad was really thorough and went over and over all the handshaking details with me. He didn't do it all at once, but there was a lot of overlap from session to session. He also didn't do it in an organized way, really. He just had gotten it into his head that I needed to know all of this stuff and would never pick it up on my own.

So he went over the rules with me. He introduced me to friends at church so I would have practice in an appropriate situation. (An appropriate situation is one where, if the child repeats the action in the same and similar situations, there will probably not be a problem with that.)

He discussed the fact that if someone was wearing gloves when you shook hands with them, you should not squeeze as hard, because they might be wearing a ring under their gloves, and it would hurt them if you squeezed.

He taught me to look for enlarged knuckles and to check to see if the other person held his/her hands in a stiff and "crabbed" position, so that I would be careful and gentle if there were signs of arthritis in the other person's hands.

He went over and over the idea that a firm (but not overly firm) handshake, brief eye contact, and a smile would make a good impression most of the time. He taught me that you cannot make a good impression all of the time, because once in a while you deal with a person who is not in a good mood or is just plain difficult, but you can do your best each time, and therefore make that good impression a lot of the time.

He talked about how, outside of the workplace and the armed forces, no one outranks anyone else, because this is the USA and we respect people regardless of the color of their "collar." Even within the workplace, once the first person has extended his or her hand, rank is not important. So when you shake hands, you give the same hearty handshake and friendly greeting to the guy who works in the metal shop and to the CEO. And don't forget that sometimes they are both the same guy, and sometimes one becomes the other.

Basically, in the course of teaching me the most basic bit of business and social manners, my dad taught me that other people have their own perceptions of us, that you should be considerate of others' physical well-being, and that you should respect everyone.

THE MORAL OF THE STORY

Teaching politeness skills is important. Teaching those skills in a way that lets your child know when and how to use them is important too.

Moreover, when you can associate useful information about why and how to be polite with simple acts of politeness, that is good.

My dad taught my brother to shake hands too. Dad didn't go into the mind-bending level of detail he went into with me, but he did talk about how to be friendly, how firm the grip should be, and when to shake hands.

My dad didn't know that I desperately needed all of the information he gave me. He didn't know that it was a huge thing for me to know that a smile and a second or two of eye contact would combine to make most interactions better.

He didn't know that it was a huge thing for me to know that other people formed opinions of me from my actions, not from what I thought about myself.

But he did know that it helps out in life to have that basic skill of greeting people in a way that communicates good social "vibes." And he took the time—an awful lot of time—to teach me.

I've gotten asked by a lot of teens and quite a few adults with autism or Asperger's how they can do what I do—how they can go out there and give talks and communicate empowering information about ASDs to people who don't understand.

I don't always know what to tell them. When a teen who refuses to acknowledge me (and turn off the gosh-darn video game) when we first meet, and then, after hearing me speak, wants to know how to do what I do, I don't know how to put into words all I want to say.

But I do know that by having strong politeness skills (most of the time), I've been able to introduce myself to lots and lots of people at conferences and seminars, including the speakers, and including the people involved in running those seminars.

If I'd waited until I knew someone could help me to be polite to them, I'd never have succeeded. Fortunately, when I introduced myself to the guy working the "bookstore" table at one particular conference, I treated him like he owned the company, which is good, because he does own the company, and I get a lot of my best conference gigs through them. Heck, he's even publishing this book.

Kindness is a Life Skill

Along with politeness, kindness is a life skill. Treating others with fairness and thoughtfulness can be pretty difficult, even for socially savvy kids. Fortunately, we on the spectrum have some advantages here: we mostly tend to really love fairness and the concept of fair play, we are good at memorizing and sticking to rules, and we have great empathy.

I just heard your forehead scrunch up. How on earth could I say that people with autism have great empathy? Lack of empathy is a hallmark of autism spectrum disorders; everyone knows that!

What is usually called "lack of empathy" is, most of the time, lack of information and understanding. When we know about what hurts other people and how they feel, we tend to be pretty darn sympathetic *and* empathetic, but we don't come by that information easily.

I've spent about thirty-seven years *consciously* observing and trying to work out typical human facial expressions, nonverbal communication, emotional reactions and behavior patterns. It is a tough set of things to figure out, and I'm still often confused. But I keep at it.

If your child can't read faces or parse verbal intonations, he can't show empathy because he can't determine who is upset and when. If your child doesn't understand that other people have their own set of feelings and reactions that are separate from hers, she also can't understand that, just because she thinks it is fun to spin and spin around the classroom, the people she slams into inadvertently are definitely not having fun.

What's more, many Aspies and auties like to spend time alone when they/we are upset. When you are easily overwhelmed by social interaction, stress makes you flee social interaction. Having that as your baseline of coping, it is hard to somehow magically figure out that many others prefer to have a buddy or sympathizer around when they feel down.

It's been said (by Simon Baron Cohen, no less) that autism is "the extreme male mind." Guys who are stressed are more likely to retreat to their caves, excuse me, rec rooms, and watch sports, absorb themselves in a hobby, or simply not do anything much for a while. Women who are stressed want to gather in bunches and cope as a group. Neither is better or worse—sometimes trying the other way is good, and sometimes going with your instincts is better.

With all of the above and more as reasons, for those of us on the spectrum, kindness is something we have to be consciously *taught*.

Kindness does go with politeness. Working on those politeness skills will help your child become more kind. But more is needed.

MODEL KINDNESS EVERY DAY

It is not necessary, or even practical, for parents to be kind to their children in the moment, every moment. It is, in fact, absolutely necessary to seem unkind to your child sometimes in order to raise a child who isn't a spoiled brat. After all, taking away privileges or sending a child to a "cool off" space may not seem the kindest thing to that child, but it is often for the best.

Modeling kindness does *not* mean being sweet and nice and oh-so-cuddly every moment of the day. It means doing the things that are kind, pointing out the things that are kind, and whenever possible explaining what is kind.

I grew up in what some call a "traditional family." My dad worked full time out of the house, and my mom was a full-time mom. Okay, every mom is a full-time mom, or at least the ones who know what they are doing, but she didn't work outside the home.

As she was wont to point out, she was not a housewife, she was a homemaker. She was not married to a house, she made the home what it should be for her family.

(For those of you interested in debating the stay-at-home mom vs. the working-outside-of-the-home mom, I would be totally happy to address that if you will just meet me in the right place for it. The line forms to the left. Of Neptune.)

At any rate, this arrangement meant that my mom did all of the cooking and most of the cleaning (except when we kids actually did stuff). And every night, after dinner, before he left the table, my dad thanked her for making the meal. In fact, for every meal she prepared that my dad ate while I was present, he thanked her.

I wish he'd told us kids we had to say thank you too. She really deserved it every darn day.

The point is that while it is not necessary to thank people every day, and while many, many people get away with not saying thank you without anyone thinking they are rude or crude, it is kind and appropriate to say thank you for things that most folks take for granted.

My parents constantly modeled kindness and thoughtfulness towards each other, not because they absolutely had to, but because they had goodwill towards each other, and goodwill towards other humans can best be expressed with kind and thoughtful words and acts.

No, your child with autism will not, in all likelihood, learn a lot of kindness skills just by witnessing kind behaviors, but it is very important to put as many examples into their lives as possible to give them a chance to see how these things work in real life.

Direct teaching, directing the child to do specific things that are kind, and teaching the child rules for kindness are important. But the constant flow of examples is very likely to have an impact.

GIVE US DATA, PLEASE!

We on the spectrum share a trait with most of the rest of the human race—we are self-centered. This is meant almost literally—my universe centers around me, and I tend to suppose that the world is a good place when I am happy and a bad place when I am depressed.

Most typical kids pick up on the fact that others' feelings of unhappiness or sadness are independent of theirs. Most typical kids learn that it is important to show a reasonable amount of sympathy in these situations. Of course, a good number of the really, really intuitively socially aware kids learn to use other kids' weaknesses as weapons and kick them when they are down, but usually that is not the problem with kids on the spectrum.

What those of us on the spectrum need is lots and lots of data. We need to be told, in words, pictures, by whatever means necessary, when other people feel hurt. We need to be told that telling other people that they are fat is unkind and unnecessary. We need to be told that if we are mean or physically hurt someone that it will make them not like us.

We need raw data on how to be kind. I had a lot of kindness pretty much pounded into me as a kid, and I am grateful for it.

My Auntie Nan wasn't aware of autism or Asperger's. She was my great aunt, and had been a teacher back in the day. She taught me to be kind in one specific way; she taught me to write thank-you notes.

How did she teach me that? First, she taught my mom and her brother, my Uncle Jim. When they were kids, they did not always promptly send thank-you notes.

After a Christmas or birthday on which she gave either of them a gift, if she didn't get a thank-you note, they didn't get a present next time.

It is a very serious learning experience to be sitting on the floor by the Christmas tree on the morning of December 25th and find you have no present from Auntie Nan. Especially if she is sitting right there. Especially if she says, "Well, dear, I never heard from you about your birthday present, so I realized you must not like my taste in gifts, and I didn't want to bother you with something you wouldn't enjoy anyway."

Brutal. Hardcore. But it worked so well that, as soon as I was old enough to write a thank-you note, my mom made me do so. She explained that I really, really had to write a thank-you note to Auntie Nan, and filled me in on the details.

Yes, it was brutal, but it taught. It is super-duper unkind not to acknowledge gifts. It is impolite too. It implies that you consider it the role of others to just shower you with presents and you don't have to do a darn thing to show any gratitude.

And somehow, sending thank-you notes has made me more grateful for getting presents. No, I am not perfect in this area. Sometimes I am stumped, sometimes I am swamped, and some Decembers I get the flu. But I do make phone calls, write notes, and otherwise let people know I appreciate them.

Of course, if your child actually can't write thank-you notes, you may have to improvise. Sometimes you don't have time to be creative, but if you can get your child to crayon pictures to send as thank-yous, great. If you can get him/her to sign or say thank-you, still great. Whatever you can do to implement appropriate signs of gratitude, you do it.

This is a kindness issue more than a manners one (although the two are deeply related in some ways).

One of the hardest areas to develop empathy or sympathy in is the area of appreciating what others do for us. After all, we are all born assuming that as soon as we want something, it is our job to scream like heck until we get it, and then simply take it when it is given.

So it is perfectly normal and natural for us, as humans, to take others' gifts for granted, whether it is our mom who makes us a peanut butter sandwich when we just can't face the tuna casserole, or a relative who supplies a vitally-needed part for our killer robot.

It can be a good thing to express to your child(ren) that gratitude is good, and that we should appreciate what others do for us. Yes, that is a good thing, but it really is a pretty abstract concept. We on the spectrum deal better with concrete stuff.

Saying thank you, writing thank-you notes, and other actual ways of expressing gratitude are concrete. If we see these concrete things practiced and are put through the paces of doing these activities of gratitude, we might just pick up on the idea that others matter.

So if your child makes his bed or picks up his toys without you having to force him to, then thank him. If someone does something nice for him, then you do need to prompt a "thank you." And thank-you notes are like affirmations—if you write them often enough, they might just penetrate your brain.

One word of warning for those whose children are technically able to write thank-you notes on their own—read the notes, especially the first few times.

A dear friend of mine, a true genius with a passel of education under her belt, decided that it was about time her son learned to write his own thank-you notes. She decided to read his notes just to make sure they were reasonably readable and clear.

What she found was that he had, on every note, carefully explained what the person needed to get him to go with the toys they had gotten him for Christmas/Hanukkah/Solstice/Whatever. He had put a great deal of thought into what he wanted for next C/H/S/W, and gave precise instructions on future buying.

My friend had to explain to him that the purpose of thank-you notes is to show gratitude, not greed, and that it is not okay to ask for more gifts that way.

Of course, in between reading his notes and having him write new ones, she nearly died laughing telling me about it on the phone, but she was not laughing when she had him write new notes.

Nothing brings a point home like having to do the task all over. He will not ever make that mistake again.

CHAPTER 21

Teach the Specifics of Kindness

Kindness is a pretty complicated concept. Being kind means, by and large, behaving in a way that takes others' feelings into consideration, doing one's best to provide comfort or assistance when it is needed or appropriate, and treating others as we would like to be treated.

In other words, telling a child with autism to "be kind" or "be nice" is like saying "now, now, learn vector calculus while juggling ten items."

Actually, saying "be kind" can be worse. At least vector calculus, juggling, and ten items are specific, easily definable things. Kindness is very hard to put one's finger on.

Because we on the spectrum have a lot more difficulty than average doing social calculations like guessing at others' feelings and knowing when it is appropriate to intervene on others' behalf, we can do a better job at being kind if we are given lots of examples than if we are given emotional orders.

It makes sense to say, "We are visiting Nana in the hospital because it is kind. She enjoys having visitors, it makes her feel a bit better, and it makes the day more interesting and less boring for her."

It makes little sense to say, to a child who balks at such a trip, "Don't be mean!" A child who doesn't know what the visit is for has no way to comprehend that it is less than kind to refuse to go.

Similarly, if your child is behaving badly towards other children, it probably won't help to say, "Be nice!" if you haven't defined what actions go with the label "nice" recently and clearly. Don't assume that a child will be able to figure out what "nice" actions from other situations will transfer to this one.

My own Nana used to get very upset when her sons fought, and would scold them by saying, "Fight nice, boys." Hey, it makes as much sense as a lot of the instructions parents give to their children.

TEACHING DISTINCT RULES BUILDS A PATTERN

You may worry that by teaching distinct rules or guidelines for kindness, you might not be teaching the overall concept. Parents have told me that they want their child to feel kind and sympathetic rather than just do the appropriate kind behavior.

While I can understand this concern, it is not necessary to worry. If you teach clear rules, guidelines, and behaviors; if you give clear information about the kinds of feelings other people have; if you keep filling in those information gaps bit by bit, then you have a decent chance that genuinely heartfelt kindness will develop.

Those of us on the spectrum are not unfeeling monsters. We are confused and upset by a world that demands things we don't understand and constantly blames us for not understanding.

If a child gets information about kindness over years of time and many situations, gradually a picture of the whole situation has a chance to build up, and the child can form a complex picture or set of pictures to associate with words like "kindness," "good manners," and "being nice."

While it would be nice to be able to just teach broad concepts of kindness and then have the child figure out the actions from that, that's not an effective way to teach a child on the spectrum.

We do better when we are given lots and lots of small building blocks so that we can create our own understanding. Providing lots of examples and clear guidelines is an important part of the process.

DON'T BLAME THE CHILD FOR NOT KNOWING

Some kids with ASDs get in terrible trouble for not knowing how others feel or not guessing right.

Parents may worry terribly about how their very young child (or child with a very young mental or emotional age) laughs when someone gets hurt. The fact is that in a very young child, laughter comes from reaction to the outward behavior that they see without understanding what it really means.

If you don't understand other people's pain either viscerally or intellectually, you are not being cruel by laughing. You're just reacting to something you don't understand.

I got the scolding of my life once when I was visiting a friend and found that her mother was under the weather. I asked what she had, and she said, "Sinusitus." I laughed very hard at the silly, obviously made-up word and she lectured me harshly on how painful sinusitus is and how insensitive I was. In reality, I was not insensitive, just clueless. I had thought she was making a deliberate joke.

And, yes, I apologized for laughing. I was old enough by then to know that apologizing is often a non-optional social convention that has nothing to do with original intent.

So don't jump to the conclusion that your child is cold-hearted, or mean, or (I've actually heard this one from a parent) "somehow evil" if he or she doesn't understand what others are feeling. Your job is to educate the child about others' feelings and not to judge the child for maturing slowly or for having to learn by rote what other kids may grasp intuitively.

LIMITS OF UNDERSTANDING

Take me, for example. I really don't have great intuitive empathy, and I never did develop the kind of innate, instinctive, instantaneous empathy that other people seem to have and autism educators seek as the Holy Grail.

In fact, other people's emotions seem pretty strange to me. I've heard a lot about people being in "denial," and I thought I understood it, but then I saw some examples of it in people I cared about, and it totally blew my mind. I do not understand how people can take an obvious fact (e.g., they have a daughter with a drinking problem) and pretend that it doesn't exist. My brain doesn't allow for it; I am constantly stuck with reality, or at least as much of reality as I'm able to understand.

There are even more strange emotions out there that are virtually incomprehensible to me. I understand feelings like happiness, sadness, anger, loyalty, love, anxiousness, depression, exultation, determination, and being hungry.

I do not understand the desire to have grandchildren, which is in so many cases more powerful than romantic love. I do not understand people who bad-mouth their spouses—what emotional weirdness permits them to air their dirty laundry in public and feel good about it?

I certainly don't understand the many complicated emotions that go on in women who are attempting to remake their mate. The emotions involved in office politics are strange to me. Other things I don't get include love-hate relationships, frenemies, and the love of buying shoes.

Actually, the list would be much longer, but most of the emotions I don't get I can't name. I just see stuff going on that obviously involves motivations that are in no way visible or comprehensible to me, and I try to get the heck out of the way.

I've been working consciously on understanding human emotions for more than thirty-five years. What chance does a child with autism have of comprehending the vast ebb and flow of complex emotional states that exists all around him?

Fortunately, you really, really, really don't need good empathy skills to be nice.

NICENESS IS NOT EMPATHY-BASED HERE

Despite all of the above, I manage to figure out people's feelings well enough to be considered kind. To do that, I have to use my own limited emotional range and apply it as best I can to others. I also use intellectual knowledge of others' feelings to help me along.

A friend had a bad cold and was busy, so I went and got him some cold medicine. Instinctive kindness? Not at all. It was thinking through the situation that got me there.

The thought process is something like this: "Hmm, Rob has a cold and colds are pretty unpleasant. He needs to get the good kind of decongestant, not that useless PE stuff. Oh, wait, he lost his driver's license, and buying the decongestant that works requires ID, so he can't get the right thing at the drugstore. Since he can't do it, I guess I'll go get some for him."

It was a logical thing, not an emotional thing. I thought through the situation and came to a conclusion. Rob's conclusion was that I was kind. I don't really see it that way.

What rules or guidelines did I need to know to get this? Well, the rules and guidelines I was taught at various times in various situations included:

- When someone has a cold, you shouldn't call their attention to how gross they are.
- When a friend or family member is sick, it is often polite and kind to help them get what they need to feel better.
- When someone has a problem they can't solve, it is kind to ask if they would like your help.

- If someone's problem upsets you or grosses you out, you should either ignore it or help. Telling them that they are upsetting you by bleeding or crying is not usually appropriate.

But, you say, all of that is too complex for my kid. He can't parse the idea of figuring out what to do in such a situation.

Well, I sure as heck didn't start with stuff this intensely complicated. I started with simple. There are simple acts that can be done to enforce the idea of being polite and kind.

For example, when a relative is sick, a child can contribute a drawing or note to go in the envelope with the get-well card.

Enforcing the rule that we are quiet when Mommy has a headache can help teach a practical attitude towards others' problems.

Enforcing rules both ways makes them more effective: when the child is sick, he or she gets special support, and when another family member is sick, the child can help in some small way to provide the same supports. This can be as small as carrying a fresh box of tissues to the sick room or as complicated as walking to the store to buy cough drops (depending on the age and ability of the child).

Explicitly linking other's feelings to the child's feelings is helpful: a child should know that another child might be just as upset at losing a game as he is/was.

Use imagination games to help: how would Thomas the Tank Engine feel if Percy did that to him? How would characters from a favorite video game handle the situation? This can work even if the characters involved would behave badly, as you can ask your child if the behavior would work, what would happen if those behaviors occurred in real life, and so forth.

A good game of "What Would Buzz Lightyear Do?" or "What Would Dumbledore Think of That?" can get the vivid fantasy-rich imagination of a child on the spectrum turned towards social ends.

DON'T FORGET THE POSTED GUIDELINES OR SOCIAL STORIES!

In addition to specific, one-time acts or guidelines that you can coach your child on, posted guidelines for various situations can help.

Guidelines can be in words or pictures, elaborate or simple. As always, avoid absolutes or non-literal language. The pictures involved can be stick figures, drawings, photographs or clip art, as long as they are clear.

Suppose, for example, that you want your child to stop blurting out things like "That lady sure is fat," or "That man has yucky skin," in public places. Then you need to post and review the rule for what we do or do not say.

The rule for that, incidentally, is an ancient and storied one that should be pounded into their little heads with love and determination.

Just in case you didn't know this one, the Rule for Thinking Before We Speak is:

Before you say anything, ask yourself: Is it true? Is it kind? Is it necessary? If it is not kind and not necessary, it should not be said.

This is the kind of rule you can post, discuss, and review with your child. Of course, your child may say it is not kind of you to tell him it is his bedtime, and you may tell him that it is nonetheless necessary.

KINDNESS AND ILLNESS IN THE FAMILY

Suppose that you want the child to behave more appropriately when a family member is sick. If your child doesn't read or simply responds best to pictures, a chart of dos and don'ts that you go over with great dramatization can be made.

A kindness chart can start with a picture of a frowny-face, a thermometer, or other similar picture at the top to indicate that someone is sick.

The list of things that person needs can be underneath, such as a finger going "shh" (or a "smiley" type yelling face with a red circle with a line through it) to indicate that quiet is needed, a box of tissues, a bed to indicate rest, a picture of a medicine bottle, and maybe a few pictures of simple chores to indicate that each of the family members must help out a little more while the person is sick.

Similarly, a list for children who read could be something like this (again, your mileage really may vary):

When Mommy Is Sick

- We use really quiet indoor voices
- We let Mommy sleep unless there is an emergency
- Daddy will make dinner on Mommy's usual night
- We can empty her trashcan for her
- We help with laundry
- We thank Mommy for all the things she does for us when she is sick (explain that it is harder for Mommy to do these things when she is sick)

This is something you may need to brainstorm with a spouse or other adults, and you never know what rules you might find out you need to add.

For example, one child of my acquaintance kept saying that his mom was "faking it" when she got sick. He had no reason to think so, but in speaking with him it came out that he was terrified of Mommy not being there when he needed her, and he also thought that when an adult was sick, they couldn't possibly do chores.

It took a while to convince him that when a snuffly, sneezy Mommy managed to get him breakfast, this did not mean she was not sick. He also needed to be reassured that Mommy being sick did not mean she would stop taking care of him forever.

I understand, by the way, how he could be fooled into thinking that Mommy wasn't sick if she did chores. After all, as a child with Asperger's, I often stayed home sick and then was told "you aren't really sick, you're obviously faking it, or you couldn't have played outside/eaten so much/moved all of the furniture in your room."

Kids on the spectrum don't necessarily have the same grasp of how to behave when sick that normal kids do. The signals from the body that tell you to rest and not do active things do not always get through in the autistic brain.

Poor body-brain communication, combined with a limited set of self-soothing skills, may mean that a child with a fever will bounce on his small trampoline for quite some time trying to "feel better."

Heck, when I'm running a fever, I often have the urge to do a ton of physical activity. My husband has often said that when I suddenly clean the whole house in one day and spend every other minute of the day doing physical activity, he worries that I'm coming down with something.

And yes, I really was sick that time my mom went out to the store and I felt that my room "felt wrong," and so rearranged the furniture, including moving the bed to another wall, while she was out. Man, did I catch heck for that!

If you are told "You can't be sick, you couldn't have rearranged your trains if you were sick," then when Mommy is sick and still dragging herself through necessary chores, then you might just say the same about her.

The lack of empathy thing cuts both ways, no?

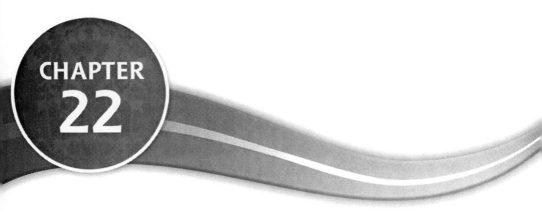

Outings Teach Life Skills

This is a tricky area. An outing into the world by a family, class, or group of friends that includes a child with an ASD can be delightful and a welcome opportunity. Or it can be an exercise in worry, stress, and desperately trying to stave off giant steaming meltdowns.

Of course, an outing into the world including only typical children, typical teens, or typical adults can also be a joy or a mess. Having a child with an ASD along just makes planning for problems and having an escape route more important.

Children, all children, learn more if they participate in field trips. These can be as minor as a trip to a model train store or as major as a trip to a gigantic theme park. One area that I'd like to strongly advocate for is the not-too-expensive trip to educational activities, such as museums, zoos, and historic sites.

Believe it or not, tons of families with kids on all different parts of the autism spectrum do manage to find ways to do these things. Okay, so they have to make adjustments, and there is a good chance that a child with autism will be slower to develop the ability to handle increasingly difficult situations. But just because a child is "behind" in his ability to handle new and different outings does not mean it is a good idea to give up.

For example, in Asperger's, the standard ratio for reckoning social and emotional maturity is to take three-quarters of the child's age. Thus, a child with Asperger's who is eight years old will most likely have roughly the emotional and social skills of a six-year-old. (Again, your mileage may vary.)

When a child (or adult) is having trouble handling the skills for dealing with new spaces and situations equivalent to that of a person several years younger, the solution is not to stop introducing new situations and opportunities. The solution is to pull back and gradually figure out the right pace for that child.

Some folks figure this is just plain unfair to any other children in the family, and even just plain unfair to the adults. After all, other families with twelve-year-olds can go on family bicycle rides without anyone using training wheels or slowing the group down so much, so it is soooooo unfair that a specific family is slowed down. All the other parents get to take their kids to the zoo without having to take elaborate detours to avoid any sight of the bird house, so it is totally unfair that this one child with autism is so terrified of birds in general that we have to be different. And all the other families get to eat the food available at the park, and we're stuck bringing food tolerable to our super-sensitive Aspie. Oh, woe is us!

The reality is that, no it isn't fair, but life has this way of being unfair all around. The reality is that there is no point in mentally hyper-awfulizing the problems of your family, your child, or your situation.

Yes, there are often serious problems and puzzles to solve in the process of learning to expose your autism-spectrum child to the larger world. And you do have the right to express your frustrations in appropriate venues.

But as Marcus Aurelius put it, "You have power over your mind—not outside events. Realize this, and you will find strength."

And don't forget the words of Terence: "There is nothing so easy but that it becomes difficult when you do it reluctantly."

In other words, even in ye olden days, folks knew that you can make a bad situation worse by focusing on how awful and unfair it is, and that reluctance to deal with that unfair situation can make even easy things hard—and hard things much, much harder.

No, I don't know your situation. But I do know that taking children outside of their usual daily grind is great for their brains and general development. If you have the urge to evaluate the chances of taking your child on outings by the "oh my gosh life is so unfair so I'm going to focus on that" method, you will focus on what you and your child can't do, which is terribly likely to lead only to dead ends. If you decide instead to focus on what you and your child can do, however small you have to start, you at least have a fighting chance at using this technique to help your child learn life skills and even get a chance for better brain development in the process.

Besides, focusing on how wonderfully easy those (generally fictitious) normal people have it will only make your world smaller. Remembering that humans have great ability to deal with adversities may well help you, inch by inch, to expand your world.

Of course, I do expect and understand that crying, bitching to your support group, and occasionally slamming cupboards will be involved at all stages of teaching life skills. But I deeply wish for you the ability to let those feelings of overwhelming frustration and worry be temporary bumps, and getting back to dealing with finding the good, the useful, and the wonderful in the process of teaching life skills to be the norm for you—if not this week, then maybe next.

START SMALL

Wherever you and your child/grandchild/student/spouse on the spectrum are in the area of developing life skills, start there. Take steps to develop the life skills involved with outings bit by bit, building up over time.

And what are the life skills that outings both teach and require? For starters, there is the ability to simply be in an unfamiliar situation. There is the ability to control oneself, even though the many shiny machines behind the counter at the restaurant may be tempting. The ability to be reasonably polite and functional when dealing with a mix of familiar and unfamiliar people. Asking for help when needed, such as going to a museum security guard and showing him an ID bracelet when separated from the family.

There are also the opportunities (and requirements) to learn to generalize those skills learned in other settings. For example, if one is at the zoo and overhears a tour guide giving information that one thinks is wrong or does not like, then one does *not* respond by saying, "NOOOOOOOOOO!"

This is, on the surface, the same as the skill that requires us to not holler at a teacher who announces a change in schedule and not to punch a brother or sister for simply contradicting you. However, there is a big difference between learning to do this (at school and at home) with familiar people, and learning to do it in new places with strangers.

Yes, this is a difficult lesson: the lesson that human beings who are unfamiliar and who act, dress, or speak differently from familiar people are, in fact, human beings. It's a hard thing to generalize.

It may be easier to start teaching these generalizations using outings such as running the weekly errands or going to the train shop each Saturday morning. Instead of expanding the child's world with a series of trips to unrelated places, start with close-by places that can be visited repeatedly.

What places are good for easy-to-repeat short outings that offer opportunities for teaching life skills? Try these:

- Public libraries
- Municipal swimming pools
- The YMCA
- Specialty hobby stores related to the child's interest (train stores, hobby shops, bookstores)
- Grocery stores

- The dry cleaner
- Low-cost restaurants, especially local independent ones
- Homes of families and friends
- City and state parks
- Biking and hiking trails
- The dog park

What do all of the above have in common? They are all places that are frequented by typical children in typical families, but that families with kids on the spectrum may avoid out of fear of "issues."

So start small and build up. Don't attempt a large-scale party for the whole family at an expensive restaurant until the child has mastered one-on-one trips to smaller, cheaper, easier-to-exit ones.

BUILDING UP THE SKILLS: START SIMPLE

While outings teach life skills, you also need to teach life skills in order to do many outings. In order to get the benefits of broadening your child's world outside his normal grind, you have to work inside it as well.

Many, many, many parents of "typical" or "normal" kids have great difficulty getting their children to behave in restaurants. Yet eating out can be a great way to learn the zillion-and-one unwritten rules about how to behave in public. Eating out can be a great opportunity to work on food-specific skills that people on the spectrum need, such as hunting down that one menu item that they can tolerate, communicating their needs to the server and others, using a public bathroom, not making faces over or otherwise mocking other people's food choices, and functioning in a situation where many other people have the same rights to service and decent treatment that you do.

So what did my folks do? If you've read the previous chapters, you know a little of the answer. They used a multi-pronged approach to making restaurant eating livable.

First, with all of us kids (me, my non-disabled sister Cath, and Jimmy), they started small. First they took us out for meals at inexpensive places like fast food restaurants. These are good places to start because if something goes really wrong, you are more likely to be able to exit reasonably easily. Okay, removing a child in the middle of a screaming meltdown from a public place is never really easy, but it is easier if the place is one where noisy children are part of the scenery, the food comes in wrappers that allow you to quickly pack it up, and no one is likely to be upset that "we spent all that money and had to leave early."

But, of course, even cheap-eats places are not free. For considerably less money, you may do well to seek out fairly regular opportunities to eat with family and friends at their homes. Supportive grandparents, aunts and uncles, or friends who have children of their own with autism can thus take part in the process of teaching life skills to children whose welfare is very important to them.

There was a long stretch of time when we had Sunday lunch at my Grandma and Pop pop's each week. This meant going from church to lunch at someplace other than home, so it meant learning to shift from appropriate at-home behavior to appropriate at-church behavior to appropriate visiting-the-family behavior. That is a bit of a triathlon for many kids on the spectrum, but since it involves all places where forgiveness can be expected and received, it's not too bad.

Sunday lunch at Grandma's did mean that I was surrounded by people who were eating food I found really gross. The usual luncheon included a platter of cold cuts and a basket of rolls so that everyone could make their own cold sandwiches.

Ewwwwwwww. To this day I find it incomprehensible that people can combine cold meat and bread and eat it. Turkey and mayo? Together? With bread? Ewwwwww.

But at lunch at Grandma's, I had to be polite and not comment on what other people were eating. I was allowed to eat my own eccentric sub-set of what was available; I took individual slices of cheese and bologna along with a roll, being super-careful not to let them actually touch each other (Your bread touched your bologna? Ewwwwwww) and ate them individually. Sometimes I went so far as to eat the one cold-cut sandwich I could tolerate, which was lebanon bologna on sliced white bread (no roll, please!) that had been buttered (keep that mayo away from me!). But I was never, never allowed to express how I felt about other people's food choices.

Eating at Grandma's regularly also provided me an opportunity to learn another important skill—helping to clear the dishes and put things away. Since no dessert (cookies!) could be eaten until everything was put away, I was super-motivated to be a helper. It's important that both boys and girls learn that, at relatives' homes, it is the rule to help out.

So the weekly lunch at Grandma's was a great place to learn to use my hard-won life skills outside of my own home and school.

Obviously, it is important to keep the level of skills needed at the child's level. A nonverbal child with poor receptive language should not be expected to sit still and be quiet for a long time while the grownups talk. I had a small "toy box" kept at Grandma's so that I had appropriate toys and books to keep me occupied when I could no longer be reasonably be expected to sit still.

Balancing the need to provide an opportunity to stretch with the need to be reasonable about a child's limitations is not a precise or easy thing, but you don't have to get it precisely right each time. You can strive to get the balance right without blaming or damning yourself when it just doesn't work out.

And yes, it is important to be prepared for more eventualities than you would with typical kids. Even at Grandma's, you may have to have alternate snacks packed in the car (in case your child suddenly cannot tolerate a food he previously liked) and a few familiar items related to a special interest.

Oh, if someone, however well meaning, tries to tell you that you can't just provide your child with alternate food and toys because "she'll have to learn to do it like everyone else sometime," just let them know that when they are raising your particular autistic child, they can make those decisions.

They, by the way, are wrong. I'm forty-four and still carry items related to my special interests almost everywhere I go: a Jack Skellington key chain, a map of Disneyland, and a few special photographs. I also frequently pack Pop-Tarts and trail mix for emergencies when I can't find food that I can actually manage to eat.

Hey, I do want you to teach life skills, but sometimes you have to make allowances for the simple human needs of a person on the spectrum, like me.

CHAPTER 23

Teach Special Skills Needed by People with Autism

Autism spectrum disorders often change over the years. The four-year-old with severe "classical" autism can wind up being a thirty-year-old with Asperger's; the twenty-year-old who seems to lack the basic abilities that lead to independence may become independent, or nearly so, at forty.

Or, a child who is classically autistic with a mental age of two when they are five years old can wind up being classically autistic with a mental age of two at forty. It is impossible to tell, really. I mean that. There is no known way to tell from the symptoms of preschoolers with autism what level of functioning or severity of symptoms they may experience as adults.

Thing is, even if a child is "recovered" at some point, that doesn't mean he or she is going to be completely free of autism-related traits. There are a whole slew of autistic traits that are usually pretty persistent over a lifetime.

People with autism don't necessarily so much "recover" as we graduate from having massive roadblocks in our every waking moment to being pretty functional but highly quirky individuals. Quirky individuals who have something along the lines of Asperger's. Fortunately, there is a good market for quirky if it comes along with a good work ethic and a large helping of basic politeness and decency.

So what does all this mean? It means that children with ASDs are often best served by learning the skills that will help them cope with being on the autism spectrum. It means that whether you are counting on your child recovering, are sure he or she never will, or fall somewhere in between, you can't go wrong teaching self-care skills and coping skills based on the persistence of autistic traits.

WHAT TRAITS ARE PERSISTENT?

Some of the most persistent traits are sensory issues (which are often mitigated, seldom eliminated); obsessive special interests (although we may well graduate from Thomas the Tank Engine to a fascination with bio-diesel); fine-motor difficulties; and a tendency to become stressed out or panicky more easily than the legendary "normal person."

This is not a complete list by any means. Some people retain their difficulty making eye contact but lose most of their panic attacks. Others find their sensory issues get better, or get worse, or just plain change over time.

No, I *don't* expect you to guess what your children's patterns of strengths and weaknesses will look like five, ten, or twenty years from now; it's not possible or necessary. What I would definitely *encourage* you to do is look at their problem areas and help them to find things that they themselves can do in the way of self-support.

THE FIRST SKILL: LIVING WITH ONE'S OWN OBSESSIVE INTERESTS

Do you happen to have a map of Disneyland in your wallet, purse, or backpack? I do; I always do. I also have a Jack Skellington key chain and a "brag book" with pictures of my husband in it.

Disneyland is one of my own special interests ("special interests" are also called "autistic obsessions"). So is *The Nightmare Before Christmas* and so is my husband.

Like many people on the spectrum, I like to have items related to my interests handy as much of the time as possible. Fortunately, I was also taught what is and is not okay to carry around all day.

The reality is that from Thomas the Tank Engine to RC fighting robots; from Bob the Builder to fractal geometry; and from Harry Potter to, well, Harry Potter, special interests remain a part of life for people with ASDs no matter how much we grow and change.

Fortunately, special interests can be a positive thing. They add zest to life, they can touch off interesting areas of research, they give us a way to soothe and calm ourselves after a bad day, and they keep eBay in business.

As many parents know, however, special interests can be problematic. Without appropriate rules, boundaries, and restrictions, special interests can create problems. The child who must watch the same video over and over; the adult who bores everyone by always changing the subject back to his topic of interest; and those of us who lug around very blatant objects and wear inappropriate attire related to the interest wind up paying a heavy price long-term for not knowing the right boundaries.

So, I have a map of Disneyland in my backpack. It doesn't invade anyone else's space, it is my own to keep and soothes me—it's a great thing. It's a place to start—teach your child that certain things related to an obsession are okay to have outside the house, and certain things aren't.

In practical terms, this means having a basket or container of some kind that holds the "little things" that a child can carry whenever he wants. Dress like Brittany Spears or Paris Hilton (there are little girls with autism who have execrable taste)? NO. Carry pictures of the same in a wallet or brag book provided for that purpose? Yes. That's just fine. In terrible taste, but fine.

CREATE A PLACE IN TIME AND SPACE

Those of us on the spectrum tend to like things that are concrete and structured; use these tendencies to create concrete boundaries and structure for special interests.

In practical terms, that means there should be a specific place where a child can have items related to a special interest; it can be the child's room, a toy box, or a special locking container just for that one thing.

There should also be guaranteed times when a child has specific access to that item, so that there is no sense that the interest is being taken away forever when it is time to drop that interest and do something else. If the child is using a visual schedule, put it on the schedule.

Why is it so important to do this? Because we who are on the spectrum need to learn that special interests are not for every minute of the day.

In my case, there were times that I was allowed to be as absorbed in my interest as I wanted, and times I had to drop it. This meant that I could bike to the library on the weekend and use most of my allowance to photocopy pictures of Fred Astaire and the Marx Brothers there. That was fine.

But I was not allowed to have my beloved books on Astaire and the Marx Brothers at the dinner table. There was just no place for that. Basic manners require that we not read, write, text, or watch TV during mealtimes with others. Not learning that can hurt a lot.

Even more helpful was that my parents taught me, indirectly, that there were spaces and places for all of my interests, just not everywhere. The only thing they could have done better on this is if they had taught me more directly, with maybe a few charts involved.

Let me lay it out for you—in my room, I could spend time and energy sorting through my photocopied pictures, I could have as many posters and other items related to my interests as I could manage on my allowance, and I was allowed to arrange the bookshelves and furniture to reflect my interests as much as I liked.

You might not think that rearranging furniture could be a special interest thing, but for a while my closet doubled as Obi-Wan Kenobi's cave from *Star Wars* (which I *refuse* to call "Episode IV: A New Hope," but that's a whole megillah I won't subject you to). There was also a period in which the furniture was set up to somehow reflect the house the Beatles "lived" in, in the movie *Help*, which meant creating a "pit" to sleep in by surrounding a space on the floor with furniture and sleeping on the floor there.

In other words, my parents allowed a *lot* of oddness and eccentricity in my room.

That's the first level to chart out: the times and places where a child can let their eccentric or "odd" interests dominate.

Then there was the rest of the house. I could bring items related to my interests into the house, and I could discuss my interests in the rest of the house, but to a more limited extent. No creating pits with the living room furniture. No *Star Wars* model kit building on any of the good tables.

One vital thing—as previously mentioned, I never had a TV in my room. None of us did. It would be financially possible to have a TV and computer in my brother's room, but that's not allowed. This puts some important limits on obsessions.

For me, the rules about exercising obsessions in the rest of the house were not laid out as clearly as would have been ideal, but my mom was able to lay down the law when needed. For my brother, things had to be made much more clear and definite.

BE SPECIFIC ABOUT BOUNDARIES

For example, when I was a kid, back in the olden days when men were men and folks smoked openly on the Tonight Show, watching a Fred

Astaire movie meant waiting until one was on TV or begging my mom to pull one of the three 35mm prints we had out of the big closet. This allowed fairly easy control of my viewing on my parents' part.

My brother was born in 1989, which meant VCRs and computers, and new rules. None of the parenting books told my mom that there would have to be a rule that said "You can only watch Mary Poppins one time per day." However, that became the rule.

Mind you, when my parents introduced unpopular rules like this—unpopular with me or with my brother—they got a lot of whining and some definite pouting and stomping around. My mom is, luckily, a master at Not Giving In, which turns out to be what it takes to keep rules like this going.

My mom and dad were, in addition, quite dedicated to the art of Creating a United Front. When a new rule like the once-daily Mary Poppins rule came out, they had discussed it beforehand and stood together on it. And if they had miscommunicated and one of them seemed to contradict the other, they would talk about it privately so they could get back to the United Front thing pretty quick.

The point is, they made the rules together and made the rules *as specific as necessary*. Telling a child with autism "you shouldn't watch the same movie so much" is not a workable rule. Setting up specific, clear limits on viewing videos is important so that the child can understand what the heck it is they are supposed to do.

IT'S NOT A SHAME

Just because I clearly believe that creating appropriate boundaries and habits regarding special interests is important, do not think that I regard these interests as shameful. There is nothing morally or practically wrong with having special interests.

What is wrong—meaning not functional—is not understanding how to best keep special interests alive without screwing up one's life, boring everyone within a ten-mile radius, or spending oneself into the poor house.

Having this particular (or any) autistic trait is nothing for you or your child to be ashamed of. Please remember that when you are teaching these particular skills.

Life Skills for the Spectrum:
Task Switching Problems and Video Game Obsessions

Difficulty switching tasks and the problem of playing video games to the exclusion of doing chores, homework, and even blatantly enjoyable non-video activities are two problems that have some causes (and solutions) in common. One of the causes that these two things can share is *hyperfocus*.

HYPERFOCUS

Despite all of our ability to follow schedules and remember what is supposed to happen when, people with autism spectrum disorders often lose track of time. This may look like a contradiction if you are not familiar with the phenomenon of hyperfocus.

Hyperfocus is a state of being that comes easily to many people with ASDs. It is a mental state in which you are so focused on the task at hand that you are aware of nothing else. It is a state of complete absorption, and can be a great way to get work done. It is related, I think, to the concept of "flow"—getting so absorbed in a task that it flows as if of its own accord.

The advantage of hyperfocus is obvious: being completely focused on a task or activity can allow you to use your full mental and physical capacity towards some end, like writing a computer program or running a marathon.

The problem with hyperfocus is that when you are completely focused on that one task or activity, you are also completely oblivious to other things around you. A child with autism who is in a state of hyperfocus may easily find himself in trouble for "ignoring" or "disobeying" instructions he truly was not aware of. Give a child with autism a really absorbing task, and he may wind up being labeled "non-compliant" that day.

When I am in a state of hyperfocus, I very well may not hear it if someone is pounding hard on the door that is only a few feet away. I realize that this is hard to understand for some people, but hearing, seeing, and responding to stimuli do not just involve having working ears and eyes, but also involve the brain. If all of the brain's resources are being allocated to one single task, they are simply not available for anything else at that moment.

HYPERFOCUS USUALLY CANNOT BE AVOIDED

Hyperfocus is not something that happens voluntarily. It happens spontaneously, and is very hard to avoid, especially for a child. In some situations, it is pretty much inevitable.

True, many of us who are on the Asperger's section of the spectrum may become aware that hyperfocus has social drawbacks, and work at preventing it in at least some situations. This is mainly done by not working on certain kinds of projects and avoiding absorbing tasks when we know we are "on call" socially or professionally.

This is, by the way, why I've worked hard at being able to work from home. When I worked in an office environment, I didn't get much done, because to actually work on a program meant that when someone interrupted me I might get upset. Working in a friendly, open workplace with lots of social activity meant being in a constant state of "busy wait."

For those of you who don't know, a busy wait works like this:

- Step One: Check to see if someone is going to speak to me or if I am required to speak to someone.
- Step Two: If yes, interact, then return to Step One. If no, go immediately back to Step One and continue.

In other words, for many years, the only way I could avoid falling into hyperfocus, and therefore not reacting correctly if I was interrupted, was to be constantly alert and anxious. And people wondered why I preferred to be alone!

YOU CAN'T PUNISH THE
HYPERFOCUS OUT OF A KID

You can't punish the tendency to go into hyperfocus out of a kid. Punishment will add anxiety and frustration to the child's life, as he just can't control the habit and the punishment is confusing and pointless.

I would have loved it if some magical pattern of rewards and losing privileges had somehow made me able to go into hyperfocus only when it was a good time for it and it was really useful. It would be lovely if a structured set of rewards could make the whole hyperfocus thing work nicely at only those times when it was opportune.

But it doesn't work to try to alter a child's involuntary brain state through "behavior modification."

Note that I say it would be nice if some structured rewards had limited my hyperfocus to opportune moments. It would be horrible to not be able to go into hyperfocus. I can't imagine the awfulness of living in a world where my attention always had to be diffuse and unfocused. I wouldn't be able to get anything really interesting done!

Both parents and teachers will save themselves a lot of unnecessary stress if they just accept that sometimes the child really can't hear an interruption. Certainly that would have saved my third-grade teacher a lot of headaches, and an added benefit is that I might not have thought her to be insane and anti-learning.

You see, I love reference books. Give me a dictionary, a copy of *Rodale's Synonym Finder* or *Bartlett's Familiar Quotations* and I am pretty much set for the day. That was true of me as early as second grade, and it was certainly true during third.

My third grade teacher had a specific drill for how vocabulary lessons were conducted. She would have us all get little school dictionaries from the side shelves, and we were to look up all of the vocabulary words. Then, when we'd had time to do that, she would go over the words with the whole class.

And every darn week, when she started reviewing the words that (presumably) my classmates had just looked up, I would be absorbed in the dictionary. It was a dictionary, for heaven's sake. It was the greatest source of knowledge available, and it fascinated me.

/fas-ə-nāt/ v. (1) to attract and hold spellbound by a unique power

So my teacher, after starting to teach, would always call on me, to check if I was paying attention. And I would never hear her.

So she would call my name again. And again. And again, louder.

Eventually, she would come over to my desk and tap me, glaring and quite angry. She would give me a short, sharp lecture about paying attention, scold me for being rude, and then continue.

Every. Single. Week.

I hated being scolded and lectured in front of the class. I hated the humiliation, and I hated the fact that it was ammo for the rest of the class to use in bullying me. It made my school life more miserable than it already was, and that is saying something.

So each week, when we went and got our dictionaries, I would try, try, try to not be fascinated. I would internally vow to look up just the vocabulary words and not to start actually reading the dictionary. I would put forth all of my mental power as an eight-year-old who didn't want to be humiliated or scorned again.

And I would fail. Putting a dictionary in my hands and telling me not to read it was like putting an unwrapped Hershey bar on my desk and telling me to take just one bite. Never gonna happen.

So I'd become fascinated. I'd be in total hyperfocus, completely embraced and surrounded by words and definitions, in a world of wonder and learning that filled me with a joy I can barely explain.

And I'd get in trouble, again. I'd get scolded and humiliated, and the teacher would get angry and frustrated.

What made me truly crazy in all of this is that I usually already knew the words we were supposed to be learning. The only way for me to actually learn new words during *vocabulary class* was, in fact, to spend some time just reading the dictionary.

To you, gentle reader, I will vouchsafe this one tip: If you are a third grader getting yelled at by your teacher for reading the dictionary during vocabulary class, do *not* offer to look up the definition of irony for her. It will not end well.

The funny thing is, every single time she tapped me on the shoulder, I came out of hyperfocus and paid attention. True, it took me about half a minute to completely get back into the swing of things, but that thirty seconds wasn't in and of itself so big a loss.

If she'd just made it a habit to tap me on the shoulder before she began the review with the class, neither she nor I would have had any reason to be upset, much less humiliated. But she wanted me to respond to her verbal directions when I actually could not hear them. She wanted me to respond in the way she thought appropriate to the stimulus she chose. It was important to her to be inflexible in this. So we both got a big headache.

As an adult, when a similar situation occurs, I could ask the person to tap or to otherwise signal me. I could also set an alarm or timer, or otherwise try to find a way to be responsive when necessary. I could even go for the dreaded "busy wait."

But as a child, I didn't have that option. The only person who actually had other options was the teacher, and she unfortunately didn't think to exercise any of them. Pity.

HYPERFOCUS SITUATION

If you know there are specific times when your child is in hyperfocus, you may need to build in coping mechanisms to deal with making the transition from hyperfocus to the next task. In fact, you may need to use literal, mechanical mechanisms, as my parents did.

When I was in my teens, after school I would go to my room, put on some music, and attempt to decompress. I found high school to be a chaotic morass of sensory and social stress, and I desperately needed to just "tune out" the world afterward.

I wish I'd known how soothing things like rhythmic movement can be, as it would have helped me feel better much more quickly. As it was, I would put on music and try to daydream up ways to solve my school problems. Pretty soon I'd be in a state of hyperfocus, mentally absorbed in reviewing various incidents from the day. This is a very stressful habit of many Aspies and auties; we try to "fix" our day by going back over it, and we wind up repeatedly re-experiencing the emotions and misery of the worst things that happen to us.

So I was in a state of profound hyperfocus each evening when my sister would be sent upstairs to get me for dinner. Evening after evening, she would totally freak me out by *pounding incredibly hard on my door*, which I would respond to by yelling at her.

Of course, she never started out to pound incredibly hard on my door. She would just knock normally at first, hoping to get my attention quickly, so she could get back downstairs, out of the "Jenn-rage zone."

But I was in hyperfocus. I couldn't hear her knock, and had no idea that it was close to dinnertime. So she would have to knock louder ... and louder ... and louder ...

Until finally the noise was so loud that it broke through my reverie and crashed into my brain like an unwelcome party guest. And I'd yell. A lot.

The fact that my sister had just come upstairs to get me for dinner (a perfectly reasonable activity) made no difference to me in this state. My whole brain had just been completely preoccupied, so I didn't have any part of my consciousness handy for the task of understanding what was going on.

What I did understand was that I'd been interrupted, which set off something very close to the fight-or-flight mechanism, and I was much more a fight than flight kind of person.

My poor sister would retreat pretty darn quickly, and I'd turn off the music and follow downstairs reluctantly. By the time I got to the kitchen, my mom knew that I'd chewed out my sister again, and I was in trouble.

So after spending an hour or two musing on the most miserable parts of my school day, then having an uncontrolled panic response to being interrupted, I'd get a quick scolding right before dinner. Many of my meltdowns occurred during dinner.

COPING MECHANISM

Obviously, it was not at all okay for me to yell at my sister nearly daily. It was wrong for me to yell at her, but it was also beyond my capabilities at the time to control myself enough to respond to her appropriately. The fact that she is, today, still speaking to me is a marvel.

It would have helped if I'd known about using exercise to detox my brain and body; it would have helped even more if I'd known about using cognitive behavioral therapy to defuse my anger. And it would have been really great if I'd understood enough about Asperger's to realize that what was happening in my brain was nobody's fault, not mine, and certainly not my mom's or my sister's.

But I didn't have those options, and my sister was naturally more and more reluctant to come upstairs and get me for dinner. So my parents solved the problem another way.

My dad went to the hardware store and got some in-room buzzers. Two buttons in the kitchen to two noisy buzzers; Dad put one in my room and one in my sister's.

This way, when my mom needed me to come downstairs, she merely pressed a button and a really loud, annoying door-buzzer type of sound was immediately very audible in my room.

I got just as mad at the buzzer as I had at my sister, but with no one around, I didn't get in trouble for feeling upset at being interrupted. And by the time I took a few deep breaths and got downstairs, I was starting to calm down. Also, since the buzzer had no feelings to hurt, my mom didn't yell at me for getting upset, so I kept feeling (relatively) calm.

No, this didn't solve the underlying problem. But it did mean that my sister didn't have to deal with my more unpleasant neurological issues quite so often, plus it got me downstairs when my mom wanted me.

Never underestimate the importance of saving the sibling's sanity!

Using a mechanical means to signal that it was time for me to snap out of hyperfocus and change tasks really helped me to cope.

The beauty of the mechanical method is that it can be used throughout life and is something many children can learn to use for themselves. Timers and alarm clocks are readily available and once a child has learned to set timers for himself, he has a life skill that is truly useful.

I use timers often to make sure I am on time for various events, and to ensure that I spend an appropriate amount of time each day on long-term projects. I know that if I want to start writing but have to be somewhere in a short time, I need to set a timer so that I won't wind up late.

So don't think this was just a case of my parents letting me off easy for my sister's sake. They may not have known it, but they were teaching me a useful skill that has served me well for decades.

Learning to Spend Time

TIME MANAGEMENT AND THE TV ALLOWANCE

My parents made a much greater effort to teach time-management skills to my brother than to me; they expected me to pick up skills from implicit teaching and general, non-specific advice. The result is that my twenty-one-year-old brother with autism, who until only a year or so ago we thought would not be able to get a high school diploma, is much better at time management and task-switching than I am, even though I'm forty-four and have a bachelor's degree in computer science.

Very fortunately, while they did not realize how poor my ability to deal with time was, they did actively work to teach me not to use all of my time for just one recreational activity. That is, my mom got sick of me watching TV all day and decided to do something about it.

You may be familiar with this scenario: one summer, when I was perhaps twelve years old, I discovered that I had never fully appreciated the wonders of daytime TV. I became entranced with the subtleties of talk shows (which at the time involved actual celebrities plugging movies or sharing recipes), syndicated sit-coms, and extremely scratchy prints of old movies playing at one P.M. on a UHF channel that could, by the painstaking adjustment of the circular UHF antenna, be received almost well enough to distinguish human figures.

(For those of you who don't know what a UHF station is, I'd like to say that I'm older than you and therefore smarter and better than you, so get off my lawn.)

I was able to watch TV from approximately 9:00 A.M. until 9:00 P.M., with only a short break to fetch my lunch (which I ate in front of the TV) and another break to eat dinner with the family (which was an absolutely *non-negotiable* requirement in our house). I also tolerated occasional breaks for our required outings to the swim club and the library—especially as the library had books about TV. I had the entire TV schedule for the greater Philadelphia area memorized. No, I'm not exaggerating that last part, not even a little. I knew what was on every channel, all seven of them, at any time of day.

(If you don't remember when there were fewer than ten TV channels that you could watch in any given major metropolitan area, turn down that darn rock 'n' roll music and put some decent clothes on.)

There were slow spots during the TV day, of course: there were times when I was deeply grieved to have to watch the Brady Bunch go to Hawaii and meet Vincent Price yet again (even though I looooooove Vincent Price), but mostly I thoroughly enjoyed my daily wallow in the glow of the cathode ray tube.

My mother deeply believed that she had tried to get me to watch less television. She would harangue me repeatedly about the amount of TV I watched, make many suggestions for other fun activities, and try to convince me to "watch less TV."

None of what she said meant much to me. "Watching less TV" is as vague a request as anyone could possibly make. I mean, if I stepped outside for ten minutes, or ate lunch in the kitchen instead of the family room, I was watching less TV, but that didn't seem to make her any happier.

Her specific suggestions for other activities carried no punch, as they were always made at what felt like inopportune moments. That is, she usually got fed up and made these suggestions at the same time of day, immediately before or during *The Addams Family.*

Hey, you can suggest a trip to Disneyland if you want, but in those pre-VCR, pre-DVD days, I was not going to miss my chance to continue attempting to commit every episode of *The Addams Family* to memory. *Pirates of the Caribbean* ride will be there in twenty years, but *The Addams Family* went in and out of the daily lineup like spring blossoming and fading. Sigh.

(If you don't remember having to watch shows when they were actually on, and not being able to see shows unless some local station decided to put them on the schedule, well, you kids today have never had it as tough as we did. And spit out that gum.)

So my mom got more and more frustrated with my seemingly endless TV viewing. I had no idea she was getting more frustrated, as my ability to read her mood was limited to those times when she gave me "the look," but she had had it up to HERE with my bad habit. And so she took action, in an ultra-clever, devious, and oh-so-effective way.

WHAT FINALLY WORKED

My mom had a conference with my dad one night, and the next day, at dinner, they jointly presented a new wrinkle on the house rules to me and my sister (same rules for everybody).

With horror, I listened to the new plan: my sister and I were to be given *TV allowances.*

Yes, TV allowances. We were allowed up to fourteen hours of TV each week, which could be, if we wished, broken down into two-hour daily chunks, or used in any way we saw fit. However, once we had watched fourteen hours in a given week, we were to be cut off—no more TV until Sunday came around and we got the new fourteen hours for that week.

Cunningly, Mom and Dad had worked out every detail of the scheme to prevent abuse of the system. So we were told that we absolutely could not save TV time from week to week. No "rollover minutes." Not never, not nohow.

This meant that there was no way to save up TV during the school year so that I could spend all of next summer watching TV (and yes, I would have done it, in a trice). Fourteen hours, each week, good only from Sunday to Saturday, then a new week started with another fourteen hours being the only possible TV time available.

There were, I was told, some possible exceptions to be made in the event that I was assigned to watch something educational for school (which occasionally happened), but it had better be something actually educational that was actually assigned.

After this detailed revelation, my sister shrugged and went back to her dinner. Not me. I was livid. I was distraught. I was in a state that somehow combined a deer caught in headlights and a full-scale Tazmanian Devil fit.

My parents, heaven bless them, weathered my rage. I tried to question every possible aspect of the new program, but it was airtight. I tried to wheedle my dad, in the hope that he would be more flexible than Mom. No dice. I enumerated the many Very Important Shows I *needed* to watch, and the dearth of other entertainments. I begged, I argued, I questioned. And they stayed in United Front Mode. No cracks in the facade, no hope of more TV.

So I gave in. Oh, sure, I complained a lot, but I knew by then that there was no hope of getting past that ironclad joint front once it had been raised.

Yes, TV was in fact my "special interest" (autistic obsession) at the time. But I gave in and watched TV only to the extent permitted. So I became less obsessed, right?

Not likely. Instead of watching TV all day, I waited anxiously each week for the following week's *TV Guide* to be delivered, snatching it from the mailbox as quickly as possible and combing through the listings at length. I spent hours "weighting" shows, determining whether to watch them by calculating a combined factor of how long they were and how important they were to me. I drew up schedules, tore them up, and drew up new schedules.

Each week, when we went grocery shopping on Thursday morning, I secretly ached upon seeing the lovely rack of fresh TV guides on display, knowing that I had to wait until ours came in the mail, as much as thirty hours later sometimes.

So yes, I was obsessed with TV. But I stuck to the fourteen hours a week.

DETERMINING THE AMOUNT OF TV

Temple says she was only allowed one hour a day. That's not bad either, but in my case my parents knew that there were shows and movies that I really liked to watch that were educational or led to interesting research on my part. They had spent years taking us to the library once a week, every week, and my dad had spent a lot of time teaching me to look up books by subject (as well as by title and author) so that I could research all of my favorite topics. The last thing they wanted to do was squelch my love of research.

Besides, watching TV as a family together was very important. If they'd put me on shorter rations, I wouldn't have gotten nearly so many useful lessons from my folks, who commented on and discussed the shows we watched with us. For example, my dad used to ask me, "What would happen if you did that in real life?" and talk to me about it to make sure I understood which of the things on TV were totally unacceptable in real life.

And there was my mom, who would provide a tremendous amount of supporting information about anyone who appeared on *The Muppet Show*. Hey, without an explanation of who Spike Milligan was, I might have grown up thinking that the members of Monty Python were far, far cleverer than they are.

And Mom was also busy exploiting my special interests for education through television. One day, she casually said to me, "Oh, would you like to see a TV show where the guy who plays Darth Vader acts without the mask?"

Would I!!!! It turned out that she had noticed that David Prowse was going to play the Duke's wrestler in *As You Like It* in the PBS/BBC "Shakespeare Plays." I was so excited that I sent away for the program guide with my own allowance money, and read up on all the plays that were being shown that season.

Fortunately for my mom's attempts to educate me, that particular production of *As You Like It* totally rocked. It was really, really, really good. I wound up becoming so darn fascinated by the whole thing that when we read *Romeo and Juliet* in my 9th grade English class, I insisted on reading from my own copy of the play, bought with my own money, instead of using the heavily censored and shortened version in our textbook. In this way I got to annoy my teacher by always volunteering to read and throwing everyone off. It annoyed the other students too, but I was happy about it. It made me feel like I was striking a blow against censorship or something.

There is a point to all of this, even though it seems I've rambled off topic a bit. It's that my parents took into consideration both the good and bad of TV viewing. They didn't just cut me off, and they gave me enough TV time that they could convince me to include some educational stuff (which never would have happened had they insisted on *only* educational TV). It was a carefully considered move on their part, and it was helpful.

Besides, it is important for children (and adults) to have plenty of non-toxic amusements they can enjoy. There are so many really bad ways for people to dispel boredom; it is bad to waste huge amounts of time on one passive occupation, but good to enjoy yourself and relax a bit every day.

Coping with Sensory Issues

Most of us on the autism spectrum do, in fact, have some sen-
sory issues. This means that most of us need to learn some life skills for
coping with sensory issues. While I know there are a lot of OTs and
families doing very cool work helping out kids on the spectrum by using
"sensory diets" and other means of mitigating sensory issues, it is pretty
unusual for sensory issues to be completely eliminated.

My mom worked on coping skills for sensory issues with me without
either of us knowing it. She herself was sensitive to being in crowded,
noisy stores and malls, as well as to annoying smells and perfumes (but
I repeat myself). So she worked out practical ways to deal with those
things and explained them to me when we used them.

For example, when we went to the grocery store quite early on Thursday morning, right after breakfast, she explained to me that we went
early because there were fewer people at the store early in the morning,
and that meant less crowding, less auditory noise, and less visual "noise."

When you have a grocery store with a lot of people in it, it's pretty
loud, and there is a lot of distracting movement. People are not at all
organized in the way they meander up and down the aisles, stopping

and starting, taking products off of the shelves and sometimes leaving random products in random places. It's chaotic, and for the child who can't deal with all that noise and motion, it's overwhelming.

Why, if my mother was handling the scheduling and was in charge of the grocery shopping, was it so important for her to explain it to me? Two reasons: one is that it meant that I could not logically whine about going first thing in the morning. There was a rational reason for doing so that I could not reasonably argue with.

The second reason is the life skills reason: if no one had explained why we went so early, I would not have realized the benefits or known what the purpose of doing it so regularly was. That would have made me much more inflexible in later life.

You see, when pretty much anyone on the spectrum learns a way of doing things that works, and works well despite all the sensory issues, communications problems, and social issues that come up for us all the time, he or she (or I) will stick with that way of doing things. The ritual itself is reassuring and comfortable, and the knowledge that breaking the ritual means anything, just *anything* could happen creates a very inflexible mindset.

It is super-hard to be flexible when the world is not designed for your comfort. A working pattern, a ritual, a consistent way of doing things, doesn't just mean the comfort of familiarity or habit, as it might to most average people. Doing things the same way over and over again provides tremendous protection from a chaotic and unfriendly world.

We live in a world full of unexpected social interactions, sensory insults, and just plain scary stuff. You might think your child should be just as happy going to the park or to the fast-food joint with the play area at one time as at another, but a lot of things vary according to time of day. The angle of the sun can be harsh and create unpleasant reflections at some times; there might be an unfamiliar and possibly hostile child who shows up at certain times on certain days; the play area itself may smell strongly of disinfectant if you arrive too soon after it has been cleaned.

When a child has some understanding of the sensory advantages of one option over another, it gives him at least a slight fighting chance to be a little bit flexible.

Because my mother explained that going early on Thursdays meant a calmer shopping trip with fewer people around, I could transfer that idea elsewhere. It is really, really hard for me to plan my shopping well enough to actually do it all in one fell swoop each week, but because I understand the principle of choosing a sensory-friendly shopping time, I don't panic when I have to make an extra trip, and I don't need Thursday to be shopping day.

If I find we are out of milk on a Friday night, I don't panic. I just think about how to get milk without facing the scary mobs of people who hit Trader Joe's every weekend. And I remember: between 8:00 A.M. and 9:30 A.M. on Saturdays, there aren't many people at TJ's at all. So I can avoid being stuck in the ritual and choose a time that meets some of the same qualifications that the "official shopping time" of Thursday after breakfast would meet.

So let your child know: we go shopping at "off" hours so that it won't be as overwhelming for you. And teach him or her that if we need to go somewhere that has bad sensory vibes, like the mall, we can go in and get out very quickly to minimize the problems.

That's another sensory lifesaver: the surgical shopping strike. This should have its own social story, but I'll leave that as an exercise for the reader and give you the parental information version. Again, this is one of those things where you will have to determine for yourself and your child which is the best way to communicate the plan: realistic pictures, a sketched map, written notes, or a verbal once-over.

If you can coach your child on the concept of the surgical shopping strike, you can make it more likely that you and he will keep it together when you need to run a vital errand in a pinch. To make it work, you have to do for your child what I do for myself—prepare him mentally for what needs to be done. The ultimate goal would be for a child to do this him/herself as an adult.

Choose the amount of information you share according to what the child can process. I will explain how I talk myself through it. Your adaptation is up to you.

First, I go over the necessity of the visit. For example: "I can [or will] wear only the underwear they sell at JC Penneys, and the only Penneys is at the mall. Since the dryer mangled that last load of clothes and I leave for a conference at 6:00 tomorrow morning, I have to go to the mall tonight."

Second, I go over the plan: "I will park outside of the food court. If that section is full, I will park across the street. I will then walk to the outside Penney's door (no cutting through the mall), and head straight for lingerie. I will hunt down the underwear and pay for it, and leave as soon as I'm done. There will be no side trips to see if Hot Topic has any new Jack Skellington shirts. That way lies disaster."

Third, I drive to the mall, park in the area where I planned to park, and review my planned trajectory. Once inside the store, I will do the most direct purchase possible: grab item, go to least full register (I will pay for women's underwear in boy's shoes if that is fastest), and get out of there.

Obviously, the places and things that have sensory issues for any one child will vary. The idea is not to regiment the child into one way of doing things, but to teach the child that there are ways to minimize sensory badness.

SMALL ITEMS: TEACH THEM

It is nice when parents are on the alert for items that can cause sensory stress and help their child avoid those things. For young children, or any really stressed-out child, often that is the best you can do, even though you might be able to provide some hints as to why you are doing so.

It is great when a child learns to look for or bring along small things that provide sensory support on his or her own. The feeling of being able to take care of oneself is pretty cool, and having one or two small items that Mom is not in charge of can really help out.

So, teach the small items. If your child needs noise-canceling headphones for some situations, store the headphones, clearly labeled, in your child's room and remind him to put them in his backpack before you leave for that theme park/airplane trip/jackhammer manufacturer's convention.

Yes, it may take a lot of years of coaching for a child to actually know when he needs to bring headphones and remember to habitually pack them. But having that little bit of knowledge can save a person a lot of trouble.

And yes, if your child tends to eat the ear pads off of the headphones, you may need to stow the headphones elsewhere and ask your friendly neighborhood OT about what kind of mouthing toys or objects your child might be able to carry.

Checking clothes for scratchy fabrics and scratchy tags is important too. If you coach your child on this—showing him what you are doing as you run your fingers over a shirt he wants to buy and rub it on your arm to see what the fabric feels like—he might start trying it himself. If he can read, you might want to teach him to recognize words such as "100% Wool" (scratchy even through a t-shirt).

If you find that putting an old t-shirt on her under her dress shirt makes her more comfortable, make sure she knows what the purpose of the t-shirt is. Otherwise she might insist on putting a t-shirt under a comfortable shirt, or even on putting an uncomfortable t-shirt under any shirt, just to do it the way she always has.

ASKING FOR ACCOMMODATIONS

"Appropriate accommodations" are big in the world of autism. The phrase often conjures up IEPs, legal wrangling, and serious debate about what is and is not implied by IDEA and the ADA.

But appropriate accommodations can be small, too, and asking for them is pretty simple. Starting when I was eight, when my dad and I were in a record store and I told him the music was too loud, instead of asking the clerk to turn it down, my dad coached me on asking the clerk to turn it down, explaining that "We are here to shop, and therefore they should make us comfortable. They want us to stay here and spend money, so it is absolutely our right to ask."

I didn't have to explain that I had Asperger's—heck, I didn't *know* that I had Asperger's, and neither did my dad. All I had to do was politely say, "Could you turn the music down so I can shop, please?"

There are a lot of little things you can ask for that might help. I learned early on that being seated next to the kitchen in a restaurant wasn't merely an annoyance for me; it really prevented me from understanding what anyone I was dining with might be saying. Too much confusing noise. So I learned to tell the host or hostess where I wanted to be seated. Often they will seat you just where you ask, and if they don't, they will usually give you a choice of a few alternatives.

I know, it is not appropriate for a young child to buttonhole the hostess in a restaurant and insist on a particular seat. And yes, there are children for whom it is far too difficult to say "Excuse me, would you mind seating us by that window over there?" But they may be able to point out where they want to sit, and communicate it pretty well, if they have support and the people with them don't act like it's a big deal, or weird, or inappropriate for that person to be doing. Most people are willing to go along with mild oddness if everyone else does too.

By the way, asking for the music to be turned down in restaurants can be more difficult than in stores. It varies by restaurant, but if the place has young, hip hostesses and plays young, hip music, a scenario can unfold that I've seen a few times.

I was at a restaurant that shall remain nameless, except it is in Brea, CA and the chain it belongs to rhymes with Schmoutback Schteakhouse. My husband and I were attempting to enjoy our salads, but we couldn't converse due to the loudness of the music. It is hard to converse when you are bleeding at the eardrums.

I called over our very nice waiter and asked for the music to be turned down. He relayed the request to the hostesses, who had the controls for the music near their station, and they turned it down a tiny notch, to the point where our eardrums where merely slightly oozing blood instead of actually shooting it out. I asked again, and said waiter bravely induced the gaggle of apparently twelve-year-old hostesses to actually turn the music down significantly for a whole two minutes.

Alas, while our waiter was elsewhere, a different song came on, and one of the hostesses squealed, "I love this song" and cranked it. It was not cranked as loud as it had initially been, but not good. I was not thrilled.

Then perhaps three songs later, another song came on that induced another hostess to squeal, "Oh, you guys, this song is soooo great," and once again crank up the music. This time I could just about feel my eyeballs vibrating from the sound, and the bats living in Bronson Caverns in the next county over were thrown into a tizzy as they came to believe that a major swarm of insects was emanating directly from our restaurant.

Eventually, I did get our waiter over, and he mentioned our plight to someone who I believe was a manager of some kind, who induced the hostess gaggle to turn the music down to something that was actually like listening to music. One or two of them did covertly look at us with what can best be described as "pouty faces," but they complied.

I could swear, however, that as we left there was a loud rumble behind us as the sound system was ramped back up into the ear-bleeding zone.

The point? Yes, you can induce many places to provide you with reasonable accommodations. While many people around us gave off audible sighs of relief when the music was turned down, apparently I was the only person who found it genuinely so painful that I could not tolerate it. But the accommodation was still reasonable, and I still got it.

And no, I haven't been back there since. I'd had some difficulty getting the music turned down (at five in the afternoon, for heaven's sake) before. One thing we on the spectrum need to learn is when it is probably better to find another place to go rather than ratchet up our push for accommodations.

Depending on the future social success of your child, you may have to explain that asking for the music to be turned down is not a "reasonable accommodation" in a crowded club jammed with buzzed hipsters in the wee small hours. In that case, the appropriate accommodation would involve putting in earplugs, using noise-canceling headphones, leaving, or, in my case, simply finding an appropriate location to remove a number of circuit breakers from the building's electrical system.

Darn kids with their rock 'n' roll.

Really, Really Big Skills That Everyone Needs

This section is about developing four very important skills and habits that help make life livable. All of the skills listed here are even more important for people on the autism spectrum than they are for typical humans.

The First Really Big Skill:
Exercise for Mental and Physical Health

This is a really, really, really big skill that everyone on the autism spectrum needs. We (like humans in general) have less depression, anxiety, and anger when we get regular physical exercise. Exercise as an anti-anxiety and antidepressant tool is well substantiated by high-quality research—and I've experienced these benefits myself and seen many family members benefit as well.

What is more, we now know that exercise promotes the growth of new neurons in the brain. That's right, exercise grows your brain!

Even better, the specific neurons that are promoted and grown during periods of exercise are much better at functioning under stress. Exercise makes the brain grow cells that function well under stress!

Who on earth would not grow themselves a better brain if given the chance? Exercise is the most awesomely powerful brain tool ever!

Oh, yeah, it also can help prevent Type II Diabetes and promote a healthy weight, improve heart and lung functioning, while improving coordination and stamina. Whatever.

It also makes the physical efforts of day-to-day living less difficult and stressful. As someone who flies a lot, I can guarantee you that you want to be as fit as you can be when dashing to make a connection through the Dallas-Fort Worth Airport.

EXERCISE AND ANGER

Many, many parents of children with ASDs become concerned when their children have serious anger issues, or "autistic rage." One of the main reasons for the seemingly disproportionate amount of anger people on the autism spectrum evince is that most of us experience and process multiple negative emotions as anger.

In other words, if people with autism are depressed, it can come out as anger. If we are stressed out, it's likely to come out as anger. If we have anxiety, are over-tired, have PMS, or are just plain overwhelmed, anger is often the primary external sign that something is wrong.

(Incidentally, many "typical" males also have serious anger as the main manifestation of depression. Men who find themselves getting angry to an extent that interferes with their lives in general should look into getting screened for depression.)

This is why physical activity is so important for those of us on the autism spectrum. Exercising can help not only with depression and anxiety, but also with insomnia, and mental blocks, as well as providing a boost when one is feeling "draggy."

IMPORTANT NOTE

If your child has insomnia, depression, crying jags, or any other serious emotional/physical problem, make sure there is nothing medical going on. It is important to make sure there is not an underlying physical problem before using exercise to promote a better brain.

This is vital: a child who has an invisible problem like an earache, migraines, anemia, or a urinary tract infection is going to be cranky, angry, and anxious. Treating that anger and anxiety with exercise would be bad. Getting the child healthy and *then* getting started on exercise is good.

HOW ON EARTH DO I GET MY CHILD TO EXERCISE?

Ah, that's the $64,000 question, isn't it? There are a whole bunch of ways to do this, and you can try as many or as few as are appropriate for your child.

Helping your child to get into a habit of exercise is a long-haul proposition. This isn't an overnight fix that you can just pop up with one day. Kids need help to add something new and interesting to their schedules. Some kids need more help than others.

One technique: show a child what to do *by example*. My parents got my brother to exercise by providing their own good examples.

My dad works out regularly and has, over the years, built up a good supply of exercise equipment, including dumbbells and barbells. No, you most emphatically *don't* need to run out and buy a bunch of equipment, but if you use whatever it is you have available fairly frequently, you'll set a great example.

Because my dad works out with weights, my brother got interested in working out with weights. My dad took charge of the whole thing by explaining to Jimmy that he (my dad) was Jimmy's trainer. Dad further explained that the rule about having a personal trainer is that you have to listen to your trainer and do the exercises the way your trainer tells you to.

This was very important, because Jimmy is, after all, male, and guys often want to use the heaviest weights they possibly can or do the most strenuous exercises to show how strong they are. Creating a clear set of rules where you have to follow your trainer's instructions meant that my dad was able to teach Jimmy to do exercises correctly before adding more weight, which is important to prevent injury.

My mom also exercises by walking every morning, so she also is setting a good example—BUT she probably could not have managed this when Jimmy was younger, as he took a lot more of her time and energy then.

This is also very important: while it is great when parents, siblings, and other family members can set a good example by exercising regularly, please don't think I'm urging you to add even more to your schedule if it is too overloaded already. Exercise is good for you, but sleep is even more important, so *don't* try to carve out an extra hour by robbing yourself of sleep.

Whether or not you yourself are able to be an example, if you can find someone else who can do so, that will also help. An older child or teen who is willing to exercise with a younger kid is worth his weight in gold. Someone from your temple, church, or other faith-group might be willing to do this; other possible places to look are local Boy Scout and Girl Scout troops and school sports teams.

LOOK AT WHAT YOUR KID IS ALREADY DOING

Some children with autism are known as "runners." When they get upset, angry, or frustrated, they run out of the house or classroom at top speed and just keep going. It can be completely exhausting to keep up with them.

So what to do with this kind of child? Well, first of all, they obviously are having anxiety or panic attacks that provoke a fight-or-flight response, so something should be done to help with that. Also, the child has a lot of pent-up energy that may make it difficult or impossible to sit still in school or at the dinner table.

What to do then? Get that kid running! Yes, if he needs to run, get him running, in a safe place at a safe time.

This is where drafting a local teen or adult comes in handy; if you know someone who runs regularly, they might be persuaded to run laps with a child who needs adult guidance. Running is a great form of parallel play, because it requires no interaction at all, but instead involves two or more people just facing the same direction and going!

Kids who like spinning things might well like a bike or trike to ride. Kids who like climbing could use extra time on a jungle gym. Kids who love water often love swimming. A child who is unable to swim may still be able to do "water aerobics" or other underwater exercises.

Do keep in mind the kinds of activity that a child seeks out or tends to thrive on. Kids who are soothed by rhythmic movement like swinging or jumping on a trampoline should be encouraged to do rhythmic forms of exercise—anything from walking to Tae Bo.

Kids who respond well to wearing weighted vests and blankets may well prefer walking with a weight vest on—they make vests designed with pockets for weights that are often sold not only at sporting goods stores but also in the fitness sections of discount stores.

And for heaven's sake, if your child is a music lover, integrate music into the process. You can walk to music, bounce on a trampoline to music—or put on inspiring music for use when doing pushups and other floor exercises. Inspiration may vary—I like Weird Al for inspiration, but a little Carmina Burana, the Ride of the Valkyries, or Lady Gaga might suit your child (or you) better.

WHAT I DO, WHAT MY BROTHER DOES

My brother and I have both massively benefited from adding lots of exercise to our lives; yes, it's that good! We've both enjoyed improved health and stamina as well as fewer angry outbursts and a improved frustration tolerance.

One thing that Jimmy and I have benefited a lot from is mixing it up and doing different kinds of exercise. We both use weights to build strength (he can manage much heavier weights than I can, but I'm still improving!). We both add in lots of rhythmic aerobic activity.

Jimmy's exercise program includes lifting weights with my dad, bicycling as much as he can, and using the *Walk At Home* and Tae Bo DVDs for extra aerobic activity.

Mind you, that program didn't happen overnight. No one set up a schedule where he had to do multiple kinds of exercise daily; the program just grew as my parents encouraged him to be more fit and as he saw them and other friends being active.

Some kids need a lot more than just encouragement and examples to get started. After all, some of us will see our parents exercising and categorize exercise as "something that parents do." And most of us don't really understand the mental and emotional benefits of exercise.

I was a lot less motivated to exercise than my brother. I was not very active growing up. Being seriously *not* athletic and picked last for teams at school meant I associated physical activity with stress, humiliation, and all the things about school that I wanted to get away from at home.

WHAT CHANGED MY MIND

I did occasionally start an exercise program in an attempt to lose weight, but it never seemed to stick for more than a few months. The results came very slowly, not at all like the many books and magazines that claim to help you "lose eleventy-two pounds in just five days or your money back!" So I thought (wrongly!) that exercise wasn't a good way to lose weight.

So as long as the only reason I thought I needed to exercise was for potential weight-loss, I just wasn't what you would call "motivated."

Flash forward to late 2006. I found an article on some research that indicated that a combination of strength training, aerobic exercise, and stretching showed great promise as a way to treat carpal tunnel syndrome and related repetitive strain injuries (RSIs). I had old RSIs from the late '90s that had never completely healed.

And at the same time, I was reading a lot of stuff on cognitive behavioral therapy (CBT) and rational emotive behavioral therapy (REBT).

For a long time I had thought, "It's no use starting an exercise program. I'll just give up after a month or so, so what's the use?"

Through REBT thinking, I figured out that my attitude towards exercise had been very irrational. I replaced my attitude of "It's no use" with the idea, "If I work out today, then I've made a bit of progress towards getting in better shape, which I want to do. It might well help with my RSIs. And not working out does not benefit me on a day when I have the time to exercise. So it would be smart to exercise."

To my own anxious thought "But what if I work out today but then don't exercise again?" I replied to myself, "Hey, I can't do anything tomorrow, or next week, or whenever, but only now. Doing this is the best thing I can do for my exercise program at the moment. And if I exercise today but never do again, how is that horrible? It would be a tiny bit unfortunate to have spent the time without more results, but not really bad."

And when I miss days or just can't exercise every day I want to, I remind myself, "Hey, humans generally can't fit everything we want to do into every day. I'll get back to it soon—but if I don't, even then it isn't a disaster. There's no use being worried, I'll just keep going as best I am able and get what I can out of it."

The reason I'm giving details here is that for those of us with high-functioning autism or Asperger's Syndrome, logic is one of the best motivators. After years of pointless beating myself up for being "lazy" or "unmotivated" to get fit, I had had no luck getting going. I felt bad about not exercising, but it sure didn't make me more motivated!

Once I used CBT/REBT techniques to argue both logically and kindly with myself, my attitude changed a lot—not all at once, and not perfectly, but a lot of change in a short time.

Not only that, but I can motivate myself more easily than ever. When I have time and energy for a workout but am not up to it, I often have a little conversation with my more irrational thinking self like this:

Irrational Thoughts: "You don't want to work out today. There's no point to it. You've been working out a long time and you don't look like a model or pin-up by any means!"

Rational Me: "You're right, I don't look like a model, and never will. But exercise is about feeling better and being fitter, not just looks."

IT: "But you don't feel like it. You know you feel down and tired and cranky."

RM: "Will I feel any better if I don't work out? Working out often makes me feel better."

IT: "It might not work and you could just still feel lousy after all that effort. What a waste."

RM: "So I'll feel lousy. At least I'll have gotten something done."

IT: "Why bother? Wouldn't it be more fun to surf the 'Net or watch cartoons?"

RM: "I have all of those cartoons on DVD. And if I work out and it doesn't work, I'll have burned a few calories and gained a little strength. If nothing else, it will help keep me from losing the strength I have. And besides, this is wasting time. If you want to argue with me, you can do it while I do bicep curls. I'm pushing the furniture back and working out!"

So if you have a child with Asperger's or high-functioning autism, please consider using logic, and/or helping them to learn to use logic in helpful ways. Rational reasons for working out are plentiful.

Oh, by the way, I was wrong about the weight loss thing. For three years after I started exercising regularly in December of 2006, I lost an average of 1.2 pounds (about 0.5 kg) per month. So while I may never be skinny, at least I'm less likely to be at risk for obesity-related illnesses in addition to feeling less angry, anxious, and achy. Not a bad bonus.

OTHER MOTIVATIONAL TECHNIQUES

Obviously, you can't hand a non-reading child a book on REBT and say, "Here, this is how to be logical and get over your silly objections to working out." Nor can you use elaborate arguments with all Aspies. Some of them can out-argue anyone, even when they are wrong.

If you have a functioning token system or "points" system, seriously consider making small units of exercise worth points. If the child sees walking, running, jumping, or other exercise as the way to earn cool stuff, he or she is going to be a lot more motivated.

Incidentally, awarding points or tokens for exercise is a good way to make the idea that exercise is rewarding literal and concrete. It isn't "just a bribe," it's a way of clarifying the hard-to-see link between exercise and feeling better.

Try making exercise appealing in other ways. You will have to figure out what your child can follow and understand in the way of helpful gimmicks.

One approach is using a pedometer. As advised in *The Step Diet*, walking around with a pedometer that tells you how many steps you take in a day can help concretize the concept of increasing daily physical activity. Also, it involves numbers, counting, and an ingenious little device that your child can have for his or her very own. Not a bad thing.

Children who love using the Internet can use Google, Yahoo, or MapQuest to map out walking routes and determine how far they are going. Using a simple spreadsheet to track progress can help those who love numbers.

And, of course, don't forget the appeal of simple paper charts and other written records the child can see and refer to. The more visually oriented a child is, the more he will benefit from seeing his exercise record and achievements in that concrete form.

USING DVDS

What I do is based somewhat on what I grew up with: I use some of the old Jane Fonda workouts that are now out on DVD (note: the ones that are not out on DVD are not necessarily up to current workout standards—research has improved how workouts are planned, so go with stuff that's been released or re-released recently).

And yes, I know some people hate Fonda with a passion; that's why the workouts can bring us all together. No matter what your race, creed, color, or political inclinations, by the time you're halfway through the ab crunches, you will really hate Jane. My husband swears that when I work out, he can hear me in the living room muttering, "Bite me, you pinko!"

My brother turned me on to another set of workout DVDs that are suitable for people who, like us, are more comfortable with something simple that can be done at a variety of levels. He learned of this exercise program at the school he attended for some years, as one of the teachers would bring these Leslie Sansone *Walk At Home* videos for the kids on rainy days.

This meant that while the kids spent their recess indoors, the video would be playing somewhere in the room and whichever kids felt like taking part could. The *Walk At Home* vids have the advantage of being based on simple movements and also of having the uber-hyper Ms. Sansone, who frequently reminds the viewer that "you can do it any way you want, you can't do it wrong, just keep moving to the music and you'll get fit."

It's only fair of me to mention that many teen and adult Aspies object to the *Walk At Home* workouts because Leslie Sansone is nuts. She is mind-bogglingly cheery, perky, and enthusiastic to the point of madness.

When I recommend these workouts to others with Asperger's, I always remind them that just because Ms. Sansone is naturally wired to be rather strange does not make her a bad person or make the workouts invalid. I strongly suspect that she cannot help her constant grinning any more than the Joker can help his. At least she's using her powers for goodness and niceness. It would be disastrous if she turned her energies to crime, as she would definitely have comic book super-villain status within weeks of doing so.

(Bonus points to anyone who actually uses Leslie Sansone as a comic-book super-villain after reading this.)

The point, for me, of using DVDs is that it enables me to work out without the problem of being in a social atmosphere. Remember, if there is more than one person in the room, that is a social situation. Gyms are crammed with social interactions. And sweaty people.

The other advantage of workouts that are on DVD or recorded from the television is that they can be repeated over and over, which is a big help for auties and Aspies like me who have great difficulty figuring out what leg is supposed to go which way. I often actually have to look down at my legs to see if the one that is moving is the same as the one I think is moving, so being able to pause is great.

Besides, we Aspies and auties thrive on repetition. Doing the same thing in the same way every day is very comforting. It becomes another reliably predictable thing in a world full of unpredictable chaos.

CAN KIDS WITH AUTISM DO THAT?

Yes, kids with autism can work out in a lot of ways. Ask any adapted PE (aka adaptive gym) teacher or certified occupational therapist.

You might also try asking Ellen Notbohm. She wrote this book called *Ten Things Every Child With Autism Wishes You Knew*, which totally rocks.

(Yes, I know that the very non-literal title of said book has made some of my Aspie peers upset, but that does not negate the awesomeness of the book. For the record, the book's title is *not* meant to be taken literally. It's non-literal communication from one NT to an audience of NTs, which is perfectly valid. And not evil.)

Ellen's son Bryce has autism and awesomeness in equal measures. I guess the awesome part is hereditary.

Bryce has done stuff that most kids with autism don't. That's not because he's "better" (well, Ellen thinks he is, but she's biased), nor because he has more ability than all of those other kids. It's because Ellen is too thick to have realized that kids with autism "can't" learn to ride a bike or be on the swim team.

Ellen enlisted Bryce's adapted gym teacher to teach Bryce to ride a bike. They figured out that he would be okay with learning indoors (in the gym) by himself (no onlookers) with just his teacher there.

It took him three fifteen-minute sessions to learn to ride a bike. He'd had lots of practice with training wheels, so the muscles were there, and he liked to ride with the family, so the motivation was there.

The only thing that had ever been missing was someone with a little expertise who would thoughtfully watch him and work with him. The adaptive PE teacher who did the teaching used her knowledge of balance issues and motor skills to give him the boost he needed.

Note that he had learned to ride a tricycle (at two) and a bike with training wheels (at four). His folks had seen fit to include him in the normal progression of physical activities for kids.

That combination of simply providing him with the basics to start with and then seeking out someone with a bit more knowledge when he "hit a wall" propelled him quite well.

An awful lot of parents and teachers don't bother to get ordinary riding toys or trikes and bikes for kids on the spectrum (and those are things that are just as good used or as hand-me-downs). An awful lot of folks just automatically assume that a disabled child will not be able to do these things.

Ellen assumed that Bryce could do it and therefore went to the trouble of providing not just the bike, but the boost. If she hadn't called in that teacher when the going got tough, if she'd just decided that "I guess kids with autism can't ride bikes," well, then it never would have happened.

No, no, I don't believe that just believing in your child alone will do it. Obviously, there are children with "floppy" muscles or severe movement disorders that came with their autism spectrum disorder, and they are unlikely to excel at, say, salsa dancing.

Yet I do know and have seen that providing opportunities and looking to help your child reach his best level will help a lot.

Oh, yes, both I and my brother ride bikes—and while he's much more "autistic seeming" and has more problems learning than I do, he sure is a lot better at riding a bike than I am.

THAT'S NOT EXERCISE!

I was asked to speak to a group of teachers who work with "gifted" grade-schoolers about the problems their Aspergian students face. When I talked about how exercise can help prevent meltdowns, one of the teachers asked, "What about a child who has meltdowns *during* exercise?"

I asked her what kind of exercise the student had been doing. Her response? "Playing baseball in gym class."

AAARRRRRGGGGHHHHH! Playing baseball in gym class is NOT exercise. Not, not, not, not, not! Playing baseball in gym class is an elaborate quasi-medieval torture in the form of combining social harassment, incredible boredom, and tremendous amounts of fear and anxiety for the majority of children with Asperger's.

The kind of exercise that promotes brain health and healthy emotions involves sustained effort over time, like walking, running, swimming, bouncing, or tumbling.

"Exercise" that is a thinly disguised social situation involving long periods of boredom, sitting on the bench, the possibility of failing one's team, and just plain not doing very much physical activity is not going to promote your child's health.

Heck, even professional baseball players don't prepare to play simply by playing baseball. They do a lot of things like lifting weights, doing calisthenics, and endless drills where they throw and catch ball after ball or run the distance between bases over and over.

But gym class and recess games simply are not likely to provide much actual exercise for the person on the autism spectrum. The social agony and terror of making a fool of oneself tend to make those events all about avoidance and intense anxiety.

And if your child is aware of the connection between looking foolish in gym class and increased teasing, he may try really, really hard to act like he doesn't care at all about the class. It's easier to cope with failing to catch the ball or perform well if you can say, "I wasn't paying attention, I don't care anyway."

Mind you, quite a few people on the spectrum are able to get exercise in group or team activities where each person is performing as an individual, such as being on the track team. Track and field is a sport of parallel play, which is much more our level than coordinating with the group, and also involves long periods of actual physical activity.

Still, be aware that your Aspie or autie may be willing to take exercise only in non-social, non-public ways. Be sensitive to your child's level in this, and don't judge a child who is not ready to get fit in public.

I myself don't like working out in front of people. While I will take walks in public, just because that's where the good places to walk are, I won't do any other exercise in front of people if I can help it.

I have a good reason for that. I wear my hair short these days, so I have to put it up in two pigtails to keep it out of my face. Two tiny, cutesy, curled-up pigtails like Gosselin Mallard on *Darkwing Duck*. And I'm forty-four years old. Does *Whatever Happened to Baby Jane* ring a bell?

The Second Really Big Skill:
Good Sleep Habits

People with ASDs often have greater than average difficulty falling asleep, staying asleep, or just plain getting enough sleep.

If this is the case for your child, you very much need to teach good sleep habits. It is a key life skill that is necessary to good mental and physical health.

Insomnia is hell. Sleep deprivation is actually used as a form of torture. And sleep really totally does in fact knit up the raveled sleeve of care. We need our sleep.

Sleep disturbances generally come in the form of difficulty falling asleep, difficulty staying asleep, or intermittent wakefulness. Sometimes insomnia stems from physical problems, such as allergy or asthma attacks. Other times it is a manifestation of anxiety, depression, or anger that the child simply does not have the right coping skills to deal with alone.

The first, most important thing to do when a child has insomnia is to make sure there are no physical issues involved. If your child is snoring or experiencing stoppages in his/her breathing during the night, that absolutely must be mentioned to your doctor. Mild snoring is probably not a problem, but mention it anyway. Loud snoring, especially if it is intermittent and suddenly cuts off, should definitely be mentioned and discussed.

Some sleep disturbances stem from breathing stoppages in the night (sleep apnea). Ask your pediatrician for advice on how to detect this; also, ask for a referral to someone who specializes in sleep disorders if you know breathing stoppage is happening during sleep. It is a serious thing to deal with.

At this point, I need to mention that I do not have formal medical training, and that while I've done my utmost to get up-to-date information from reliable medical sources, this book is not a substitute for individual medical care and treatment.

So please do read on, but please also be aware that you may need outside help for this one.

Serious sleep research is the source for most of my data here. It backs up what I've experienced as someone who has had intermittent insomnia since the age of six. I've learned to deal with it, and believe that your child has a great chance of learning to deal with it too. Heck, you might even manage to get some sleep yourself.

FIRST ON THE INSOMNIA TO DO LIST

One of the most important things to do when helping a child with insomnia is to make the bed a place for sleep. *A child's bed should not be a place to lie awake for hours.*

The more time a child spends lying awake in bed, the more strongly the child's body and brain are programmed to see the bed as "the place to lie awake in."

When someone (child or adult) is having difficulty sleeping, it is important that they not lie awake in bed for more than about twenty to thirty minutes. If you put your child to bed, and twenty minutes later he is still awake, he should *get out of bed* for a little while and do some soothing activity.

Most often the activities recommended are things like reading, crayoning, knitting, sketching, or some otherwise sedentary activity that will help the brain stop focusing on the stress of the day and the problem of insomnia.

For those of us on the autism spectrum, another kind of activity that may help with insomnia is rhythmic movement. Swinging, bouncing on a trampoline, or even a walk may help.

Usually, for non-autistic people, exercise at bedtime is very much not recommended. However, for some of us on the spectrum, the soothing, repetitive nature of a nice rhythmic activity can really calm the whole nervous system and help us feel calmer and more "together." It's not a time to lift weights or to go for a "personal best" time as a runner, but gentle rhythmic movement can do wonders.

In my own case, when I've been having bad bouts with insomnia, I find that taking a walk after dinner or other rhythmic movement early in the evening can get this effect going earlier and therefore save the difficulty of doing such activities in an apartment where my husband is trying to sleep.

I cannot express strongly enough how important it is to *get out of bed* and do a *soothing* activity—even if that activity is just sorting special-interest items, looking at a picture-book, or daydreaming. The more time you spend lying awake in bed, the more your body reacts to getting into bed by waking up and being super-alert and tense.

Special-interest items are especially good for distraction from insomnia. If the child can get focused on the pleasant aspects of a special-interest item, that can allow them to get away from thoughts and mental images about the stresses of the day or their worries for tomorrow.

Not only does taking a break from lying in bed help with anxious thoughts, making an insomniac stay in bed awake is sheer torture for him or her. Trust me, I know. There is little worse than having to stay in a bed that you can't get comfortable in, where there is nothing to do but wish you were sleeping and count the minutes.

When I'm having serious insomnia, every so often there is a night when I just know I'm not going to sleep. When that happens, I know that I might as well get up and read or even watch TV. If you know you have hours of sleeplessness to kill, staying bored and uncomfortable in bed is just awful.

And there is nothing so hopeless and futile as lying in bed awake, looking at the clock and thinking, "If I fall asleep right now, I can get six hours of sleep ... if I fall asleep *now* I can get five and three-quarters hours of sleep ... if I fall asleep within the next minute, I can get five and a half hours of sleep ...."

It really pays to be super-flexible about letting a child get out of bed. You can specifically restrict where they can go and what they can do if they are awake in the middle of the night—no jogging outside or drum practice, please!—but make sure they can leave the bed to do self-soothing activities.

If a short list of self-soothing activities (in words or pictures) is posted clearly, and the items needed for those activities are available in the room, you as a parent might be able to let a reliable child handle this him- or herself. Don't make the "insomnia activities list" too long—if the child gets caught up in the trap of trying to choose from myriad possibilities, it will only aggravate the situation.

IF THEY CLIMBED TO THE TOP OF THE EMPIRE STATE BUILDING AND JUMPED OFF . . .

In the world of teendom, we worry about peer pressure. In the world of insomnia, I worry about well-intentioned pressure due to the use of bad information.

If all of your friends, your OT, your speech pathologist, and your parapro all give you (unintentionally) clueless advice about childhood insomnia, should you follow it? Well, if they all jumped off the Empire State Building, would you do it too?

Sadly, sometimes I hear from parents who tell me that really smart, reliable teachers, behaviorists, and other professionals who work with children on the autism spectrum have told them to keep that kid in bed no matter what.

Unfortunately, sometimes professionals pick up wrong information about areas outside of their expertise. Hey, I'm really good with anxiety management in Asperger's, but I don't know a darn thing about basketball.

Most professionals who work with children on the autism spectrum have never had the time to hunt up published studies, check out Web sites from serious sleep researchers, or otherwise really dig up the best data for the job. That's okay. Just be aware that someone who is a generally awesome speech-path might have picked up some non-optimal ideas in unrelated specialties like sleep disorders.

WHAT OTHER RULES DOES SLEEP FOLLOW?

One rule that parents and children hate to implement is a really good one that I am truly sorry to have to tell you about.

Life is easier if on Saturday and/or Sunday, little Insomniac Isaac or Sleepless Susie can sleep late. It takes away the need for both parents and child to go through the whole horrible waking-the-insomniac thing. It means Isaac or Susie can "catch up" on much need rest. Everybody likes sleeping in!

And sleeping in is bad for insomniacs. Unless the child is ill or is truly severely sleep-deprived, sleeping in is bad.

Insomniacs have a better chance at getting some sleep at night if they go to bed at the same time every night and wake up at the same time every morning.

The body's clock just does not allow itself to be set for sleeping until 7:00 A.M. for five days, sleeping until noon on Saturday, and then sleeping until 9:00 A.M. on Sunday. Nor for any other similar permutation.

The body will learn the best sleep habits if it gets to hit the sack at the same time and get up at the same time each day. The body is not concerned about the work-week or a three-day weekend. It is just concerned with the rising and setting of the sun and the rhythms of day-to-day living.

Going to bed and getting up at the same time every day does not, unfortunately, guarantee an end to insomnia; however, regular times for going to bed and rising can definitely help get the brain into the pattern of sleep.

Since children (or even adults) may have a very hard time grasping the benefits of getting up at (approximately) the same time every day, rewards may have to be built into the system.

This may mean offering a premium for getting up early on a day when there is no school. If you have to take away the joy of sleeping until noon on Saturday or Sunday, try to plan a pleasant activity or small reward for the child that they get to enjoy early in the morning.

Earning points towards desired items or activities by getting up can really motivate (some) kids.

Having a pleasant activity or giving points for rising on time can help give the child something positive to focus on during the waking-up process.

Remember, insomnia is worst when a child is anxious or depressed, and lack of sleep creates anxiety and depression. When an insomniac is first awakened, they are very likely to immediately be focused on that feeling of anxiety or dread. The bed and sleep are a great escape from the harsh world. Giving children some sort of pleasant thought to hang on to can give them a little ammo when they try to bestir themselves.

BUT I CAN'T WAKE MY CHILD UP!

There are parents who find that they simply cannot wake their insomniac child on time, sometimes just on the weekends and sometimes on weekdays as well.

It is hard to get your child on a regular sleep schedule when you can't get him or her out of bed.

My mother's solution to dealing with my super-cranky and ultra-resistant early morning attitude was to get me an alarm clock of my own. That was when I was in second grade.

Sometimes an alarm clock is better than a person. Alarm clocks don't get angry, they don't threaten, and they don't plead. They don't do any of the emotionally loaded things that can increase anxiety or upset the child further.

Some children (like me) are not able to modulate their voices and behavior when they are first waking up, simply because their brains are not yet fully functioning when they first awake.

An alarm clock (or two) can protect parent and child from each other in those situations.

Yes, I did mention the possibility of two alarm clocks. It's a great system that many of us with Asperger's or high-functioning autism have discovered as individuals. Great minds that hate to get up in the morning think alike.

The two-alarm clock solution involves getting two plain old cheeeeep digital alarm clocks. The first one, on the child's night table, is set for perhaps thirty minutes before the child has to arise. I myself prefer forty-five minutes before.

When the first alarm goes off, the child hits snooze. And hits snooze. And hits snooze.

The second alarm clock is a little farther away (distance depends on the individual) and should be quite loud if at all possible. That alarm is set for the actual time the child needs to get up.

The usage is simple. The child gets partly woken up by the first clock and hits snooze repeatedly. But waking up just a bit for each snooze will (usually) get the brain just a bit more awake each time.

By the time the second clock goes off, the child knows that it is time to get up and that he/she has to gosh-darn well schlep over there and turn the darn thing off.

This is not completely foolproof. After particularly exhausting days, I have been known to hit the snooze button a lot of times before I even consciously know that an alarm went off. I have even had the first clock go off, hit the snooze, and then gone in search of the other clock and *unplugged it* before it could disturb me.

But this works for me when I absolutely have to get up on time and can't mess around with hitting the snooze ten or twenty times.

A POSSIBLE GIMMICK

There is, I should mention, a thing called Clocky®. Clocky is an alarm clock that as of this writing costs about $60. (Too rich for my blood.) It can be ordered from Edmunds Scientific, among other geek sources.

Clocky is a gimmick, but may be worth trying for some stubborn sleepers. Clocky is on wheels and is self-propelled. When Clocky sounds the alarm, it then jumps up to three feet and starts rolling. It is supposed to run away and make you chase it.

This is by no means a blanket endorsement. I have not tried Clocky, and online reviews are mostly pretty decent but somewhat mixed.

I do think it is worth noting that the problem of getting up in the morning is so widespread and severe that there is an actual market for a runaway alarm clock. At least those of us who can't wake up easily know we are in good company.

WHAT ABOUT THE OTHER CHILD?

Oh, dear. When another child has to share the same room or is sleeping close enough to hear the alarm, you may have to have a little talk with him.

If it is possible to reassure your other children that insomnia intervention and alarm clocks are designed to help the whole household, please do.

Don't tell any non-disabled child that "we always have to be extra nice to Martin because he's special." While it is important that they understand that each child will get as much of what he or she needs as possible, no child should have too much responsibility for a sibling.

Instead, tell them that, unfortunately, little Martin (or big Martin) can't do certain things without a lot of help, and that helping Martin should help the whole family. Offer earplugs and a shoulder to lean on. Let your non-disabled child know that you care about his/her needs, and are trying to figure out how to be as equitable as possible.

Oh, and do remember to offer those earplugs. And do let siblings earn points (both figuratively and literally) for helping Martin and for helping parents with Martin.

OBVIOUSLY . . .

Some other things that seem to be so obvious, but are often overlooked:

Don't allow the insomniac child to have caffeine after 4:00 P.M. Caffeine is not just in coffee, but also in most colas (you can buy non-caffeinated colas), chocolate, iced tea, hot tea, and some over-the-counter painkillers.

That's right, some kinds of aspirin, acetaminophen, and ibuprophen have caffeine added. It speeds up the effect of the painkiller. Just check the label—if caffeine is in there, it'll say so in the "active ingredients" list.

Additionally, medications that have ephedrine, such as the original Sudafed, Claritin-D, and just about every other decongestant that actually works, can really keep a person awake.

In my case, I learned the hard way: I like Sudafed as a decongestant (well, the store brand "compare to Sudafed" version), but it does *not* go well with tricyclic antidepressants, including Imipramine, which I take.

If you take a decongestant at the same times as you take a tricyclic antidepressant, you get to be *really, really, really alert and awake*. Wow!

So do be careful to avoid giving a child with insomnia any drug or substance that might cause them even more trouble in sleeping.

And in even more so-obvious-that-it's-often-overlooked news, when you do that initial check-up with your child's doctor to make sure the insomnia doesn't have a medical cause, *tell the doctor* about *all* the medications, supplements, and vitamins the child is taking. Those things are an important part of a child's overall health profile, and the doctor should take them into account.

(EARLY) NAPS ARE OUR FRIENDS

While getting up on time is generally important, naps can be very beneficial. Staying awake all day is not necessary or helpful.

Generally, when it comes to naps, earlier in the day is better. If a child gets home from school after 3:00 P.M., that may well be a bad time for a nap.

Still, if the child is going on very little sleep, they may need to grab what sleep they can when they can. Don't begrudge an exhausted child a nap when staying awake gets painful.

One thing few non-insomniacs ever seem to know is that lack of sleep can beget lack of sleep. The more I make myself stay awake all day, the more my brain gets into the groove of avoiding sleep at all costs. Once you've been made to stay awake for a long time, it can be hard to get the brain to disengage from that mode.

So naps can help break the cycle of non-sleep. And when your child has been getting less than six to seven hours of sleep a night, getting adequate rest any way possible is more of a priority than avoiding sleeping at the "wrong" time.

HOW MUCH SLEEP, ANYWAY?

Children from two to eighteen need anything from eight to eleven hours of sleep. A ten-year-old will probably be fine on eight hours. Many sixteen-year-olds will be significantly less functional on anything less than nine.

Yes, teens do worse in school when they get less than nine hours of sleep. Really.

The problem is that how much sleep is needed varies from age to age and from person to person. It can be very hard to tell how much sleep to insist on—although, again, that initial doctor visit can get you vital information that is germane to your particular child.

Sadly, children and teens are usually really terrible at determining how much sleep they need. This is one of those areas where the grownups have to be "mean" sometimes.

As a teen, I had horrible insomnia. I would fall asleep sometime around two in the morning, drag myself out of bed at 6:00 A.M. for the early bus so that I could get to school choir rehearsal, and I considered that I was getting by pretty well.

I did everything wrong. I was always tired when I got home, so I would often have a snack and then lie down with the radio or headphones on and obsessively go over what went wrong with my day, sometimes just plain lying awake on my bed until dinner.

I'd feel logy after dinner, then watch TV for as much of the evening as was practical. I'd go up to my room sometime between 9:30 and 10:30 P.M., but go to bed sometime between 9:30 and 12:30 P.M. Then I'd ruminate some more on my bad day, toss and turn, try to make myself sleep by thinking of the word "sleep" obsessively, and generally stay wide awake.

In the midst of those days, I did do some chores, read some books, do some homework, and keep myself fairly well occupied. But since I had little in the way of really engaging physical and mental activity after school, I spent a lot of time in bed being awake, and did nothing that really helped me unwind or avoid ruminating on things that made me anxious, I just didn't sleep much from, say, October 20th until perhaps April or May of any given year.

What would have helped? Here are the things that I would recommend for me as a teen:

- Daytime walks to get some sunlight so that my body would be more fully awake when I was awake.
- Some consistency in when I actually went to bed for the purposes of sleep.
- A schedule (with a bit of flexibility built in) so that I would have consistent times for working on homework, and consistent limits on non-activities like rumination about my day.
- No iced tea or cocoa after about 4:00 in the afternoon.
- Self-applied cognitive behavioral therapy, as it is explained in this book, for both anger and anxiety.
- A dual alarm clock set-up as described above.
- Some kind of useful volunteer work on weekends or even one or two days a week after school, so that I could have a positive experience of fulfilling a useful function and learning new skills.
- Appropriate exercise.
- And for heaven's sake, no lying in bed awake!

A NOTABLE ABSENCE

You may have noticed that I have not mentioned my brother or used him in any examples in this chapter. That's because not only has he has not had insomnia, he also gets up in the morning on time, bright, cheerful, and full of energy.

I am convinced that at least part of the reason for that is that he has always been encouraged to be self-accepting, and has realistic self-esteem that comes from hard work and accomplishment. Because of those things, he sees the day he is waking up into as a good thing.

Yes, I think the fact that he has avoided the kind of severe, intense, long-term anxiety and depression that I've gone through helps immensely with his ability to get to sleep and to wake up and face the day.

That is one of the reasons why, despite all of the well-founded and useable advice on insomnia I've put into this chapter, I would strongly urge parents of children with insomnia to, over time, find ways to deal with the underlying causes, such as anxiety, anger, depression, panic attacks, and difficulty processing stress.

For all of that, I'd like to refer you to the sections of this book about anger and cognitive behavioral therapy.

Cognitive behavioral therapy (CBT) doesn't just work for me; it has been shown in multiple studies to work for children on the spectrum who have the cognitive ability to understand the basic concepts.

It has also been shown to work for "typicals." Just in case having a child with autism has in some ways added to your anxiety and stress.

As the section on CBT points out, Tony Attwood has two workbooks on CBT designed for kids who are at a grade-school level intellectually. (Actually, if you ask me, the books are good for older people as well, they just haven't been formally tested for use with adults.)

So if you can, please take advantage of those things that can help decrease the underlying problems that cause insomnia. It can help a lot.

Oh, and one last time—don't forget that doctor visit at the start! It would be just heck to go through all of these processes and then find out the insomnia is a side effect of the child's medication or other physical causes.

The Third
Really Big Skill:
Dealing with Mistakes
and Failures

This is the first of two skills that involve concepts that require really good communication for teaching, BUT any child with autism whose parents and teachers understand these concepts is very likely to benefit tremendously.

In other words, even if your child doesn't or cannot understand it, you and your child will both benefit from your own understanding.

In yet other words: trust me; this is a good thing.

MISTAKES AND THE AUTISM SPECTRUM

Those of us who are on the autism spectrum are often very upset by mistakes and failures (or perceived failures), whether our own or others'. We often overestimate the seriousness and extent of mistakes and failures, and seldom understand the necessity of doing the hard work that results in mistakes and failures.

Yes, I said the *necessity* of the hard work that *inevitably* results in mistakes and failures. Without mistakes and failures, there is no progress.

Look at a human baby learning to walk. Humans spend a lot of time learning to walk badly before they learn to walk well. They also do a huge amount of falling on their bums. They get frustrated by their own inability to creep, crawl, walk, or travel in the direction they want to go as far as they want to go. They make horrific noises of frustration, suffer a lot of bumps and sometimes bruises, skinned knees, and the like.

Then, as small children, they continue to struggle with many simple motor skills: using crayons, dressing themselves, learning to write letters and numbers, and a host of other simple activities.

In fact, most small children are extremely good at making mistakes and failing. If they weren't, they would never get anywhere or learn to do anything.

In fact, failure and mistakes are the price of success.

Learning is a mistake-littered process.

Marie Curie, Albert Einstein, Thomas Alva Edison, and The Beatles are all examples of people who worked incredibly hard and put in untold hours of "dues paying" to become successful. Talent is great, but without that harsh trial-and-error phase, it doesn't bear fruit. And guess what? Almost all human beings who have any measure of success wind up doing the same.

WHAT DO YOU MEAN BY "SUCCESS?"

If I say mistakes are necessary to success, then I had better define success. For some of us, "success" means financial or professional success. For others, "success" means learning to care for ourselves in the most basic ways.

And for all humans, or at least the ones smart enough to be lucky, success is not a fixed point. For those of us on the spectrum, success, however defined, does not occur by a specific date or in a specific way.

The adult with autism who is struggling to function in even the highest quality group home at twenty may be independent at forty. There are children with autism who struggle to communicate in even the crudest way at ten who are able to type clearly and completely independently at thirty.

And sometimes success is very modest and simple. Succeeding at actually asking a girl out, regardless of whether she says yes or not, is a huge milestone for many high-functioning people on the spectrum. Being able to help get out the ingredients for dinner, or to participate otherwise in their own care is a major success to be treasured for others.

And finding ways to make sure their adult child with autism will be decently cared for after they are gone is a huge success for many parents, and one which is seldom reached without many, many false starts, wrong turns, and difficult decisions. Mistakes and failures on that journey are common, but not insurmountable. They are just part of the path.

There are people with autism, and also people not on the spectrum, for whom getting up in the morning is an act of great strength and courage.

So when I say that risking mistakes and failure is an important part of success, I mean all of the above kinds of success and many more. I'm not just talking about super-duper life success. I'm talking about the many kinds of success in life.

MISTAKES, AND FAILURES, AND STRUGGLES, OH, MY!

But alas, we on the spectrum dislike making mistakes and failing. No, *dislike* is the wrong word. Most of us hate and fear mistakes and failures to an almost pathological degree. Given the choice between risking failure and staying inert, we often not only choose to remain inert, but fight like hell to remain inert.

If the choice is between the video game that has a clear path to conquest or the math worksheet that is likely to result in mistakes, we choose the video game *not only* because it is colorful and fun and full of cool stuff, *but also* because it is *safesafesafe*.

After all, most of us are pretty good at video games, and the things we are best at are the ones we favor. The more innate skill we have, the less we have to struggle and therefore show what we consider to be weakness.

Many, many, many of us on the spectrum will choose almost any distraction or activity that involves a low risk of failure over any activity that involves making the kind of mistakes that are necessary for learning.

Fortunately, when it comes to auties who have low testable IQs or are considered to be "very involved cases," there is a great tendency among parents and teachers to combat this problem, even though they may not know that that is what they are doing.

For a child who is considered slow or seriously disabled, there is much more likely to be a constant stream of praise for *effort*. From very early on, they have a good chance of hearing things like "Good try!" and "Wow, you really tried hard, that was great," and "I'm so proud of how hard you worked," and, "Oh, that was a mistake, let's figure it out together."

The more "low functioning" a child is, the more likely they are to get praised for their efforts just as much as their successes. And those kids more than deserve it. In a world that is super-bewildering and often totally unsuited to their needs, they deserve to be congratulated when they reach out and actually are willing to join in that world.

The higher functioning kids (and adults) on the spectrum also deserve that kind of praise, but seldom get it. And even some of the kids with low testable IQs miss out on the kind of encouragement and praise that make a person (any person) more likely to take the risks involved in trying to learn a new task.

The psychology professor and researcher Carol S. Dweck, PhD, has researched and written about this phenomenon at length, and what she has learned/taught should be presented to all parents of any children, but is ultra-super-hugely-ultimately-infinitely necessary for parents of children on the autism spectrum.

A LOT OF DWECK

Dweck is among those who have studied in detail two seriously hard-core attitudes or "mindsets" that humans have about learning—one is called the "fixed mindset" and the other is called the "growth mindset."

While there is a lot of well-established research and plenty of detailed constructs about these two mindsets, for this book I'm going to go with some personal examples. I grew up with my parents and teachers promoting a fixed mindset, and my brother grew up with our parents and his teachers promoting a growth mindset. There is a big difference.

I grew up in a world where intelligence was something you just had (or didn't have) innately. When I started grade school, I was bored and frustrated a lot of the time. I could read earlier and faster than the other children, I could figure out math problems better, and I turned my worksheets in at lightning speed. Yay for me, right?

Not quite. A lot of adults let me know, in one way or another, that the reason I did things so darn easily is that I was smarter than the other children. I was gifted, darnit.

Heck, my dad was constantly going nuts over some little thing I had done that was advanced for my age. He didn't notice the things I sweated blood over, but only those things that seemed effortless and instantaneous. The appearance of no effort was the thing that won the most attention.

So my personal, internal definition of smart became something like this: "You are smart because everything at school is easy for you. If it is hard for you or you make a lot of mistakes, then you are not smart. The smarter you are, the easier everything is. And when you are smart, things just come to you. One try is all it takes to be smart. More than one try is for stupid and incompetent people."

This is what is called a fixed mindset. In a fixed mindset, a child (or adult) believes that intelligence is something you are just given (or not given), magically, at birth. In the fixed mindset, you either have it or you don't. Every chance you get to fail is a chance to show you don't have it.

So guess what? I became insanely anxious about mistakes. While my dad seldom or possibly never gave me positive feedback for effort, he did get upset if my grades dropped at all. So I knew that mistakes were bad, very bad, and missed problems were horrible, very horrible.

I also knew that it was just as bad to get a B as it was to get a C. Working hard and getting a B got the same exact feedback as not working and getting a C. Work was absolutely worthless.

From being a golden child of brilliance I moved quickly and precipitously to being a problem child who "wouldn't try" and "made no effort."

Of course I made no effort! Effort was terrifying. Trying to study or work on a particular problem caused panic attacks I could barely tolerate. The sensory and social issues of every day at school were overwhelming and draining to start with; why on earth would I try to work up the energy to put effort into my schoolwork when I was not only already exhausted but also *absolutely knew* that if I didn't get it the first time, I just didn't get it.

To me as a child, a mistake was a sign not only of temporary failure, but also of being stupid. If I got a problem wrong, I hated it when the teacher went over it with me. After all, getting it wrong was the measure of my innate ability. Going over my mistake seemed to me to be just the teachers' way of rubbing salt in the wound: "See, here's the right answer which you'll never, ever, really understand because we had to explain it to you so very carefully. There, there. There are plenty of jobs in fast food."

No one ever worked on study techniques with me. It was assumed that as a "gifted" child I would just learn to study. But learning was not really part of my school experience much of the time. I only learned what I could pick up without risking those anxiety attacks from trying things that I could make mistakes at.

The assumption was always that I could easily understand how to get through the school day, how to play with others, and how to do well academically without any outside help or realistic encouragement. For the record, "You could do so well if you would just try a little," is *not* encouragement. When a child is already exhausted from trying to cope with a school situation they have almost no handle on, "try just a little" has no meaning. Try what? How much is a little? What did they want me to do?

Additionally, when it came to the social world, teachers assumed that my problem was entirely a lack of effort. They were working on a similar "fixed mindset," but in the social arena. They assumed that people just "get" a certain amount of social understanding, and that the amount given is roughly the same for everyone. Since I had no innate understanding of how to play with children, their communication of a fixed mindset concept made me more and more determined that I simply could not socialize successfully.

So I grew up in a world where I was a genius if I got something right the first time, an idiot if I didn't, and where there was nothing I could do about it except desperately hope that if I paid heed to my gut and the anxiety attacks it generated, I could avoid mistakes and failures well enough so that maybe no one would notice that I was stupid in huge areas of life.

JIMMY'S WORLD

My brother Jimmy grew up in a different world than I did, and I'm not just talking about the twenty-three-year difference in our ages.

Jimmy's difficulties with others making mistakes and with making mistakes himself were regarded as serious problems that had to be dealt with immediately, frequently, and persistently over time. Lucky duck!

Where I grew up with adults constantly reinforcing my idea that mistakes and failures were tragic, my brother grew up with adults constantly working on making him more able to accept and deal reasonably with his own and others' mistakes.

Jimmy had great difficulty understanding that if the server at a restaurant got his order wrong, it was not a serious problem and could be fixed easily. So my dad and mom spent a lot of time teaching him the appropriate, polite responses to others' mistakes. By enforcing behaviors on Jimmy's part that indicated the mistake was not a big deal, they forced into his consciousness that mistakes are not a big deal.

Mind you, this was never easy. Jimmy has had a lot of difficulty developing a non-fixed mindset, being as he has an autism spectrum disorder. It has been really hard for him to understand that mistakes are simply a natural and often necessary part of life.

Even today I'm not sure Jimmy has fully accepted the necessity of mistakes. He has the classic problem we with ASDs tend towards—he can easily focus on his (or others') mistakes to the point of obsessing on them.

While Jimmy does have that "autistic" tendency to be upset by mistakes and by unfamiliar territory, our parents and his teachers have made the world he lives in as safe as possible for mistakes and therefore for growth. The huge effort they have made to do this has fostered in him a very different mindset from the fixed mindset. Instead, he has a growth mindset, in which talents, intelligence, and skills *grow* out of trial and error and out of sheer effort.

Yes, I do envy Jimmy for growing up with the people around him determined to foster this kind of mindset in him. For a child to know that the amount of ability, skill, and knowledge he has was not fixed at birth, but is flexible and can grow with effort, is an incredibly valuable thing.

I have been able, as an adult, to foster more of a growth mindset in myself—not perfectly, but then again, growing myself a growth mindset is a process, not a once-and-for-all thing. A growth mindset can be cultivated from a very small seed of knowledge. A few of those seeds are my next topics.

WAIT A SECOND—MISTAKES ARE NECESSARY?

One of those wonderful seeds is a simple one: understanding and accepting the fact that mistakes are a necessity of life.

And yes, once again, I really do mean that. Mistakes are absolutely necessary, and allowing for them is part of a functional life.

Think about the many things that simply couldn't be done if mistakes were not allowed. No one would be able to learn to read (they might make an error) or calculate unless they were savants. In fact, no one would be able to teach or learn anything, because those are mistake-prone activities. We'd pretty much have to just plain ban humans altogether to prevent all mistakes from happening.

Of course, mistakes are tremendously important in areas such as experimental sciences, education, and relationship growth. The only way to avoid mistakes and failures in those areas would be to ban all progress in all of them!

As Einstein said, "If we knew what we were doing, it wouldn't be called research."

And yes, Einstein and other "biggies" of science have all had their own failures—sometimes spectacular ones. Einstein succeeded wildly beyond all possible expectations in 1905, and made contributions that cannot be overstated. But he didn't just think up general and special relativity as instantaneously perfect ideas; he had to work hard to develop those theories and the proofs that went with them.

At the same time, he spent a large chunk of his later life, right up to his death, trying to figure out a way to force the universe to be much more orderly and predictable than it is—which he couldn't do, because the universe is no respecter of persons. So he actually failed a lot. But if he had not risked failure a lot, he'd never have been Einstein in the first place.

If you prefer applied science to the theoretical, it was Thomas Edison, a great experimenter in the practical applications of science, who said, "I have not failed; I have merely discovered 10,000 ways that do not work." That's not even close to a complete count of the failed experiments at his labs.

All of human life would have to come to a standstill if we wanted to avoid mistakes. The fixed-mindset people often do come to a standstill themselves, avoiding anything new, different, or challenging because they don't see mistakes as vital and important. In fact they often are so afraid to make a mistake, so filled with anxiety that they make mistakes in thinking and actions precisely because their anxiety about mistakes is so intense it interferes with good thinking!

THE GROWTH MINDSET

Growth-mindset folks may not exactly enjoy their mistakes, but they don't fear them too much either. People who have developed a growth mindset are able to make reasonable precautions about mistakes: for example, they may use flash cards in academics, making their mistakes at home before the test to avoid making similar mistakes on the test. Or they may simply be sensibly alert to their surroundings and take non-toxic precautions to protect themselves.

The growth mindset is based around a few solid facts. The most important one is this—the brain has a lot of plasticity (ability to change). While there are changes that are too great to achieve—yes, the person with a testable IQ of 60 who makes it a goal to learn vector calculus is doomed to failure—it is extremely possible to make your brain better than it is. Every new thing you learn, every new skill you develop, causes new pathways to form in your brain.

This means that trying new things, studying, or working at a new skill will actually improve your brain's functioning and build up your brain, just as exercise builds up muscles.

The brain really is an amazing thing. It generally rewards effort and persistence. That's a good thing that any human being can exploit to his or her own or others' benefit.

Kids who know and believe that they can positively affect their own intelligence and ability do better than those who mistakenly believe that intelligence and ability are fixed quantities.

What's more, kids (and other people) with a growth mentality are more self-forgiving, more forgiving of others, and more able to cope with life's disappointments. If we see ourselves as people of potential, who might just be able to learn something and have some ability to improve, we are more able to deal with the inevitable bumps (or chasms) in the road.

HOW TO ENCOURAGE A GROWTH MINDSET

You can't instill a growth mindset in a child, much less a child with an ASD, in one moment or day. Those of us on the spectrum are often particularly stubborn about believing that mistakes are tragedies and failures are horrific.

It is absolutely possible to cultivate and grow a growth mindset in a child (or adult) over time. The technique is similar to the "catch him doing something good" school of thinking, where you give praise for positive actions more often than you give negative feedback for negative actions.

The way to encourage a growth mindset is to catch your child making an effort and to assume effort as often as possible. At the same time, you try to catch mistakes and identify them as interesting, useful, and solvable.

Try statements like "wow, you really worked hard on that and I'm proud of you," "I'm sorry, those problems were too easy—how boring," and "hey, there's a mistake we can learn from—isn't that great!"

At the same time, avoid fixed mindset style praise. Even if you have the smartest little Aspie kid on the block, avoid, avoid, avoid statements like "you're a genius," "you have an innate talent," and "you were blessed to be gifted."

Specifically, good praise is saying something like, "Wow, you did a good job at that, you must have worked hard," *not* "wow, you did a good job at that, you must be smart."

For heaven's sake, don't tell your child he's smart. If I run into one more egomaniacal little Aspie whose parents have praised him until he's an obnoxious jerk who won't lift a finger to do schoolwork, I am going to start knocking heads together!

Of course, with kids who are distinctly non-gifted, you may well have an easier time convincing friends, relatives, and teachers to use effort-oriented praise. When a child struggles to speak, it is pretty obvious to many (not all) people that it is great to say, "wow, you tried really hard, that's so great!"

Regardless of testable IQ or how "disabled" a child is, reward effort with praise. When a child struggles, he or she deserves credit for those struggles.

Talk about mistakes in a positive way, even if you find it odd to do so. Say things like, "Oh, I made a mistake, how interesting! How do we fix it?" No matter how silly you think it is, it is important.

BRING IN THE VISUALS

Making charts of progress can be a concrete way of showing how effort over time pays off.

While it is nice when someone can make a lovely scrapbook of a child's progress, all that is necessary is some visual way of showing how hard he or she has worked.

Heck, we as adults look to do this all the time. Exercisers are often urged to keep workout logs to help them stay motivated; businesses post staff awards and "best practices examples" that the public will never see but the staff will. Visible notice that effort has been made is good.

These rewards should be centered on effort. A child should get gold stars or points or happy-face stickers for atrocious piano practice so that he will understand that the struggle is being rewarded long before he actually gets good.

For myself, I keep notes in my organizer to help me mark my progress. Different highlighter colors indicate different areas of effort.

So each day that I've worked on this book, even a little bit, I've written the words "Life Skills Book" in my organizer with a checkmark and highlighted it in yellow. That way I can look back and see that the more yellow highlighting I add to my planner, the closer to done the book is.

Similarly, I highlight all workouts in green. That means that when I'm discouraged, say because I've missed a week of exercise while busy or sick, I can look back and see that, yes, I've lapsed in my workouts from time to time, but came back up to my previous level when I reapplied myself.

Heck, for me, having a planner is a way of keeping track of what I have done more than what I'm going to do. A special calendar or notebook can track a child's efforts using colors or stickers to make those efforts visually obvious.

And by "efforts" I mean practicing, studying, reading, words they have attempted to say to the best of their ability, days when they did their time in OT or speech class, or whatever it is they need to spend time on to learn. The effort is all.

REWARD, REWARD, REWARD CALM HANDLING OF MISTAKES

Not only is it necessary to point out and reward effort, but for those who panic over mistakes, it is necessary to build in rewards for simply not freaking out when they get one problem on the worksheet wrong.

I don't mean that all children should get medals simply for coping with a "B." But any child who is deeply upset by errors needs help and support to learn to handle mistakes.

Handling mistakes calmly is a vital life skill, work skill, and people skill. Every aspect of life is better when you can deal with your own and other's errors calmly. Employment in particular is often contingent on dealing well with mistakes.

If you give clear rewards for calm, cool handling of mistakes, then you get a chance to encourage the child to really use any technique he can remember, create, or otherwise muster. There's not much point in teaching coping skills if the child doesn't get lots of praise for applying those skills, however slightly.

Tony Attwood recommends a simple points system for kids with Asperger's who freak out when getting back tests with—horrors—a less than a perfect score. It involves giving two scores when a test or worksheet is handed back—one is the actual academic score earned, the other is a score for how the child reacts to getting the test back.

Attwood's approach can be used with a variety of children on the spectrum, since it works on the same principle as a "token economy" (where a child gains or loses tokens for good or bad behavior). If the child is already getting points or tokens for positive behaviors, add handling mistakes as a potential area for earning those tokens.

Heck, for kids with Asperger's, just giving them a rating in points for a behavior can be motivational, without the token economy. For some reason, we just love getting good scores on *anything*. When one of us gets a piece of paper that says, "Jennifer's Calmness Rating for Today is 5 Out of 5," hey, that's a big win!

So this particular technique that I'm shamelessly cribbing from Attwood was designed for the many, many children who get angry, upset, loud, and generally hard to deal with when they make an error or get a test back with an imperfect score.

Parents and/or teachers wanting to use this technique will need to explain to the child in question that she will be scored on her reaction to getting a test or worksheet back. If she is calm and does not fret or yell at all, she will get a perfect 5-point score. If she is a little upset and perhaps pouts or temporarily refuses to participate, then she will get a 3 or 4. A really bad tantrum/meltdown/hairy cat fit will result in a score of zero or 1. The score will be given promptly so she can tell how she has done.

It often (not, unfortunately, always) is amazing how well children react to this technique. Auties and Aspies are as competitive as any children, and love to "win." It also helps that if the test score is bad, the child is given an immediate chance to score better on the difficult task of being calm. The child can think, "Well, I didn't get 100, but at least I can get a perfect 5 on my behavior if I don't pout."

WHAT NOT TO DO

I would be remiss if I failed to provide you with an example of What Not To Do.

When I urge you so strongly to reward effort, I don't mean that you should reward only perfect efforts that follow the prescribed pattern the child has been taught. If they try to do what needs to be done, they deserve some credit.

My second grade teacher, Miss G, was a wonderful woman, even though she frustrated me often. I really did like her, and she really was mostly a lovely and intelligent person, but she did one of the stupidest things any teacher could do to an Aspie.

In my second grade class, we would have little games and competitions where the teacher would give us points for what we remembered or what math problems we could do. I liked playing—as long as I won. When I lost, I raised high holy heck, with meltdowns that really upset my teacher and classmates.

To me, losing those competitions was disastrous. If I won, then I felt I was smart, for a few minutes at least; if I lost, it was a tragedy, because I had been shown to be stupid in front of the whole class. Getting back a test with a mistake in it was disheartening, but at least the whole thing hadn't been seen and participated in by everybody else!

Losing was tragic, it was overwhelmingly humiliating, and it also involved not getting whatever little prize the winner(s) got—stickers or a small toy or novelty eraser. What I wanted with a novelty eraser anyway, I don't know. Things like that matter more when you're seven.

Miss G talked to me over and over again about my meltdowns. She talked to me about being a good sport, that it was okay to lose sometimes, and that being calm when I lost was the mature thing to do. That last one got me—I wanted to be mature and grown up. If she'd also told me that handling losses calmly showed intelligence and was something that many adults failed to do, but that she knew I would be able to learn to do, well, then she would have been the perfect motivator!

Fortunately, just telling me that calmness in the face of defeat was mature and good manners was enough. I worked really hard at not melting down, and tried with all of my might not to freak out.

One morning, we had a little competition, and somehow, miraculously, I worked out a little strategy in my head that genuinely worked for me. I was calm, I didn't yell, and I behaved exactly as Miss G wanted me to.

As we were all going out to recess, Miss G called me over and asked to talk to me. She warmly congratulated me on my calmness and good behavior.

I, happy at the praise, decided to let her in on the secret of my success. "It's okay to lose," I told her. "I mean, it's just a stupid little toy, I don't need it or anything. It isn't such a great prize."

Miss G looked at me a bit askance. "Sounds to me like sour grapes," she said.

I didn't know what "sour grapes" meant, so she told me the Aesop tale of the fox, unable to reach a bunch of grapes he wanted, who declares they must be sour after all. She explained that my disdain for the prize I normally would try so hard to get was just my way of putting down the winner instead of accepting my loss graciously.

I was crushed, utterly crushed. I had worked so hard to find a way not to melt down, and my miraculous way of being okay with losing was simply not good enough for her. It wasn't enough for me not to have a meltdown, to please her I had to think correctly and be totally internally gracious too.

I never trusted her after that. I tried a lot less hard for her too, and felt that I could not ever rely on her to tell me what she really wanted. She'd said she wanted me to be calm, I'd worked my frontal lobe off finding a way to be calm, and it wasn't good enough.

And why should I believe her if she said she'd be happy if I would go to the math workstation more often? After all, if I worked hard to change my habits to please her, she'd probably just tell me there was something even harder I had to do to deserve even one tiny bit of praise. I was left with no motivation, no trust, no belief that school is anything but a pit of mind-games that no one can win.

What is really ironic about the whole thing is that my basic idea was sound. It really wasn't worth getting all worked up about one game and a little prize worth a few cents. It really is good to remember when the thing you've lost isn't so great as to be worth mourning over. It wasn't such a huge thing, and it wasn't worth getting worked up over, and she managed to tell me that looking at it from that point of view wasn't okay at all.

Yes, it would have been even more mature if I had somehow decided that the toy was a lovely prize that I would really have liked, but that it was, in the scope of life's vicissitudes, not important enough to sully myself with bad sportsmanship. But honestly, for a seven-year-old kid with Asperger's, "It's just a stupid prize that isn't all that great, why would I yell about it," is pretty good.

So for heaven's sake, when your child takes small steps towards trying to live up to your requests and coaching and handles a mistake, an imperfect test score, or a change in schedule decently well, don't cavil about the details. Praise the effort, reward the behavior, and leave working out the fine points as something that can be done when there is time and energy to burn.

The Fourth and Final Really Big Skill
Understanding Cognitive Behavioral Therapy Concepts

This is possibly one of the most useful skill sets for those people on the autism spectrum who can acquire it. Even if you cannot fully communicate these concepts to your child, if you understand and can apply these even a little, it can help you and your child a great deal.

Cognitive Behavioral Therapy (CBT) is a form of psychotherapy has been empirically and clinically shown to help with toxic anger, anxiety, depression, panic attacks, insomnia, and obsessive-compulsive behaviors.

So what the heck is it doing in a book on life skills for kids with ASDs?

It turns out that the basic concepts applied in CBT are really, really useful for kids on the autism spectrum and their parents, and can help those who are trying to learn life- and work-skills such as learning to solve problems calmly, dealing with changes in schedules or expectations, and avoiding and mitigating meltdowns.

Since it is vital for kids on the spectrum to learn how to handle life without screaming meltdowns and with the ability to cope with schedule changes, being able to apply the ideas that come from CBT is a huge life skill.

My personal favorite kind of CBT is Rational Emotive Behavioral Therapy (REBT), which is a heck of a mouthful, but has really coherent, logical concepts that are pretty simple. It also has the advantage of being a way of problem-solving that doesn't have a bunch of touchy-feely stuff attached.

Then again, many people feel that basic CBT is not touchy-feely enough! That is, people have some difficulty with a kind of therapy that is not based in fuzzy-wuzzies or lots and lots of talking it out.

People on the autism spectrum, however, are often not so good with touchy-feely. We also have the problem that, when the people around us try to solve all of our problems and over-protect us, we get pretty messed up.

While the terms CBT and REBT are may seem jargony or even sound a little imposing, the actual ideas involved are pretty simple. Children with good receptive language can learn the basic ideas involved without too much trouble.

Of course, *simple* is not the same as *easy*. Learning to apply the simple concepts can take some hard work, and is not always possible. When neurological and sensory issues abound, sometimes even the strongest, most determined child cannot use tools like these at the drop of a hat.

In other words, if you teach your child these concepts, don't expect perfection overnight. It takes time for even typical adults to learn to really use this stuff, and every step forward counts.

Even if your child is too young for the concepts or has poor receptive language, or otherwise can't learn this stuff, these are ideas that can save *your* sanity. If you use these ideas to reduce your anxiety and stress levels, then not only will you be in a better position to teach, but you will also have a chance to get familiar with applying the ideas so that when your child is ready for them, you will totally have them down pat.

WHAT'S THE BIG IDEA?

The big ideas behind cognitive behavioral therapy are that (1) what you do affects how you feel; (2) what you think affects how you feel; and (3) you have a good deal of ability to change what you do and think and therefore how you feel.

This is important, important, important. Humans in general and, in particular, modern Western humans, generally think that their feelings are truthful, meaningful reactions to their environment. That belief is often double for us on the spectrum.

In reality, as Albert Ellis and Robert Harper wrote, "All your feelings (just because you honestly feel them) are authentic. But none of them is absolutely and certainly 'true.'"

Let's take a person with Asperger's—say, me. When I get really angry, my natural, normal human assumption is that there is a *reason* for my anger. The angrier I am, the bigger I assume the reason must be. For years, I would respond to anger by expressing and "venting" my anger, in the belief that it was important to "get it out" so that the problem could be solved. This approach is normal and natural for humans, and it is pretty darn useless.

While loudly venting anger, acting panicky when anxious, and refusing to cooperate when depressed are simply what many humans do, these are generally counterproductive activities.

Oh, it makes good sense to go for a run or walk or otherwise physically burn off the adrenaline rush that can come with anger or panic. But yelling and panicking "to get it out" have a strong tendency to make people even angrier and more panicky.

And those of us on the spectrum are often unusually good at yelling, panicking, and generally expressing unhealthy negative emotions at full gale force, thus reinforcing the negative emotions.

When a child with an ASD is angry, anxious, or worried about a situation, the results can be pretty extreme. Sometimes it is necessary (*very* necessary) to alter the situation so that the child can function.

But at the same time, even children can learn to mitigate and dissolve these problematic emotions—at least some of the time.

You see, that statement above, about how our thoughts and actions profoundly affect our emotions, is key to this whole thing.

Let's say you get cut off in traffic—a real close call that gives you a scare and a burst of adrenaline. If you start cussing the other driver out, and I ask you what made you angry, you would say, "I'm angry because that bleeping jerk cut me off!" And you'd be right— partially.

Yes, that immediate impulse to anger or panic did come from the other person's actions. But any yelling, flipping off, or cursing that comes out of the deal is not his fault.

Yes, I said that angry behavior is not the fault of the person who did the stupid thing that triggered the initial impulse of anger.

After the first second, it is your own thoughts and actions that make you angry. And while it would make no sense to be happy you were cut off, there is a world of difference between being enraged and simply being annoyed and frustrated.

So imagine the guy cutting you off, and you yell and flip him off. At that point what are you thinking?

- "What a jerk!"
- "He could have got us killed!"
- "How dare he cut me off!"
- "Driver like that should be shot!"

So you and I, like everyone else, have a natural tendency to take it personally and think very angry thoughts when we get cut off. Some people think so angrily that they wind up getting road rage and may create a serious incident or accident.

In the world of CBT or REBT, we recognize that rage is totally, totally useless in these cases. It does not make the other driver drive more carefully, it does not improve road safety, and does not make us feel good. It might even cause an accident, as a really angry driver who is focused on one incident may not pay good attention to his driving.

As an Aspie, when I get angry, I get really angry. Also, my anger at others for doing stupid, thoughtless things can add up over time, so I can even wind up collecting grievances against others, against all humanity, and against the world. Totally toxic.

So what to do? Well, to start off, when I get cut off on the freeway, I play a little game. The game is called "How many reasons can I find?"

So when I get cut off, I think:

- "He didn't see me."
- "Maybe he has a large blind spot in that car."
- "He's late for a job interview."
- "He's going to the hospital."
- "He's desperate to get to a bathroom."
- "He was distracted by the kids in the backseat."
- "It had nothing to do with me."
- "A miss is as good as a mile."

Then I flip the stations on the radio to find something to sing along with and just forget the whole thing.

Of course, if the person who cut me off was weaving wildly or otherwise showing signs of really being out of it, I might have to pull over and call 911. But most of the time, no action is needed. I just need to remind myself that there are a million reasons that people accidentally cut others off every day, and none of them have a darned thing to do with me personally.

So this is a really simple demonstration of how a cognitive behavioral approach works. By changing my thoughts and my actions—by thinking calm thoughts and not yelling or gesticulating—I can change my feelings.

THE BASIC THEORY: ABCS

This basic theory of CBT is usually put in the form of ABC.

"A" stands for Actuating Event or Adversity; this is the trigger for an emotion or behavior.

"B" stands for Beliefs: what you think of the event, what significance you put into it.

"C" stands for Consequences, meaning the way you feel and act.

For example, if the A is a call from your child's school saying you have to come pick her up, your C might be to feel overwhelmed and depressed. That's natural enough.

This is because of your Bs. The A alone isn't enough.

If your Bs are:

- This is humiliating having the school call me like this.
- They probably think that I'm a terrible parent.
- This teacher is nothing but trouble.
- Why can't my child just get through one week without this nonsense? It's never going to stop.

Well, then, naturally and normally you will feel overwhelmed and depressed. But what if you had a different set of Bs, like this:

- My child is having a hard time during the day. We need to do something about this.
- Parenthood can be really difficult. I need to call my local ASA group for support.
- I sure don't like this happening again, but we will find a way to work through it.

- This teacher (or aide, or situation) seems to be a bad fit for my kid. Maybe we need to do something about that.

- Boy, this is a big pain.

That second set of Bs is neither super-cheerful nor Pollyanna-ish, but it is realistic and not as disastrous as the first set. You wouldn't feel happy about the problem (that would be unrealistic), but you'd feel okay. You would be much more likely to feel things like a healthy level of frustration and irritation, but along with that you'd be more likely to have a healthy determination to change, and the belief that you could learn to change the situation and/or cope with this for a while longer.

Rational, self-helping beliefs, thoughts, and actions can make the difference—even in seriously bad situations—between healthy negative emotions (frustration, annoyance, sadness) and unhealthy negative emotions (rage, hate, despair, depression).

Think about it: one person who loses a family member to a particular disease or type of accident may "crawl into a bottle" indefinitely; another may devote time and energy to curing the disease or preventing that type of accident in order to help others. The main difference is not in the situation, but in the thinking of the people involved.

No, I most certainly do not think (nor does CBT or REBT teach) that most people can easily change their thinking or just magically cope better. It takes hard work—often very hard work—to think rationally instead of irrationally.

SIMPLE?

So CBT is all about looking at your (or your child's) underlying Beliefs about a situation and switching out any that are Irrational Beliefs (IBs) for Rational Beliefs (RBs).

Sounds simple enough, and in a way it is simple. Simple, but, again, not so easy. Almost anyone with just a bit of "theory of mind" can learn the concepts, but learning to apply them takes time and real effort.

If you ever find you want more detail on these concepts, there are many books, both large and small ones, out there that cover cognitive behavioral therapy and/or rational emotive behavioral therapy in detail. There are some suggested ones in the "resources" section at the back of this book.

A detailed survey of CBT and REBT is beyond the scope of this book, much as I would love to go on and on. What I want to get into here is how these ideas can help you help your child.

LOOK FOR YOUR CHILD'S ABCS

There are a lot of kids (and adults) on the spectrum who have serious issues with anger, anxiety, and depression. My first round of serious clinical depression that lasted more than a few weeks was when I was seven. Unfortunately, these problems are no respecters of childhood.

On the one hand, much of the anxiety and depression that affect children with ASDs stem from the stress created by social isolation, sensory issues, and difficulty understanding the "unwritten rules" that govern much of human behavior. Those are all things that can and do need to be addressed by parents, schools, and professionals working with these children.

At the same time, the anxiety, depression, and anger that plague many of us on the spectrum are worsened and sustained by Irrational Beliefs (IBs) or simply mistaken ideas.

Looking at the ABCs of your child's emotional situation can give you key insights to help him or her cope.

In his excellent book, *No More Meltdowns*, Jed Baker gives an example of a young boy, Kevin, who would hit and yell at other children during recess almost every day. From seeming totally calm, the boy would go first into violent anger and then into a total meltdown. Poor kid—he was stressed out, he was stressing others out, and the only thing his school knew to do about it was to constantly increase the intensity of punishments and/or rewards. But you can't "fix" a behavior you are punished for if your basic Beliefs about the situation are toxic.

Baker went out on the playground with Kevin to observe what was going on firsthand. Kevin went over to two other children who were playing checkers and asked to play. The other children told him, "No, we just started."

So Kevin pushed one of the checkers players over.

Baker was able to interview Kevin and find out what he thought had happened. When the other kids told him he could not play, Kevin thought, "They hate me!" And he reacted violently.

This is a prime example of how Beliefs trigger Consequences. If Kevin had understood that you don't interrupt a game of checkers in progress, and that he couldn't possibly play with either child until the game was done, his reaction might have been quite different.

Dr. Baker was able to work with Kevin and teach him rational beliefs (RBs) about playing on the playground. Parents can do this too if they look to the ABCs of their child's behavior.

(*Note:* Jed Baker's book uses the letters A, B, and C in their behavioral meanings: Antecedent, Behavior, Consequence. If you get his book, remember that it's a different context and you'll be okay.)

Often a child with Asperger's or autism will do things that seem to make no sense or occur for no reason. Parents and teachers will look at the Activating Event and the Consequences and find no link—or they may not even see that there *is* an Activating Event.

When you realize that it is really, really easy for those of us on the spectrum to pick up Beliefs that don't work out very well for us, you can start looking at problems like anger and anxiety differently.

For example, common Irrational Beliefs among people on the spectrum are:

- It is a disaster if people don't play by the rules as I know them, with no exceptions, even if it is a casual game.

- Everybody at school hates me all of the time.
- If the other kids tease me it means there is something seriously wrong with me.
- If a teacher corrects me, it is because she is mean and hates me.
- If a teacher gets one thing wrong, like changing the schedule without warning me, she is a liar and completely unreliable. (The C for this may be not listening to the teacher ever.)
- Being in a constant state of intense anxiety is absolutely necessary to help protect me from bullies.
- Life will never be any better than it is now.

These are easy beliefs to come by. When you get teased a lot, it is easy to believe that everyone hates you all of the time, that you are a loser, and that you are stupid. It is very unlikely that a child will, on his or her own, guess at the reality that bullies are narcissistic people who wrongly believe that they are better than others, and that bullying behaviors are a sign of something wrong with the bullies, not the bullied.

It is also hard for children on the spectrum to understand that the reason other kids may go along with bullying is not because they "hate" the child with an ASD, nor because there is something wrong with the child with an ASD, but because those "typical peers" are also afraid of the bullies and go along with them to avoid being bullied themselves.

When kids on the spectrum get bullied, they can wind up feeling very much that something is wrong with them and that the other kids *all* hate them *all* of the time. Then, when they report the bullying and there is the usual backlash, the spectrum kids will also feel that the teachers or principal has deliberately duped them, or is stupid and useless.

Reporting bullying is a nasty Catch-22 for many children on the spectrum. Not reporting it will result in teachers simply not noticing it; reporting it will result in punishment for the bullies, which leads to severe retaliation against the bullied child, and rather extreme (and believable) threats about what will happen if they "tell" in the future.

I kid you not—when teachers and other adults encourage kids to report bullying, they seldom have an effective anti-bullying plan in place, and the backlash from the bullies can be massive.

There is also the fact that if a child is bullied regularly, the *bullied child* is the one who is usually sent to therapy or social skills training, thus making it clear to just about everyone that the victim is the one who has something wrong with him or her.

It is easy to see how a child on the spectrum can easily develop self-defeating Beliefs. Their experiences can easily teach them Irrational Beliefs, and they can easily find support for believing irrational, self-defeating things in their everyday experiences.

Those Irrational Beliefs then create more stress, which fosters more and stronger IBs, and things can go to heck fast.

Why am I going on so much about a topic that is so grim and fore-boding? It is *not* to make you feel helpless or hopeless, but to help you ferret out these toxic beliefs and combat them.

Once you know the Irrational Beliefs involved, you can combat them with Rational Beliefs. Rational Beliefs must be presented in a calm, supportive, firm way, and often must be repeated and reviewed frequently.

Rational Beliefs to counter the above IBs might include:

- It is boring and time-consuming to argue about the rules in a casual game on the playground. It is okay to let small mistakes and confusions about the rules go.

- Nobody is perfect all of the time. My teacher knows a lot of important things despite making mistakes sometimes, and I can still learn from him/her.

- If kids pick on me or bully me, it means they are egotistical, scared, or just plain foolish at that moment. Even if they are usually smart, that doesn't mean they are right to bully me. In fact, it isn't really about me very much of the time.

- Some kids pick on me sometimes. I can avoid them when that happens.
- When a teacher corrects me, it means she knows I can learn.
- I can be alert to bullies without being on "red alert" all of the time.
- Sometimes life is hard, but it can be good too. Life will not always be as hard as being a kid is.

Try to find ways to get these things through to your child. Unfortunately, every child is different; some children who seem less "smart" can easily take on rational thoughts, and some who seem like "geniuses" are stubborn about their misery-creating beliefs.

Talking with your child on a regular basis can be a big help. Use actions as well as words to communicate.

Listening is important too. If your child can't talk or won't talk about certain things, then "listen" to his or her behavior. Behavior is a powerful form of communication. Silent children can speak volumes with what they do.

MY MOM SAVES MY LIFE WITH A POWERFUL "B"

Rational Beliefs are so important and useful that they can save a life. I know, because my mom saved my life with one.

I've mentioned that, in the process of growing up with undiagnosed Asperger's, I went through a lot of clinical depression in my childhood. I seriously considered suicide when I was in second grade, but rejected the idea. This was largely because I read Ann Landers religiously, as well as reading as much of the newspaper and news magazines as I could. From these sources I learned that suicide hurts all of the people left behind, and I really hated people who caused others pain. So I checked out what my life expectancy should be and decided to just tough it out.

Unfortunately for me, we were a church-going family. By my mid-teens I had figured out that if I were to die, God would take care of my family and make everything all right, so I occasionally wavered on the suicide thing. After all, "all things work for good for those that love the Lord," right?

(This is a pretty good example of how kids on the spectrum can take what you think is straightforward, positive information and then take it to the logical conclusion you never would have thought of. Tuck it in the back of your mind for future reference, just in case.)

But my mother was able to keep me alive without even knowing that any of this was going on in my head. She did it by determinedly planting a powerful Rational Belief in my mind, one she repeated over and over in some detail, until it took root and wrapped itself around my thinking.

When I found school, dealing with other kids, and the stress of growing up to be just too much, my mom would frequently remind me of this:

- "Some people are good at being kids, and some are good at being adults. While there are people who are good at both, they are in the minority. You are terrible at being a kid. You have no real talent for elementary school (or junior high, or high school)—it just doesn't work for you, but it doesn't have to.

- "Fortunately, childhood only lasts a few more years. You are going to be great at being an adult, and you will get better at it with time. You have good adult skills.

- "Don't worry about being a kid. Being an adult is most of your life. There is every chance that some of those kids who are on the football team or cheerleading squad are going to always look back on high school as the best years of their life. What could be sadder? To have three years of the second decade of your life be IT? Wouldn't it be much better to have a life that improves over time?

- "You are terrible at being a kid, but you will be great at being an adult. Just remember that and hang in there."

That is a truly powerful set of Rational Beliefs. The idea that getting through childhood is temporary and that life can and often does improve over time is a great one.

She was right, incidentally, about some of those kids who were thriving in junior high not doing so well for the rest of their lives. Bullying, cliques, and social snobbery work well in the world of K-12, but can easily result in chaotic and toxic lives for adults. Bullies in particular tend to have higher rates of alcoholism, divorce, and unemployment than average once they grow up.

Heck, even in the unreal world of "reality" TV, we can watch people who are clique-ish and vicious social climbers and see that those people are seldom happy and always on guard against the next person who might knock them down. That's the problem with making your life into one long game of "King of the Mountain." Unless you forfeit your "right" to keep playing, you are always looking over your shoulder.

So yes, RBs are so important that they can save lives. Similarly, IBs like "Nobody cares about me and everyone would be happier if I were dead," can take lives.

Planting as many RBs as you can find time for can help make your child more able to cope with life. Keep an eye out for those IBs when you have the chance. Look, listen, and be ready to reinforce RBs as often as necessary.

You might just save a life.

Postscript

I wrote the outline for this book at Temple's behest in June of 2009, when I was forty-three and my brother Jimmy was twenty years old. At that time, we didn't know whether or not Jimmy would be able to actually graduate from high school. For a long time, it had looked as if that would never happen.

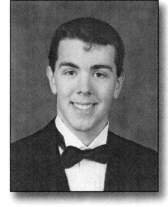

In June 2010, at the age of twenty-one, my brother, James Henry McIlwee, received his high school diploma. We were all thrilled. My dad even asked the school if the grades Jimmy was getting were equivalent to a "gentleman's C." The response was that, no, Jimmy's grades and qualifications for graduation were completely on the up-and-up.

This fall, as this book goes to press, Jimmy will be taking both academic and life skills classes at the local community college.

Just recently I received an email from Jimmy containing this poem about his journey. It told us more about how he perceived his own life than we'd ever guessed.

(And for anyone who's thinking of writing in, we're aware of the link to the song "Don't Write Me Off" from the movie *Music and Lyrics*. The final product here is 90% Jimmy's words and 100% Jimmy's sentiments. So if he wants to go a little bit "Weird Al" on it, none of us need mind.)

Don't Write Me Off
by James H. McIlwee

It's never ever been easy for me
To find the right words to say.
I could only use phrases from shows on TV.
Did I think of anything else? No way!

I've been watching Blue's Clues and Thomas and Friends…
But it just got dull and insipid.
The way my old life was came to an end.
I no longer watch shows for kids!

I used to wear red all the time
But now I can even wear blue,
And I can also wear black which is not a crime
And white, green and gold too.

Since you all helped me, my whole life has changed.
It's not just my bedroom you've all rearranged!
I can also play video games on my new Wii
And use other ways to exercise my body.

I can talk on the phone. I can play guitar.
I can listen to music performed by Rock Stars.
I know I've blown more chances than as much as I should get
But I must say, "Please don't write me off just yet!"

A Mini-Glossary

Asperger's Syndrome: an autism spectrum disorder that occurs in people with normal or above-normal testable IQs that is sometimes referred to as "the geek syndrome." People with Asperger's Syndrome are generally verbally adept but have difficulty understanding and developing nonverbal communication. Other symptoms of Asperger's include (but are not limited to) sensory issues, social difficulties, literal or rigid thinking, being rule-bound, and slow or "different" emotional development.

Autism: A neurological disorder or state of being that usually involves difficulty developing speech, social awkwardness or failure to develop socially, poor ability to read people, and emotional immaturity or simpler emotional development. Autism can also involve sensory issues, poor motor skills, speech disorders, odd or repetitive speech patterns, lack of reflexes, and a whole mess of other things.

How much of a disorder or handicap autism is varies a lot; the severity of each symptom and the problems that stem from it can be minor or major. Autism may or may not be accompanied by mental retardation (low testable IQ).

Autism spectrum: This term refers to the wide range of "autisms" that can include anything from a child who is unable to speak or communicate to a child who is hyper-verbal and seems to be a walking encyclopedia. The autism spectrum includes diagnoses such as autism, Asperger's, PDD: NOS, autism spectrum disorder, and autistic-like behavior.

The common threads that run through the autism spectrum are difficulty in communication, difficulties with reading faces or perceiving others' emotions, slow and/or different emotional and social development, and a heightened interest in objects, categories, and order.

Autism Spectrum Disorder: any disorder or syndrome that is on the autism spectrum. This includes autism, "classical" autism, high-functioning autism, PDD:NOS, Asperger's Syndrome, and possibly others.

Autistic Obsession: An old-fashioned term for special interest.

Classical autism: is not an official diagnosis, but is used to refer to any form of autism that seems very severe and includes a distinct lack of speech development, stereotypical "blank" facial expressions, low level of interaction, and poor receptive language. If the child does not speak but does rock and head-bang, the chances are that they will be thought of as having classical autism. (Please note that head-banging is often a symptom of an ear infection, frequent severe headaches, or migraines, and should result in a full medical evaluation!)

While it used to be thought that having "classical" autism meant that a child was uneducable and even "hopeless," this is now recognized as a load of BS. Many children with some or all of the symptoms of classical autism can learn quite a lot and may surprise the heck out of you. Even those who stay pretty severe often wind up being able to communicate, do laundry, go bowling, and otherwise have lives.

If any doctor tells you that, since your child has autism, you might as well just institutionalize him or her, find another doctor. That doctor is at least thirty years behind.

High-functioning autism: a term often (but not always) used interchangeably with Asperger's Syndrome. Usually people with a diagnosis of high-functioning autism have a significant speech delay but an average or above average IQ. Technically, according to the

DSM IV, any person with autism and a testable IQ of over 70 has high-functioning autism, but the term is seldom used in day-to-day life to refer to people with IQs of under 80.

Many people with high-functioning autism started out with a diagnosis of just plain autism and worked their way up, so to speak. Also, people with high-functioning autism may have severe, persistent issues with language processing and sensory issues that are often (not always) more severe than those usually expected in a person with a diagnosis of Asperger's Syndrome.

Please note that these boundaries vary greatly. Different geographic regions and different diagnosticians may typically favor their own distinct diagnostic patterns. What is Asperger's in Maine may be high-functioning autism in Illinois, or vice versa.

Intelligence: Usually this term refers to the kind of intelligence that is tested by standard IQ tests; however, intellectual intelligence, academic intelligence, social intelligence, verbal intelligence, visual intelligence, spatial intelligence, and emotional intelligence are all separate functions, and any or all can be at very different levels in a given individual. In people with autism spectrum disorders, these intelligences often vary widely.

Neurotypical: Short for "neurologically typical," this term refers to any person who does not have any kind of autism spectrum disorder. The implication is that the brain of the non-autism-spectrum person is somehow more typical in its configuration and function than the brain of a person on the autism spectrum. Unfortunately, we do not have tremendously well-defined parameters for either typical or autistic brains.

Note that this term is not very precise: it seems a bit silly to refer to someone who is not on the autism spectrum but does have a seizure disorder "neurologically typical." Certainly there are individuals out there who have had large sections of their brains removed due to tumors, who therefore have very atypical brains, but who do not have autism.

Still, if you see someone called a "neurotypical" or "NT," it just means that they don't have an autism spectrum disorder.

Normal: Sometimes folks describe people without autism as "normal," as in "Billy has autism, but his sister is normal." The problem with this is that we really haven't figured out what "normal" actually is—and sometimes what seems most normal is not really the greatest thing.

The usual substitute used by professionals and others in the autism field is "typical," as in, "In our social skills class, we have five children with autism and five typical peers." The objections to typical are the same as the objections to the word normal, but since we have to call people without ASDs *something*, we usually go with typical.

Obsessions: There are two kinds of "obsessions" that are frequently brought up when discussing autism. The first is the "special interest obsession" or "autistic obsession," which is an intense, focused interest (see "Special Interest").

The second kind of obsession is the sort that occurs in obsessive-compulsive disorder (OCD), in which the OCD sufferer will obsessively wash his or her hands; align toys, shoes, or other items compulsively; clean things repeatedly and with little reason; or otherwise repeat seemingly unnecessary and meaningless actions without being able to stop. OCD is also characterized by intense anxiety about anything that interferes with the obsessive behaviors.

Please note that while these two kinds of "obsessions" are not directly related, they can both occur in a person with autism spectrum disorders at the same time. OCD requires professional psychological intervention, often a combination of medication and cognitive behavioral therapy.

Parallel Play: any kind of play that is done in parallel, that is, next to and at the same time as another person, but not in interaction with them. Forms of parallel play include finger-painting, swinging on swing sets, many home improvement projects, and watching the Super Bowl.

PDD:NOS: This stands for "Pervasive Developmental Disorder: Not Otherwise Specified." PDD:NOS is a label that is used because the set of disorders that make up the autism spectrum are not well defined. When a clinician feels a child is "almost autistic" or that the person being diagnosed does not fit into a specific diagnostic niche (like autism, high-functioning autism, or Asperger's Syndrome), the diagnosis is generally PDD:NOS.

Sometimes the diagnosis PDD:NOS is given because the diagnostician thinks that the word "autism" will freak out the parents or caregivers of the child. That is, sometimes it's a sneaky way of cuing people in to the child's autism spectrum issues without saying the "A" word.

Depending on the specific case, a child with PDD:NOS may do well in a program designed for children with autism, a program designed for children with Asperger's, or a little of each. Fortunately, no one ever has to actually teach, raise, or "treat" a label; one can only teach, raise, and treat human individuals.

Receptive language: the degree of ability to receive information in a verbal form. Some children have sensory issues or other difficulties that make it almost impossible for them to make sense of the spoken word; others can make out the words just fine but can't put very many of them together meaningfully. Determining how much of your language your child is able to receive on his wavelength can save you a world of grief.

Self-efficacy: A sense of one's competency at a specific task or process. Self-efficacy is generally based on real experience: once someone has successfully done a task, he or she will have a sense of self-efficacy in that area. Self-efficacy is completely independent of self-esteem; a person may have a very high sense of self-efficacy but a low sense of self- esteem.

Special Interest: This term usually refers to the intense, focused special interests children (and adults) with autism have. The object of the interest or "obsession" may be anything from elevators to Thomas the Tank Engine to fractals. Many adults with autism spectrum disorders are particularly obsessive about science fiction and/or comic books. San Diego's ComicCon is one of the favorite gathering spots for adults with (possibly undiagnosed) Asperger's Syndrome.

Testable IQ: A number generated by standard IQ tests, usually including but not limited to the Stanford-Binet test. IQ as usually tested is generally (not always) a good predictor of success in primary school.

Visual Schedule: A schedule that uses a series of pictures to indicate the order in which activities will occur and possibly the times at which they will happen. Usually this consists largely of a poster or card with a strip of Velcro™ on it, and pictures of activities with Velcro on their backs, so that the pictures can be arranged on the strip in the correct order each day.

Recommended Resources

Autism Society of America

www.autism-society.org
Phone: 301.657.0881 or 1.800.3AUTISM

The Autism Society is a great place to start getting information on autism and finding a local support group.

(Please note that the Autism Society does *not* supply treatments, diagnoses, or legal representation.)

Asperger's Syndrome (Understanding It)

Asperger's Syndrome: A Guide for Parents and Professionals
    by Tony Attwood, PhD

Asperger's Syndrome: Diagnostic Assessment DVD
    by Tony Attwood

Autism Spectrum Disorders (All Types)

Thinking in Pictures: My Life With Autism
    by Temple Grandin (expanded 2006 edition)

Ten Things Every Child With Autism Wishes You Knew
    by Ellen Notbohm

Ten Things Your Student With Autism Wishes You Knew
by Ellen Notbohm

1001 Great Ideas for Teaching and Raising Children with Autism Spectrum Disorders by Ellen Notbohm and Veronica Zysk

Cognitive Behavioral Therapy: Information and Resources for Parents to Understand and Apply CBT

Exploring Feelings DVD by Tony Attwood
(Note: While this is a useful presentation, it is absolutely *not* needed if you want to use Tony's workbooks, which are in the Workbooks for Kids section, below. The workbooks stand alone just fine!)

Feeling Good by David D. Burns, MD
This is the now-classic book on CBT and is awesome. Do not be cowed by the length of it: it is designed so that you can read only the parts you need, but there is lots of extra information if you find you want more. Also, it's cheap. Awesome!

A Guide to Rational Living by Albert Ellis, PhD and Robert A. Harper, PhD.
What do you call a brilliant therapist who writes the best books on any of the cognitive behavioral therapies but has the bedside manner of a cranky crocodile? Albert Ellis. Not recommended for fragile, precious snowflakes.

Cognitive Behavioural Therapy for Dummies by Rob Wilson and Rhena Branch
Seriously. This is a great resource that is available cheaply on used-book Web sites.

Cognitive Behavioral Therapy: Workbooks for Kids on the Autism Spectrum

Exploring Feelings: Cognitive Behaviour Therapy to Manage Anger
  by Tony Attwood

Exploring Feelings: Cognitive Behaviour Therapy to Manage Anxiety
  by Tony Attwood

Asperger's…What Does It Mean to Me? by Catherine Faherty

Employment for People on the Autism Spectrum

Developing Talents: Careers for Individuals with Asperger Syndrome and High-Functioning Autism by Temple Grandin and Kate Duffy

A Foot In the Door: Networking Your Way Into the Hidden Job Market by Katharine Hansen
  (This book is not about autism, but is all about finding the "back doors" into jobs, which is the method that works best for people on the autism spectrum.)

Just for Fun

Laughing and Loving with Autism
  compiled by R. Wayne Gilpin

More Laughing and Loving with Autism
  compiled by R. Wayne Gilpin

Much More Laughing and Loving with Autism
  compiled by R. Wayne Gilpin

Any book by Dave Barry. No, Dave Barry does not have any kind of autism spectrum disorder or anything like that, but you might need a break, and his stuff is really funny.

Medications for Autism Spectrum Disorders

Thinking In Pictures: My Life With Autism by Temple Grandin, 2006 Edition, Chapter 6 "Believer in Biochemistry"

Taking the Mystery Out of Medications in Autism/Asperger's Syndromes by Luke Tsai, MD

Meltdowns – Surviving and Preventing Them

No More Meltdowns by Jed Baker, PhD

Asperger Syndrome and Difficult Moments by Brenda Smith Myles and Jack Southwick (Note: "Difficult Moments" here is used to mean "giant hairy cat fits from heck.")

Sensory Issues

The Out of Sync Child by Carol Stock Kranowitz, MA.

The Out of Sync Child Has Fun by Carol Stock Kranowitz, MA.

Asperger Syndrome and Sensory Issues by Brenda Smith Myles et al.

Social Skills for Adults

How I Raised Myself from Failure to Success in Selling by Frank Bettger

How to Win Friends and Influence People by Dale Carnegie

Unwritten Rules of Social Relationships
  by Temple Grandin and Sean Barron

Reading People
  by Jo-Ellan Dimitrius, PhD and Mark Mazzarella

Social Stories – How to Create and Use Them

www.thegraycenter.org

The New Social Story Book: Illustrated Edition
  by Carol Gray

Understanding How People with Autism Think

Thinking in Pictures: My Life With Autism
  by Temple Grandin (expanded 2006 edition)

Pretending to Be Normal: Living With Asperger's Syndrome
  by Liane Holliday Willey

The Curious Incident of the Dog in the Night-Time: A Novel
  by Mark Haddon

Visual Supports – How to Make and Use Them

www.icontalk.com
(Barbara Bloomfield)

*Making Visual Supports Work in the Home and Community:
  Strategies for Individuals with Autism and Asperger Syndrome*
  by Jennifer L. Savner and Brenda Smith Myles

Visual Strategies for Improving Communication
  by Linda A. Hodgdon, M.Ed., CCC-SLP

Index

If you liked this book, you may also enjoy these great resources!

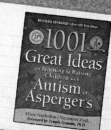

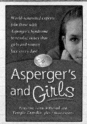